For the generation of leaders yet to be . . .

may you find yourself on these pages and, in so doing,
liberate your voice with hope and resolve to lead as you
have always imagined leadership could be.

Table of Contents

Acknowledgements

M ost authors would admit that any literary endeavor requires a team of people. This project redefines team. Were the cover to be representatively true, it would have the names of all those whose stories grace the pages ahead. Still, many have made this project possible, to whom we are deeply grateful.

The MJ Murdock Charitable Trust, especially Terry Stokesbary and Mary Hill, for believing in the project of developing emerging leaders through their generous grant to Mars Hill Graduate School. Thank you Terry and Mary—your vision, support and friendship have meant the world to us.

David Fisher, whose independent student leadership project forms the structure around which this book is organized. Your brilliant insights and willingness to dig deep into these stories will allow the voices of these men and women to be heard with greater clarity and power.

Sarah Steinke—thanks for your great editorial support and gifts—your polishing made this project shine so brightly! Your work was amazing.

Joshua Longbrake—for your brilliant eye that captures the world in light . . . thank you for sharing your gift with the world on the cover.

And most importantly, to the brave and generous women and men whose stories compose this book—we are humbled and privileged to have held your stories, and we hope you feel they have been honored tenderly and valiantly. Thank you for everything you taught us about leadership. May your voices be that much more powerful, vibrant, and clarion as you engage the world in the noble endeavor to change it for good.

Ron would like to thank:

Tom Ryan. Your partnership on this leadership journey—in the classroom, at the keyboard, at the conference table, over late coffees and dinners, and over the barbeque has been a holy gift to me. What a privilege to work alongside such a brilliant emerging leader and even more, a dear, dear friend. You have taught me a great deal for which I am endlessly grateful.

I have had the good, good fortune to have been accompanied by some of the most gifted emerging leaders who will unquestionably continue to change the world. They have changed much of it already where they have lead, and they have certainly changed mine. Their friendship continues to bless my life by the day. I could fill pages with many names, but for now I will name a few who have made indelible marks and taught me copiously about leadership. To each of you, my heartfelt thanks. Cathy, Paul, Joel & Brooke, Tim & Cote, Jon & Annie, Crystal, Jeremy, Josh L, Justin B, Justin M, Jay & Heather, Jarrod, Paula, Blaine, Ben K, Ben H, Zach, Nathan, and Greg—know this: the world will be that much closer to heaven because you have lead in it.

Josh E. For the faith to pray a simple prayer years ago that changed the course of history, mostly mine. Working alongside you in the grand pursuit of transformation—of the world's, and our own, makes life so, so good. Macheeto awaits.

And to Barb, Matthew & Becca, all my love and gratitude for being the most wonderful family a man could ever want.

Tom would like to thank:

Ron Carucci. You've been a dear friend and have shown faith in my leadership when I had little. Thanks for your perseverance and pursuit of my giftings, and for the ways you dream bigger than most of us can handle.

Keith Anderson and Steve Garber. Rarely are books like this individual endeavors, and your fingerprints are on this text as much as mine are, for each of you have left indelible marks on my soul. Your wise, patient, thoughtful, and contemplative spirits are models for my own life. As you have each pushed me into deeper thought and deeper life, you have also taught me what it means to be a man of faith. To say "thank you" somehow doesn't do justice to the depths of my gratitude. But thank you.

Dwight Friesen. You have been both a professor and a colleague to me, and I'm grateful for our teamwork in and out of the classroom. You've helped me become a far better educator and thinker because of our time together.

Jess. What can I say about the love of my life? Your support and encouragement amazes me each day. Thank you for being an important "teammate" during the uncertainties of this season. I love you more than you'll ever know.

Introduction

by
Thomas R. Ryan & Ron A. Carucci

Does the world *really* need another book on leadership?

And worse than that, another *Christian* book on leadership?

The last thirty years have proliferated a veritable cottage industry on leadership development, with thousands of texts touting secrets, steps, habits, laws, principles, and other formulas promising an almost instantaneous boost to one's leadership skills. For Christians the choices are even more vast, with a litany of texts touting the biblical way to lead, or the Christ-centered way to lead, or the most "spiritual" way to lead.

If we're honest, most of us who've read any of them would concede that too many of them are useless. The promises they make of catapulting one's leadership can never be kept, and their easy-to-follow recipes prove hollow and delusional, separated from the real world by galaxies.

Still, the need to prepare tomorrow's leaders has only grown more acute, with today's leaders wringing their hands in frustration and anxiety over just how to reach a generation of women and men who are more different than they care to admit. The media is dominated with public leadership failures, leaving tomorrow's leaders that much more jaded when considering leadership opportunities. And worse, their voices continue to grow more faint as they lose hope for being able to follow the dreams they were told to follow, the calling they were told God gave them, and to make the difference they were told they could, and would, make.

So, yes, frankly, we believed the world needed *this* book. At the conclusion of the book, we hope you will conclude similarly. But that will ultimately be your decision.

As men who hail from different generations, we bring a combined set of convictions about why we believe in the importance of tomorrow's voices. We have taught leadership at the graduate school level together for four years and have learned much along the way about the emerging generation of leaders entering the world. For this text, we will simply serve as your hosts for the real authors of this book. But we each have had formative experiences that have prepared us to blend our voices as a combined "John the Baptist" of this book—announcing the arrival of tomorrow's leaders to you, and hoping to prepare you for their entrance into your world.

Tom's Story

Several years ago I was a student at a moderately sized, Christian liberal arts college in the Midwest, majoring in political science but earnestly attempting to work out the meaning of my faith in the world at large. I was heavily involved in student life during my time there, having been regularly identified by various staff and faculty members on campus as a "leader." It was the first time in my life that label had been explicitly attached to me, and I remember thinking that it felt odd. What do you mean I'm a "leader"? What exactly is a "leader"? I couldn't tell you what a leader was, and I was quite sure that I lacked whatever it required. But the importance of developing students on campus as "leaders" was becoming a major emphasis for those staff and faculty I respected and admired, and they made sure I was aware that I had leadership gifts, which I needed to cultivate.

As I moved into my latter years on campus my leadership positions became more visible, and yet I was still left mostly in the dark about what good leadership required. For all the talk on campus of "the world" desiring quality leadership from college graduates, the lack of any definition left me mostly confused.

Apparently I simply had "it" and no one could tell me what "it" was.

Shortly after graduating, I was hired by a multi-national insurance and financial company. It wasn't glamorous work but it was a stable career with a stable income and allowed me the chance to garner some real-world experience. It was also, given the rhetoric of my previous four years, a chance to demonstrate to the world that I had the leadership skills they desired. I looked forward to not only leading, but learning from my managers and supervisors about the specific skills needed to lead in a corporate context. Though I couldn't articulate it then, I was hopeful that I would be shown quality corporate leadership to integrate with those loosely defined skills I had learned in college.

It didn't take me long to realize that to be a leader and to be *in leadership* are two entirely different things. Some of the people who had formal leadership positions really had no business leading a team in the first place, and I once again was forced to wonder what it took to be a good leader. The meetings they ran were chaotic, their voices carried little weight in the room, and they garnered little respect from their peers. It took some time for the sobering reality of the situation to hit me, and for the third time I was faced with the question, "What does it mean to lead well?"

I have worked in a variety of corporate and ecclesial contexts in the years since graduating college, and I've continued to wonder about the attributes of admirable leaders. The book you hold in your hands grows, in part, from those evasive answers about good leadership. It's likely you have had your own experiences when you've been led well and times when you've felt like the leader was simply unqualified. But the disconnect I have felt between a leader's position and actual leadership gifts is a very real tension, particularly for this emerging generation of leaders. They feel something of the same gap that I saw and carry profound baggage from leaders who've demanded a top-down, military-directive style of leadership. What once passed as a given or "best practice" in leadership is being called into question, and a younger, emerging generation of leaders is asking (and demanding) something different.

As Bob Dylan sang, the times they are a changin', and our philosophies of leadership are no exception.

Ron's Story

I have spent my career consulting organizations of all kinds on the topic of leadership. I have led organizations and written about leadership to a great extent. The more I have led, the more I consult and write, the less I feel I know. Several years ago I wrote a book entitled *Leadership Divided: What Emerging Leaders Need and What You Might Be Missing* (San Francisco: Jossey-Bass 2006). It was born from several years of research on the impact relationships between leaders have on the performance of their organizations and communities. The book focuses primarily on the extensive differences between generations, and the strain those differences have on the ability to form meaningful relationships. My hope was to draw riveting attention to this gap, encouraging incumbent leaders to better understand emerging leaders, and vice versa, helping them see one another in a different light, and ultimately, to facilitate stronger more vibrant relationships between them.

I was not prepared for the impact of this unfolding conversation about tomorrow's leaders, mostly on me. Since the book's launch, my convictions for the importance of effectively preparing tomorrow's leaders have multiplied exponentially. Of this I am sure—this generation has been uniquely prepared by God to bring about his kingdom in ways we have never seen. And in order for them to take on this daunting mantle—one they are eager and passionate to don—they will need help, support, and preparation that they are, for the most part, not getting. And if they don't get it, the transformative work they have been called to do will be risked.

If this happens, the consequences would be catastrophic. For the church, the Christian faith, the world.

So when the opportunity to create this book arose (you'll hear the specifics of that story below), I was compelled. Because it isn't going to be my voice conveying to you the crucial importance of what tomorrow's leaders are yearning for. It will be theirs.

You will hear directly from passionate, gifted, anxious, cynical, and hopeful emerging leaders. And I feel enormously privileged to be part of facilitating their introduction to you. I had the good fortune to work with these young leaders on the journey of their graduate studies, and frankly I learned more from them than I ever offered them. If you let them, they will rend your hearts as they did mine. They will open your eyes and mind as they opened mine. And they will instruct you ever so tenderly, yet firmly, on just how you can best help them realize their fullest potential, thus ensuring your legacy. Outside their potential, your legacy is nothing. Fueled by their potential, your legacy is eternal.

So prepare yourselves well, fellow inquirers of leadership. The experience you're about to have with this book can transform your life, and the world in which you lead, beyond your imagination. You get to decide if it will.

Your Story

Now that you've heard our stories, you need to think about yours. For this material to penetrate your mind, heart, and soul the way we believe it has the potential to, it's important to understand the assumptions and expectations you bring to your leadership endeavors. To whom do you look for leadership inspiration? How would you characterize the disciplines, philosophies, or values of those leaders you most admire? And as you look toward cultivating this next generation of leaders, who are you looking for? Your ability to accurately assess and articulate some of your assumptions will make your reading of this text immensely more enjoyable and effective. And it will, we believe, honor our deepest hopes that you earnestly converse with the voices in the text.

You have had numerous formative experiences that have shaped the way you lead. Some were epic and unforgettable moments. Others came and went without being noticed as formative until years later. The mosaic of your own leadership story will get both strengthened and deconstructed in light of the essays in this book. They will both affirm and unnerve you.

So pay attention to yourself and your reactions as you read—
we encourage you to write in the margins how you're responding
to each of these essays. These stories will likely provoke much in
you, whether anger, pride, frustration, happiness, defensiveness,
pity, or confusion. How you are responding to these essays will
reveal much about the ways *you* view leadership and, ultimately,
how well you are listening. Don't waste time defending leadership
principles you have long held dear. Don't spend an ounce of time
refuting points with which you disagree. And don't be lured into
undue guilt for harm you may come to realize you have unknowingly caused. To succumb to any such reactions completely misses
the point of the text. For they are reactions that close your heart
and mind. Instead, cheer when your leadership principles can
be strengthened through expanded perspective and interpretation. Be curious when passionately expressed convictions seem
in tension with some of your own. Grow in compassion with the
heart breaking stories of abused power and arrogance that have left
some of these young leaders despaired. And as you learn, resolve
that you will do whatever you can to come along side them and fill
their sails with gusts of hope. To be sure, the burden of this text's
efficacy lies squarely on your shoulders.

These essays are not the final, authoritative say on this generation of leaders, but we do believe they are strongly representative
of the emerging voices of tomorrow's leaders. They articulate some
important experiences that are worth hearing, and proffer some
hopeful and brilliant solutions for more honoring, effective leadership in the future.

The Story of This Story

Like most everything you read, these essays and this book
grow out of a specific context. In order for you to more fully
comprehend some of the language, vocabulary, and specific
phrases used in the following essays, there are a few things we'd
like to bring to your awareness.

The essays that follow are the result of a three-day intensive
leadership course offered at Mars Hill Graduate School (MHGS).
Located in downtown Seattle, WA, Mars Hill Graduate School's

raison d'etré is to train men and women to be competent and insightful readers of the biblical text, the human soul, and the broader culture, in order that we might more fully experience God through transforming relationships. MHGS offers three distinct Master's degree programs in Counseling Psychology, Divinity, and Christian Studies, and is committed to a holistic vision of education which sees one's spiritual formation as intimately tied to their academic growth. Therefore students in each degree program are invited to spend significant time wrestling with not only the course material, but to pay attention to the ways their minds, bodies, and spirits are being formed by the material they study. It is a dynamic education process, one which develops graduates who are deep thinkers, compassionate and insightful listeners, and people who demonstrate relational depth and character.

In the Spring of 2008—amidst dreary, overcast Seattle skies—forty students, representing all three degree tracks, gathered together for the first in a series of three courses in our Leadership curriculum. Our primary focus for the course was on making them more aware of the strengths and liabilities they bring to leadership (Leadership 1). In subsequent semesters they would continue their work by examining their proclivities and behaviors while working with teams (Leadership 2), and learning how to facilitate broad systemic change in organizations (Leadership 3). Since this first course asked them to wrestle with their own particularities as leaders, many of the discussions and much of the content focused on their previous experiences or conceptions of leadership and both the problems and promises of those experiences. The format was highly interactive and provided a great deal of space for self-assessment and reflecting. We spent three days together wrestling through the harm of their leadership experiences and wondering about ways to lead that would embody a more compassionate, holistic approach and that would honor the cacophony of voices in the room.

Prior to the course beginning we asked students to submit a one- to two-page essay chronicling their experience in leadership, and to keep a journal about a particular leader of their choice for one month. The hope in this pre-class assignment was twofold: first, we wanted to hone their attention on what they value in leaders and what shapes their expectations of those leaders. Secondly, as teachers we make a concerted effort to tailor our course around some of the specific leadership questions and concerns in the room. For a generation of leaders who feels largely neglected and overlooked because they value different things from their leaders, it was crucial to us that they hear the weight of their own experiences and be forced to wrestle with them with integrity.

During the week leading up to class, we communicated often with each other about our impressions from the course essays, and we were overwhelmed with the amount of cynicism, betrayal, and contempt our students had both received and dealt as leaders. We had a hunch that our group was suspicious of anything having to do with leadership, but the realities of our students' stories and words were dark and heavy.

In response we felt that the final course assignment needed to be different than most. Rather than asking our students to simply recap their learning through a paper or recite how they had been influenced by the material, we felt that it was crucial to their development to make their stories count in a way that they hadn't before. So we asked them to write "Leadership Stories from the Future," essays that are both reflections of where they've been as leaders and earnest hopes for change in how leadership is done. Our hope was to get them thinking generatively and positively toward a future of leadership to which they could truly and passionately give their lives, and one which kept them from sinking into an abyss of leadership disillusionment.

When we told them of our intent to publish their essays, some began to cry in disbelief that their voice could actually matter that much. As you will see, the results are nothing short of stunning, and we sincerely hope that you allow each of the students' stories to shape both the ways you lead and the ways you'll interact with an entirely different generation of leaders.

The Language

In the essays, you will hear students sometimes refer to specific content from the course. We asked students to engage a variety of methods and tools to assist their reflection, including several tests aimed at making them more aware of their assumptions and behaviors in leadership, and invited them to earnestly wrestle with their results in their essays. We also relied on three texts for the course along with a scattering of biblical texts to guide our time. The tests and the books are referred to by shortened names throughout the essays, so here is some brief background into their uses.

DiSC Classic Personal Profile System by the *Center for Internal Change Inc.* (Minneapolis: Inscape Publishing, 2001). The DiSC is a personality profile test that examines behavioral proclivities and patterns for certain environments and, based on the results, determines which environments are most beneficial for success. The test assigns participants a letter (*D, I, S,* or *C*) based on their responses, and each letter corresponds with a general pattern of behavior. To be assigned a *D*, for example, means that a person's primary emphasis is "on shaping the environment by overcoming opposition to accomplish results." People who fall in this category tend toward a more dominant, action-oriented style of leadership that demands immediate results. Those in the *S* category, for example, will emphasize leadership that "cooperates with others within existing circumstances to carry out the task." Those who score an *S* often possess a very different demeanor than those with a *D* and will typically demonstrate more patience while "creating a stable, harmonious work environment."

It is important to note that no letter's behavioral interpretation is better than another. It isn't, for example, better to be a *D* rather than an *S*. But far more, it is one's responsibility to fully live into the results, wondering about the ways it can be leveraged for the good of one's leadership, while also thoughtfully considering the ways one can do harm with it and working to mitigate those tendencies.

Like many personality tests the DiSC deals in generalities and is most effective when applied to a specific context—like one's office or family system. And as you'll see, our students found their results to be tremendously helpful in their growing understanding of their behavioral and leadership patterns, and they reference their DiSC results often.

Personnel Relations Survey by Jay Hall, Ph.D. and Martha S. Williams, Ph.D. (Waco: Teleometrics International, 2000). If the DiSC is designed to reveal one's behavioral tendencies and their environmental preferences, the Personnel Relations Survey was created to hone in on the particularities of those results. The test seeks to understand the ways one interpersonally relates to their superiors, their subordinates, and their peers by measuring the degrees to which one knows one's self and is known by others. The results are offered through the prism of the Johari Window, which describes our relational tendencies by examining one's "arena," "blindspot," "façade," and "unknown." And the size of each area will vary depending on one's relational context—one may have a larger blindspot with their boss or a larger façade with their peers.

Understanding how well we know ourselves and allow ourselves to be known can say much about what we value in our leaders and in our own leadership. For our students this was an important test that revealed some key ways they operate within leadership. You'll see that many of them refuse to be known by others as much as they would like, making it an important area of growth for them.

Leadership Jazz **by Max DePree** (New York: Dell Publishing, 1992). Leaning on the metaphor of jazz music, Depree invites readers to consider leadership as an improvisational art. To be effective leaders, he argues, one must be connected to one's voice and touch, and continually seek to find creative and innovative solutions. It is a rich text with far more than can be captured here, but it was a crucial text for our course.

Leadership and Self-Deception: Getting Out of the Box **by the Arbinger Institute** (San Francisco: Berrett-Koehler, 2002). Perhaps the book we relied on most, this text, written in a narrative format, traces the development of a disgruntled and temperamental senior manager named Tom. While Tom is ostensibly successful in his career at the fictional Zagrum Company, he has been asked by Bud and Kate (two long-time leaders of the company and veritable institutions at Zagrum) to spend a day with them. What transpires is a discovery into how, despite Tom's best intentions, his work, family, and peers are suffering under the weight of his leadership.

The text introduces two important concepts: self-deception and out-of-the-box thinking. Self-deception occurs when we see matters from only our perspective, when we close ourselves off to any realities outside of our own. This leads us into self-betrayal when we willingly betray our best intentions by consistently pointing to the other as the cause of the problem.

Conversely, to work and exist "out of the box" is, contrary to popular wisdom, something of an antidote. It requires that we see the other person as a person, not as the source of the problem, and work to see a variety of viewpoints and realities at play in any given situation.

Leading with a Limp by **Dan Allender** (Colorado Springs: WaterBrook Press, 2006). Written by Allender after close to a year of leadership research, this book explores how we can learn to lead from our places of individual weaknesses. Much thinking about leadership implicitly demands a demonstrated perfection no real person can achieve, and Allender calls us to embrace those weaknesses we are constantly at work to cover. Most leaders suffer from feeling beat-up, abused, and lonely, and the only real response for each of us, Allender says, is to flee. He offers some helpful paradigms for what often provokes our feelings of inadequacy in leadership — betrayal, crisis, complexity, and others. Allender goes on to offer some wise reactions to these feelings, which allow leaders to both embrace them for what they are and move to a place where they aren't undone by the weight of the emotion. By meeting betrayal with gratitude, for example, we can begin to move past the enormous betrayals in our midst and live more fully into the grace of God.

The Stories Ahead

You hold in your hands a sacred book. We don't mean "sacred" in the sense that it is imbued with any special truths otherwise inaccessible to you outside of scripture. But rather, this is a sacred text because the stories it contains are sacred. What awaits you in the following pages are stories of loss, heartache, untold sorrow, and untold joy from young, wounded leaders. They are people for whom leadership has lost some of its once-inspirational appeal, for whom leadership no longer holds the power, prestige, and privilege it once did. They've been disabused of those notions partially out of experience, but also because they are eager to find a different way forward—a way that honors both who they are as people and who *we* are as a community working together toward a common purpose.

Leadership has often been defined, though not always intentionally, as a highly individualistic endeavor centered around one person, with an occasional hat-tip toward their followers. The stories that are told in the following pages have experienced this leadership-as-solo-act approach—they have even tried to emulate it to the best of their abilities—and have found it wanting. Instead they are working to imagine a new way forward, a more relational way of leading that leans on the expertise and voices around them, a vision for leadership that values each voice in the room, where they become curators of a conversation rather than the dictator of a particular view.

We don't offer these voices to you lightly. We hope you'll read them with the seriousness and honor they deserve. They are strong. They are powerful. They are sometimes harsh, perhaps even shrill. They are still forming. Sometimes less precisely articulate than you might prefer. And they are brilliant. They are a gift directly from heaven if you allow them to be. And so, as we have asked you above to honor your own story in how you read this material, so too are we asking you to honor theirs in how you read them.

As you venture forth into the wilderness of these emerging leaders' stories, we hope you do so with an open mind and heart, a willingness to learn, and most importantly a willingness to reflect on and transform your own leadership. Where have you sympathized with them? Where have you been the object of their frustration? And where can you advocate for this generation, challenging them to push beyond their scorn for leadership and laboring with them to facilitate change?

Let the Stories Begin

The essays you're about to read have been written by good, good people. They are men and women passionate about seeing the Kingdom of God reign on earth through justice and righteousness, and despite their hesitations about leadership, are daring and bold enough to still try, and try again. While you may not meet these students specifically in your life and work, we promise that you will meet young leaders like them. Take their stories, and your responsibility to further shape them, seriously. Be insatiably curious about their questions and commitments, and wonder deeply about the ways you can step into their stories and support who it is they hope to become.

A decade from now, you will tell the story of your own leadership, and the legacy you have left behind. It will undoubtedly include the mark you've left on those who came after you.

It is our fervent prayer this book will profoundly inform the trajectory of that story.

With our deepest regard for your courage to read on,
Tom & Ron

Seattle, WA
June 2009

Chapter 1

Stories of Inquiry:
Redefining Leadership

*I tell you the truth, if you have faith as small as a mustard
seed, you can say to this mountain, 'Move from here to
there' and it will move. Nothing will be impossible for you.*
—Matthew 17:20

If tomorrow's leaders have made nothing else clear about themselves, it is that they are insatiably curious. Having grown tired,
perhaps even cynical, at the model of "leader as answer giver,"
they are far more receptive to deeper questions than time-tested
answers. The timeless question of "what is leadership" forms
the foundation of this opening chapter. These four young leaders
search earnestly for a redefined leadership that fits the vast expanse
of how they hope to lead, and the voice they hope to discover in
that leadership. You will see the disdain for traditional hierarchical models of leadership that have so long troubled emerging
leaders. You will see the wrestling of contrasting views on leadership with little need to land on one model or another. You will see
vulnerable expressions of discovery that leadership is a difficult,
even isolating endeavor. You will read of the formative moments
that shaped leadership in these leaders long before they had the
remotest inkling of their pension to lead. You will see a far greater
comfort with paradox than has traditionally been the case in main-

stream views of leadership. These leaders can hold the brutal realities of human failure and still ask the question, "In what can I hope?" As has been the case with past generations of leaders, they have no need to draw black-and-white contrasts, draw the line, and close the conversation. And finally, you will see keenly into where these young leaders are placing their hope for leadership in the future, into which they are stepping.

As you read, we encourage you to test your own hypotheses of leadership against the unfolding leadership landscape these leaders suggest as a possibility. It is a reimagined leadership that is far more relational, inclusive, ambiguous, and curious. It may depart radically from the foundational principles of leadership you have held, and it may, in fact, liberate aspirations you've kept protected from the harsh realities of today's leadership that might too quickly reject them.

To be sure, your leadership assumptions will be tested in some way as you read. When you feel that pinch, what will you do? It is likely you will feel tempted to rigorously defend the articles of leadership to which you have loyally adhered, even biblically justified. Watch carefully that you don't dismiss too quickly views that could transform yours, bringing you closer to the gospel and closer to a more profound capacity to transform others.

Daniel, a student whose story you will soon read, puts it quite well when he says, "The end goal of [tomorrow's] leaders isn't an end goal at all. They are concerned with relationships in process, and they see their influence and the structures in which they lead as tools by which they can engage in relationships. For leaders who dare to enter crisis with humility and openness, there is hope for redemption . . . it is with great hope that we look to the future of leadership, believing that pain and crisis can be met with humility and openness that bring life and draw us into realizing our full humanity in relationship with God and others."

May your own definitions of leadership undergo significant reformulation as you read and ponder the inquiries of these leadership stories from tomorrow.

Carl

In hopes of a more profitable dialogue, I would like to first delineate two presuppositions that I bring to this discussion on leadership. The first is that I do not believe leadership to be a distinct quality or learned skill. I believe it to be an ever-changing aspect of personality present in all people. The so-called leadership qualities of a given person are a combination of that person's giftedness, experience, passion, and vision, as well as her woundedness and limitations. Secondly, my understanding of leadership will continually evolve and change. While the words on these pages are my current thoughts on this topic, it is doubtful that I will have the same ideas in six months or five years.

What does it mean to lead in today's world? To be sure, much ink has been expended in the answering of this question. My challenges in approaching this topic are threefold: 1) Defining leadership in a meaningful way, 2) Discerning the considerable distortions Western culture lends to the discussion of leadership, and 3) Understanding how scripture might inform leadership in present-day contexts. movement / voice / risk

In approaching the challenge of definition, my first move will be to surrender. Though this may seem a curious choice, I will take instruction from the philosopher Jacques Derrida and admit that the limitations of language and its inherent distortions prevent definitive descriptions of *any* concept, leadership included.[1] Therefore, in this preamble, I will consider a conversation about what leadership might be. If one is to look online under the entry *lead* in Oxford's American Dictionary and Thesaurus, the following words will be found: guide, conduct, show, usher, steer, escort, pilot, shepherd, accompany, cause, induce, prompt, move, persuade, influence, promote, provoke, stir up, arouse, instigate, effect, create, and produce. Clearly, the concept of leadership is multifaceted, and yet as I read this list, three ideas (words, themes, energies?) come to mind. They are *movement, voice,* and *risk.* I will return to expand on these three shortly.

The second major challenge I face in this conversation is my embeddedness in this individualistic, male-dominated, consumeristic, media/corporate/government/military-driven culture. Five years ago, if I were to confess my list of great leaders across history, names like Alexander the Great, Caesar, Napoleon, Washington, Lincoln, Roosevelt, Patton, Eisenhower, Reagan, and Iacocca would have been present, to name a few. And while I hesitate to disqualify any of these men as leaders, I cannot help but notice the themes of power, fame, strength, and gender. True, I do not represent Western culture, but I am certainly a product of it, and I would be surprised if these men did not show up on many leadership lists made by Americans. How, then, can I "tease out" these distortions from what I find to be a truer sense of leadership?

To that end, I will turn to the third challenge in my discussion of leadership. If it is true (and I believe it is) that leadership has been greatly distorted by Western culture, where might I turn to find wisdom and direction in this task? I believe that the Old and New Testaments, appropriately contextualized, can shed considerable light on this topic. Sadly, however, these texts have often been misused and distorted themselves in the service of those (often Western men) who wish to control others by power. Therefore, I write with great humility and an awareness of the harm already done, as well as the perceived irrelevance and/or danger many believe to be contained in the scriptures. Nonetheless, I will attempt to discern and communicate how these same texts might inform a redemptive dialogue on leadership.

Voice

If it is true that leadership has much to do with *influence* (a word derived from the Latin *into; to flow*), then what exactly is *flowing* from a leader, and why would that be good? I concur with the author of Genesis, who describes God's reflection on the creation of people as "very good."[2] Additionally, the Psalmist writes that people are "fearfully and wonderfully made."[3] These descriptions are important because the voice that I bring to leadership can be good only because I have been created in the image of God. Here, theologian Jurgen Moltmann is instructive in his elaboration of *imago Dei*. He writes, "As his image, human beings represent God on earth; as his similitude, they reflect him . . . To be an image of something always means letting that something appear, and revealing it."[4] My position is one that supports this concept of *imago Dei,* the belief that it is truly the goodness of God reflected in all human beings, and that this goodness is expressed uniquely in each individual person.

Because of the effects of sin on creation, our unique voices are a mixture of glory and depravity. How, then (if at all?) can we discern the beauty and goodness in our own voices, while embracing our brokenness with care? David Benner writes of the importance of self-examination by what he calls *transformational knowledge.* He writes, "Truly transformational knowledge is always personal, never merely objective. It involves *knowing of,* not merely *knowing about.*"[5] This *knowing of* can occur only in the context of honest, vulnerable relationship in which feedback is actively sought and welcomed. Through this process of self-examination, our deepest passions and desires can be identified (though not separated) within the matrix of our disappointments and darkness. There we can begin to find the unique words of hope and courage we have to speak to the other.

Movement

Nothing happens without movement. The word *lead* itself is a verb, implying that leaders must fundamentally be movers. This does not simply mean motion but implies deliberate action. One of the primary functions of a leader is to help others to move from their current location to a better one. Obviously, this means more than just physical location, but includes attitudes, beliefs, goals, vocations, and relationships, just to name a few. How then might movement be an important aspect of leadership?

It has been said that "you can only take a person as far as you have gone yourself."[6] The implication is that as a leader, I must be the first one to read the book, see the therapist, organize the protest, take the class, admit my failure, or initiate the difficult conversation. It is this instigation of movement that not only enables my growth but also serves as a model and an encouragement for others to grow.

An additional barrier to movement in my life has been the fear of failure. A critical aspect of movement in leadership is that of normalizing failure and seeing it as critical to growth. Michael Jordan, agreed by many to be the greatest basketball player of our time, missed over nine thousand shots during his career and failed to make game winning shots twenty-six times. In reference to those statistics, he remarked, "I've failed over and over again in my life, and that is why I succeed."[7] All great leaders embrace their inevitable failures as essential to growth.

Risk

Closely tied to the notion of movement is the reality that movement involves risk. Why is it that leaders must be the first to do those difficult things mentioned above? If there were no risk involved, wouldn't everyone just do them? It is the willingness to risk that allows the leader to move into places of instability, unfamiliarity, and chaos that few are willing to go. When we move into the unknown, we risk embarrassment, disappointment, pain, and failure. Most importantly, we will always struggle with the shame that accompanies all of these. Although a great deal of healing can take place in regard to our shame, ultimately we are faced with the issue of trusting that our risks are worthwhile in the face of this shame. The opposite side of this risk involves faith. All effective leaders must have some level of faith to be able to move into the unknown. This union of risk and faith often demands that leaders will be led to action considered unusual, or even bizarre, by some. Here Søren Kierkegaard offers helpful guidance. He writes, "For the movement of faith must be made continually on the strength of the absurd."[8] Is leadership a risk? It is more. Is it faith? Yes, and more. Is it vision? Of course, and much more.

It is true that failure will come to those leaders who move and risk. But this failure is indispensable to the wise leader. Not only will they learn from their mistakes, but they will have the opportunity to grow in humility and compassion. While at first blush these may seem to be extraneous qualities for a leader, such is not the case. Writing for the Harvard Business Review, author Jim Collins cites personal humility as one of two distinguishing characteristics for outstanding leaders.[9] My addendum would be that it is a desirable characteristic for all people.

Cultural Distortions

While it is impossible to remove myself from the context of Western culture, I believe it is essential to have an awareness of what I consider to be distortions of true leadership. In a culture that is informed more by reality television and *Cosmopolitan* magazine than classic literature and art, the definition of leadership seems to have devolved into something much different than what I believe it could be. Therefore, I will instead use the term *false-leadership* to signify the modern day aberration it has become. False-leaders lead by power and manipulation, and often get their power due to charisma or physical attractiveness.[10] Fueled by the media and our "cult of personality," those attracted to false-leadership are often motivated more by narcissism and insecurity than by vision and mission. This awareness is critical in that it gives the wise leader the knowledge that good leadership in Western culture may not resemble our popular notions of the title.

Here again, scriptural texts are helpful. The paradoxical message of grace informs the reader that real power resides in weakness.[11] The departure here from cultural norms is drastic, but good leaders *must not be bound by cultural norms*. It is no exaggeration to say that sometimes good leadership will involve quitting a job, leaving a church, or working fewer hours in the service of self-care. These types of actions are not often considered the actions of a leader in twenty-first-century America, and yet if leaders limit themselves to cultural expectations, they have already lost the battle.

Much remains to be said in this conversation. Issues such as consensus leadership, the role of community, and ecclesial structure in relation to leadership require further exploration and discussion. To be sure, leadership is a complex domain, and any redemptive dialogue about it will require openness, curiosity, and a critical assessment of current cultural norms.

Daniel

As we lean into the future of what Christian leadership will look like, one thing is certain: a tide has turned—though the question of where it is going has yet to be decided. What face will leadership take among those who simultaneously reject the objectivist underpinnings of the modern project while constructing their lives on (and delivering their messages through) the technological and cultural fruit of the very system we claim to reject? To say we are postmodern is to define ourselves against that which we see as an inadequate system for understanding and organizing life and truth. We must move beyond the project of naming against and turn to naming what it is that we are for. We look at the world handed to this younger generation with the hope that things can be changed. We see the future of leadership as the work of an orchestra, to take old instruments, notes, and themes, and play a new song. Our inspiration is theological, relational, communal, and built on believing the impossible. This is our song.

In talking to young people who demonstrate the capacity to lead in this changing context, certain themes become apparent. One such theme is the near universality of having been harmed by someone in leadership. This is the generation that came of age amidst a barrage of corporate, pastoral, political, and ecological crises. More than the high-profile fallouts, everyday leaders, from the workplace to local congregations, have been doing what we all do best—letting people down. It is this factor that may be the single greatest catalyst for a hopeful new vision of leadership. The failure of leaders has birthed in many young people a wariness of leading. We have been wounded, and we would rather not step into roles where we know we may harm others. This mentality has led to two revolutions: one theological and one structural.

The theological revolution begins with our understanding of the leader as self in relationship with God and community. Leading is less about building a legacy and more about journeying together for the purpose of transformation. In my personal experience of leadership among Christians, I have been deeply harmed when leaders' personal goals have been presented in terms of the will of God. Too frequently, in Christian leadership, the power that a leader holds over those being led is misrepresented as spiritual authority. Among those who have been the victims of abusive leaders who have led in God's name, there is a deep reconsideration of what spiritual authority means.

We are turning toward the gospels for a picture of leadership and spiritual authority from which we can model our own ways of influencing others in relationships. It is in the gospels that we find accounts of the incarnation of God among humanity. God clearly has greater power, more insight, and better motives than humans, and we find God leading us into relationship through the incarnation of Jesus Christ. God not only becomes one of us, but as Paul describes it, Jesus "did not consider equality with God something to be grasped, but made himself nothing, taking the very nature of a servant, being made in human likeness. And being found in appearance as a man, he humbled himself and became obedient to death—even death on a cross!"[1] Jesus did not grasp for the power that he already held as God. Instead, he lowered himself as a servant—this is the theological model for dealing with power upon which this future leadership will be built. The future leaders do not distinguish a difference between servanthood and leadership, and it is this lack of distinction that is beginning to reconfigure the relational and organizational structures in which these new leaders will serve.

The structural revolution is built on this theology of living with and for others. It is a way of realizing a true sense of self only through the pouring out of self on behalf of the other. While this theology may not always be clearly articulated in organizations, it has been realized in many new expressions of church, organizations, and networks that are leading the charge of creating change in our culture. The incomprehensibility of the structural revolution, to older generations of leaders, is that on the surface there appears to be no structure. The truth of the matter is that younger leaders believe that hierarchical and even team approaches to leadership have been undermined by their frequent inability to hold difference well, respect all members of a community, and deal with power following the self-emptying model of Christ. Perhaps one of the most easily cited examples of the failure of this model is in the pyramid scheme businesses that flourished around the childhood and adolescence of many young leaders. Seeing structures where the people on top profit from the people who are getting things done has caused this generation of leaders to turn toward new ways of conceptualizing organizations with ethical concerns of equality, justice, and sustainability.

In order to understand these new structures we must familiarize ourselves with a new vocabulary for understanding the concept of structure itself. Instead of envisioning a building with supports, joists, walls, and floors, we may need to open ourselves to different possibilities. An example of a different kind of structure that is capable of fulfilling many of the same needs as that of a traditional building is a tent. Tents can vary in size, be subdivided, and give shelter. Tents differ from buildings in several key ways as well. If you are looking to have a corner office on the seventeenth floor, a tent is probably not the structure for you. Neither is a tent suitable for maintaining confidentiality—thus making a tent an ideal structure for those who value transparency. If the members of an organization abide in and constitute the structure of the organization, it becomes clear that in both models—building and tent—there are roles to be played. A building needs a foundation, walls, and a roof. A tent needs stakes, poles, and a canopy. The first is constructed on a value of stability, endurance, and definition whereas the second assumes desired adaptability, motion, and malleability. It is not that younger leaders are abandoning buildings altogether. Instead, younger leaders are learning that in a culture of change, survival and health in relationships and organizations depend on a leaders' ability to adapt rapidly to implement a variety of structures.

There are other structural metaphors for understanding this revolution. Many are borrowed from nature and technology. Indeed, many of the most recent technological innovations have been modeled on organic systems that exist in the natural world. One conception that has recently been successful is decentralization. This method has been used with great success in online data storage. Another manifestation of this is the decentralization of the power grid. It is not coincidental that the advent of moving from centralized carbon-based power sources to decentralized sustainable energy has coincided with the structural revolution. Both are motivated out of similar concerns. Coal, nuclear, and large-scale hydro-electric power solutions will not keep up with the future demands for electricity, moreover, they pose serious ethical dilemmas by their very structure. For this reason many consumers are taking matters into their own hands by either going off the grid or selling green power back to the grid. In the same way younger leaders are reading the signs of the times. We see that the old structures can no longer provide for the needs of people in our societies. We also recognize that there are certain inequalities and practices built into this old system that violate their ethics and theology. Some are opting out while others are attempting to live out our theology and ethics in a way that infuses the old structures with the life and possibility to slowly change directions.

The arena in which these two elements—servanthood and adaptability—come most into play for leaders is when they are confronted with crisis. The character of a leader and their ability to lead well without harming others in an attempt to maintain control are revealed in the crucible of crisis. There is often a question in the back of leaders' minds that sounds something like, "How will I respond if a crisis occurs?" This question does little to prepare a leader for the actual situations of crisis that are certain to occur. Truly, it is the leader who shapes how a crisis will impact relationships and organizations. By regularly making choices to step outside themselves and broaden their window of openness to others through self-disclosure and welcoming feedback, leaders can learn the dexterity and humility necessary to confront crisis with grace.

A helpful way to consider how future leaders will understand crisis is to look at the short stories of Flannery O'Connor. In her stories O'Connor is infamous for bringing her frequently grotesque southern characters to uncouth moments of redemption. In one of her most noted stories, "A Good Man is Hard to Find," O'Connor drives two nameless characters, who serve as mirrors in which we see ourselves, toward a moment of crisis. In the story, the grandmother encounters an escaped criminal known as the misfit. At the moment of crisis, the misfit is about to kill the grandmother.

At that instance the grandmother, who has been largely self-consumed, reaches outside of herself and sees the misfit as human. When faced with crisis she allows it to call her to a place of being fully human and in her response she is able to humanize the other. This does not prevent her from being killed, but it allows her in her death to truly live. She does this by reaching out to touch the stranger and speak to him as one of her own children. In doing this she invites the stranger to something new and creates a moment of crisis for him. She is calling him to a new and different way of relinquishing power and becoming human—unfortunately, his response is to shut down the possibility for life by shooting the one who brought about his opportunity for redemption.[2]

This is the same challenge faced by each leader. When crisis arises a leader may respond defensively, often bringing pain and destruction, or they can choose to open up to the possibility of change and new life. As leaders we have the opportunity to view each crisis as a sort of Flannery O'Connor moment where crisis truly offers us a choice between life and death. Success for future leaders will be defined by stepping boldly and humbly into crisis by seeking to serve the other by adapting both systems and relationships for the sake of stepping into moments of reciprocal transformation.

This brings us to a final description of how these future leaders will serve. The end goal for these leaders is not an end goal at all. They are concerned with relationships in process, and they see their influence and the structures in which they lead as tools by which they can engage in relationships. For leaders who dare to enter crisis with humility and openness, there is hope for redemption. When structures reflect the values of servanthood and adaptability, the winds of crisis provide leaders with moments for repentance and transformation instead of death. It is with great hope that we look to the future of leadership, believing that pain and crisis can be met with humility and openness that bring life and draw us into realizing our full humanity in relationship with God and others.

Joshua

Being twelve years old is terrible and awesome in the same moment. When you are twelve you get to play all the time. Everyone loves to play. When you are twelve you go through puberty. *Puberty.* I know. You can feel your voice crackling or your hips growing right now. No one in the history of the known world has enjoyed puberty, and when you are twelve you don't really know exactly what puberty is, but you know you hate it. My love/hate relationship with leadership started right around the time of my hate/hate relationship with puberty.

In my elementary school we had this rule: for every piece of playground equipment (kickballs, tennis balls, et cetera) that got kicked or thrown onto the roof at recess, the student would be charged twenty-five cents. I don't know what the teachers were thinking. Maybe they thought that it was still 1965 when a quarter could buy you a year's worth of life insurance, but a quarter to a sixth grader meant jack. *Ooooohhh a whole quarter? Wow. Thanks for letting me mow your gigantic yard for a quarter, Mrs. Jensen.* So, like any adventurous twelve-year-old boy would, I got all of my friends to kick every kickball, throw every pinky ball, and whip every Frisbee we could find onto the roof. I told everyone, *If we all do it, who will they blame?* Sounded logical to me. It turned out that my teacher decided to blame me. Go figure.

Mr. Wilhite pulled me out to the hall during class to tell me that what I had done was wrong, that I was going to get charged the majority of the cost, and that I was leading other kids down a negative path. *I'm not responsible for the other kids,* I told him.

"But the decisions you make will affect others. You're a leader out there in everything you do," he said.

"I don't want to be a leader," I told him.

"You don't have a choice," he said, with that look that only teachers know how to give, the kind of look that says, *This is an important moment.*

This one moment in my life, standing there outside my classroom with Mr. Wilhite, has had a tremendous impact on my life. For me, there is no divide between my life as a leader and my life

as a spiritual person. My leadership decisions and lack of decisive-
ness are all deeply spiritual. If I truly believe that I am made in the
imago Dei then I must come to a more full understanding that my
spirituality and my leadership decisions cannot be separated.

Past informs the present and leads into the future. That story on
the playground and Mr. Wilhite's words inform how I think about
leadership today. The actions I take today, and the actions I don't
take, lead into who I will be as a leader of others as I get older.
When talking about leadership in the future with my peers, cynicism is by far the drug of choice. You can shoot up anytime you
want, and you don't get those nasty scars on your forearm. Win/
Win. And I admit, I've got my invisible scars on my arm as well.
But when I project into the future of leadership, for me and for the
church, I see hope in a new way of leading. I see the old paradigm,
the top-down, head pastor a.k.a. CEO model, as one that is going
to fade away. And even if it is not going to fade away as a whole,
my hope is that I can lead in a community where, in some way
or another, power can be distributed amongst a team of men and
women who are interested in creating and sustaining communities
that are living on behalf of one another.

I believe that this type of community, a new community, will
need new voices. These voices, men and women who are envisioning a new faith, will need to be working out of the positive and
not the negative. It is so easy to be against—against this movie,
against that book, et cetera, I believe one of the easiest things to
do as a leader is to make your voice heard by being against something. If recognition and fame is what you're after, being *against* is
a great way to be heard. But the future of leadership relies on being
for. What would it be like if faith communities were constantly
creating goodness, pointing out truth, and celebrating those who
are making the world a better place in which to exist?

A certain pastor of a large church wrote a very popular book
a few years back. It was number one on the New York Time Best
Sellers List, and all types of people were buying the book to
learn how to live a better life. Then another pastor, one just miles
north of the first pastor, wrote another book that, essentially, said
why pastor no. 1's book was heresy. Pastor no. 2 had set out to

40

be against from the beginning, and he set that example for his community. The people in pastor no. 2's church are likely of the mindset of pointing fingers at what they consider to be false, as opposed to pointing out what they believe to be true or good or whole.

I think this was a bad leadership decision on the part of pastor no. 2. There are times, admittedly, when I think it is good to point out what is harmful or unjust, but this was a media move to sell a book. I don't want this to be the future of leadership. I don't want to be leading with people who are constantly raising a negative voice. I want to be leading with people who seek to claim truth where they see it. In 1 Corinthians Paul writes to the church and tells them that "all things are yours," no matter who teaches it or where it comes from.[1] If it is true, then it is yours. As a leader, I will point out truth where I see it, claim it, and teach others to do the same.

With these hopes come discouragements as well. In our leadership class we took a number of personality tests to see who we are and how we interact with others. One of the tests we took was the DiSC, which tells the test taker a number of things regarding how they do and do not deal with conflict. I had taken tests like this before, but never this particular one. After I took the test, my results told me, literally, to go back and make sure I hadn't made any errors in computing the totals, because my ending data was not calculable as it stood. *Ah. Great.* At first this was frustrating, and then after a few seconds it was still frustrating. I want to better understand who I am, especially in regards to how I deal and don't deal with conflict. How a leader addresses conflict seems to be one of the most important aspects to be aware of and develop. My test told me that it didn't understand me. When I talked to my professor about this, he helped me understand that a few recent circumstances in my life, all highly stressful, probably played a part in how I took the test, which made sense to me.

And as I've thought about it further, it seems like these sorts of small road blocks, tests not computing or results failing to add up, are regular occurrences in the life of a leader. These will happen. So, to get a more broad scope of leadership, for the same class, I observed a leader in my life for about 40 days and recorded what I saw.

What I noticed in this leader was their overall consistency. While he didn't know I was observing him, taking notes about his decisions and his interactions, what I saw in this leader didn't surprise me. He didn't let the small, incomputable parts of data get to him. He has been leading long enough, it would appear, to see the small bumps in the road and be able to navigate them well without being so affected that he is unable to lead. I can so easily get thrown by the details, especially when I feel attacked. The leader I observed seemed to remain very steady on the outside, and I gained from this.

I do not know what leadership will look like five years, ten years, or even ten days from now, but I believe that I know what I want it to look like. Embracing my call and reluctance to lead, my desires of what I want community to look like, and observing others in their leadership roles will play intricate parts in my development. I do not take them lightly. I have high hopes for who I will be as a leader, and I will pursue those hopes with passion. I don't know any other way to live.

Jon

A two-hour-long leadership team meeting has just ended, and it seems like nothing has been accomplished. Frustrated and tired, I feel useless and like I have no idea what I am doing. I'm only twenty-four years old and in my second year as the youth director at a fifteen hundred-member, mainline, suburban church. The expectations are starting to weigh heavy on my shoulders. Parents want special attention given to their child. Church staff members want to see a growing youth program with more youth and more events. The youth just want someone to listen to them and spend some time with them. In fact, they've all tried the flashy youth groups in town, and they hated them because nobody would spend any time with them. I feel caught in the middle. I strategically announced at the beginning of my time there that I would not make any major changes for a year and that I was committed to being there to see the current freshmen graduate high school. These were not bad moves, but the year had come and gone and changes needed to be made. The only problem was that my youth leaders, students, and parents would not tell me what those changes were.

Maybe this is a typical problem in leadership, but I felt completely alone and isolated in my struggles. It was my first full-time job, I had little practical support from my board or pastor, and I was beginning to drown. I felt like I was doing all the right things, at least according to the books I had read up to that point. Delegation. Empowering leaders. Ownership. Humility. I knew not only irrefutable laws but also the indispensable qualities *and* the seven habits of being a good leader. I was a leader for sure, but only in title and in character. I was a good guy with a good heart. I think I even did a good job appearing as if I knew what I was doing and calm during conflict, but on the inside I was a perfect storm of confusion, doubt, and fear. Eventually, it became too much and my job performance suffered and my desire became little more than a pilot light in my soul.

Stacy stuck around after the meeting, the last one to leave as always. She was a mother of three youth, and had been a volunteer over the past several years under at least six different youth direc-

43

tors. She knew. I am sure she could see it in my face and in my energy level. Yet she was always there to encourage me. She had the perspective of many years. She had seen leaders come and go; some didn't care, some didn't know the first thing about teenagers, and others were just passing through to more important church jobs like associate or senior pastor. I asked her how she thought the meeting went, and politely she expressed that it was good. I could tell that she was frustrated. I knew that she wanted more for her kids and for the entire youth group. She had been through so much with them. I felt like this was her youth group, but she silently wanted me to take it and make it mine. Both of us wanted the other to be the leader, but only one of us should have been. I knew of course that I was the one who needed to take the wheel, but I was content to try and stay in the background and allow the team to come up with a vision and direction; after all, I would leave some day and they would remain. It needed to be their group not mine. I was blind to see their plight and Stacy's frustration. They wanted a leader to give them vision and the tools they would need to bring that vision to reality. I was failing them, and Stacy told me that night. She expressed to me that it was unfair for me to put the burden of leading the youth ministry on her and that it was my job. She didn't have the skills, but that I did. She said I had great ideas, but that I was waiting on something and that *she* was tired of waiting on me.

Stacy's words that night cut deeply. They hurt, but I knew they were said out of love and genuine care. They were also said out of frustration and exhaustion. We both felt the same way and for the same reasons. We were waiting on each other to take the lead. Her words, though I don't remember them verbatim, have haunted me for the past five years and will continue until I am either dead or senile. Some leaders burn out their employees or volunteers

because they give them too much stuff to do that is meaning-less and mundane. I burned out my best leader because I put too much responsibility on her. Responsibility that should have been mine ended up being no one's until it was too late. At that point in my life I was too arrogant (or ignorant) to accept her words and

OK for me to be me —

to bring my voice

change. It wasn't until about eight months later that I began to see more clearly.

It was one of the few days that I woke up excited during the past couple of years. I was going to have lunch with a man whom I had grown to respect as an emerging leader and was secretly hoping he would take me under his wing and pass on his wisdom to help me with my leadership struggles. I think Bob agreed to have lunch with me specifically because I wanted to talk about my leadership struggles for I think he probably had similar ones and was hearing stories of pain from young leaders all over the country. I wanted to know how to lead from the back, or maybe in the middle, because it seemed like he was able to do it that way. He took me to a great Mongolian BBQ place and we sat down and talked for about an hour. He seemed to know not only the staff but also some of the customers, and though he did acknowledge their presence with quick, yet genuine greetings, his full attention was on my story. As our conversation started coming to a close, he could tell that I wanted a way out of leadership. He knew I was scared, and he even agreed I had good reasons, but he told me that his church existed the way it did because his fingerprints were all over it. "I bring myself to everything I do there, Jon," he said in a matter-of-fact tone. "Our community is just as much marked by me as I am by them, if not more." In that moment I knew that it was okay for me to be me, and for me to bring my voice. It was okay for me to leave my mark. But I had a lot of work to do before I would even begin to know how to do that.

In the days before I ever started doing ministry as a vocation I was being trained as a leader. I was being trained at conferences, by best-selling books, and by campus student-life leaders. Leadership, at least the way I heard it, was about being right, saying the right things, developing the right programs, and drawing the biggest crowds. I was also taught about servant leadership and building relationships, but really they only seemed like the means to the ends mentioned previously. To me this seemed disingenuous and even manipulative, yet it seemed like the only option at the time. Bob's words flew in the face of everything that I had been indoctrinated with, yet his words felt so true. I also felt a huge burden lift off my shoulders—the freedom to be myself felt like a shot of Red Bull; it gave me wings.

There was only one problem: I didn't know who I was or how to use my voice. These were questions that I was going to have to wrestle with, but if I was going to get the youth ministry back on track I didn't have the kind of time I knew I would need to engage in this self-reflective project.

After my only lunch with Bob (he never became the mentor I wanted) I attempted to truly lead. I was taking Stacy's words to heart and jumped back on board. But like trying anything new there were a lot of bumps in the road, and ultimately there was too much baggage to save what was left. Three years into the project the church board, with the help of our community antagonist, let me know that my attempt at youth ministry in their church had run its course and effectively it had failed. But for me the journey to discovering my voice and my identity had just started, and it has been the most important path I've taken in my leadership development.

Now, I am in Seattle enrolled in a master of divinity program that focuses on personal transformation. I am also at a local church where I have taken on various leadership roles, some of which I've done well with and others which I've been less than comfortable with. Three years into this process and I am finally beginning to understand who I am and feel more comfortable with my voice and what I bring to the table. I have a long way to go to undo the buttons, straps, and zippers of the layers of leadership that I put on over the years so I can lose the façade and be who I am leading from a posture of knowing myself and using my voice.

I used to take tests like the DiSC and would come out as a *D*, which is dominant. However, I am not a *D*, and I really doubt I ever was, but that is what leadership seemed to be about in those days, so that's what I was. I am truly a *C*, meaning I am a listener, and more subtle than dominant. I like to take my time making decisions, weighing the pros and cons. I value quality, not quantity, and I am a team-oriented person rather than a lone ranger. These qualities at one point in my life were not available categories for leadership. But now I know that I am a leader, and I am in some

46

ways quite the opposite. The difference really is that in my past I was trying to be something I'm not, and now I am becoming more comfortable with who I am, thus allowing instruments and tests to be more of a confirmation of many things I already know as opposed to telling me who I am or should be.

During a board meeting at my previous church we reached a unanimous decision: we would ask a member of the community to join the board as a consultant because of his experience running a nonprofit and for his strengths in developing systems of organization and communication. As the leader of the board I knew that my role would be minimized, but I was excited about moving forward with a new person who seemed to be strong in areas where I was limited and had little experience. I made the initial contact with him, and we met up for lunch at a little Greek restaurant. As I explained to him what the board was asking for, I could see the gears turning in his brain. After I finished giving what I thought was a very comprehensive and well-spoken proposal, he paused for a moment, looked me in the eye, and then began his counteroffer. I was not really prepared for a counteroffer. Our board was asking for his help in continuing to create a healthy faith community of which he was an active participant. It seemed he came prepared with a plan of his own. He began by saying that he needed a title and that he needed full authority from the board to make decisions about policies and structures. He agreed to serve a six-month term and would then leave the position to do other things. There was something in his words that did not feel right to me. His insistence on having a meaningful title and his use of the word *authority* particularly left a sick feeling in my stomach. Obviously, this changed things significantly, and I would need to go back to the board with his proposal.

In this situation my intuitive sense was that something was not right. However, I was locked in on the fantasy that this person could really help our board and our church. Maybe I was even looking to him to be a kind of savior because I seemed to be taking the group only so far. Maybe he was the one to take it the rest of the way. Then came the questions of power and authority. It seems that these are the areas that most concern emerging generations

Power
+
authority

of leaders. We have seen power abused in politics, businesses, family structures, and churches. Why do leaders need to have titles or power? And how exactly is it that one has authority? It seems authority is given to us, not imposed on those around us. My vision and a hope for a new kind of leadership involves setting aside the need for authority and power for it seems that if we are good leaders those will be appropriately placed in our hands. Bob, the leader I mentioned above, has significant authority in his community, so it is not that authority is wrong or that power is inherently bad, but it is about the way in which those elements come to fruition in a community as well as how they are stewarded by the leader who receives them.

After talking with other board members about the counterproposal everyone seemed to be okay with his plan. I was hesitant to express how I really felt, and I just chalked it up to my own issues and struggles with leadership. I chose not to raise the questions that were burning in my heart, and we decided to accept his offer to come on the board. We created a position and title that would give the entire community the impression that he, in fact, was in charge. We gave him the green light to do what he needed to do, and he invested himself heart, body, mind, and soul into his project. He worked tirelessly and made significant progress. The board also invested more time and energy into this six-month project. We overcame some significant difficulties and a couple of crises. But roughly four months into it things started to unravel. Some decisions were made that some people on the board didn't really agree with. Then one person got burned-out. Then another. Then my term came up, and I did not want to stay on for another term, so I eventually got out. At the end of the project, the board was left with half the number of members and no leader. We had become totally dependent on one person.

The point really is not about authority structures. There are probably times when a person needs to be calling the shots and making decisions for the good of a community. The thing that is really interesting to me is that I did not follow my intuition. I do not say this to say that I was right and the other guy was wrong and should have never been allowed to join the board, but I do mean to say that there were other ways to handle the situation that would have been more appropriate. I could have at least asked the questions that were troubling me. I could have brought my voice, and then if the board still wanted to go in that direction, then I would have had a whole set of options available to me, such as stepping down from my position altogether and handing it over to him. Instead, my hesitancy led to my own frustration and burnout, and potentially harmed other board members in similar ways.

Beyond knowing myself and bringing my voice I don't really know what leadership is. I hope to learn skills that will help me as a leader, but if those types of skills exist they are only meant to support who I am as a leader. I cannot attempt to fit into some sort of prefabricated model of leadership, because the organization will suffer and I will surely suffer from damage caused by retrofitting. The old adage is true that a square peg cannot fit into a round hole, but sometimes it seems with leadership the call is to round off the edges, or make the square a little bit smaller, just get the peg inside the hole. I don't want this to be the case, because our edges are beautiful and make us who we are, and I don't want them cut off. So why not create new forms of leadership so that pegs of all shapes and sizes can lead without changing who they are? It is time for creativity and imagination and for new kinds of leadership to be realized.

Know yourself
Bring your voice

Chapter One Questions for Reflection

1) What formative experiences and teachings most influenced your current assumptions and definitions of leadership?

2) What leadership assumptions and definitions did you find being tested as you read this chapter? Which stories did you relate too?

3) How might your own philosophies of leadership change as a result of what you read in this chapter? How might this modify how you lead?

4) Who stands to benefit the most from these modifications?

Chapter 2

Stories of Shattered Ideals: Disrupted Paradigms

You brought me out of the womb,
you made me trust in you,
even at my mother's breast,
From birth I was cast upon you,
from my mother's womb you have been my God,
Do not be far from me,
for trouble is near, and there is no one to help.
—Psalm 22:9-11

The late Dr. Stanley Grenz liked to say that to be 100 percent Christian means that we are to be 100 percent human, that as we embrace the fullness of our humanity we also embrace the fullness of our faith in Christ. It was a not-so-subtle reminder that our humanity is explicitly tied to our faith as Christians, and as we seek to deepen our faith, we ought to also be hard at work at exploring the depths of our own humanity. Each of the essays in this next section wrestle with the darkness and depravity of our humanity and its impact on our leadership.

Do you remember when you first stepped into leadership? Do you remember why you chose to lead? Or the feeling when you were chosen by someone else to lead? For many of us the first step into leadership is filled with a sense of honor and pride (and even excitement, perhaps) as our peers look to us to navigate the choppy waters of a new idea, process, or goal. Indeed, there's something inherently thrilling—even intoxicating—about the privilege of power being bestowed upon us. Yet for anyone who has spent time leading knows, the luster of the position quickly dissipates as we're confronted with the sober complexities of real life. The isolation of the position quickly becomes apparent, and we realize that we are in charge not of a robot, but a living, breathing, dynamic system with its own sinful proclivities and character. What had once seemed like a dream job is now seen for what is: a job with demands we can't possibly meet and more work than we can possibly complete.

The stories of this shalom shattered are likely very similar to some of your own, and they are heartbreaking every time we hear them. It is easy to dismiss this generation of emerging leaders as entitled, brash, idealistic, or simply out of touch. And you might be right to call us that. But every story is situated within a context, and the essays that follow give painful contours to a generation of leaders that feel burned, isolated, and victimized by their own attempts at leadership. They have stepped into this position we call "leader" with the best of intentions and have exited leadership scorned and unsure of their capacity to endure the heartache leadership ultimately requires.

For students in our class the reality of the dirt and muck of leadership is compounded by the expectations of a traditional leadership structure that devalues their personhood while expecting a standard of perfection. Each came with painful stories of hoping they could be themselves in leadership—faults in all—only to wind up being dismissed or banished because they were *too* broken. As you will see, they are good people who made earnest attempts to lead in the ways traditional leadership asked them to lead—impersonally, professionally, and by leaving something of the essences of their personality at the doors. But as each of them contorted their bodies to fit what they saw as an ideal model of leadership, they were left with bruises, torn muscles, broken bones, and shattered hearts. Simply said, they worked to contort their bodies in ways they were never meant to be bent and therefore suffered the consequences. Sarah writes about the cost of this leadership beautifully when she writes,

As I have thought and prayed about some key points to leadership, I am struck by the great need for grace and for leadership in my own life. I look at [my] story and see that I am not that different from my pastor. I have hidden my pain and hurt. I have taken other burdens upon myself without allowing myself the space to grieve or to even need. In fact, I fear needing others. I am scared that they will find me weak or, even worse, be turned away and off by my need and weakness. Imagine, though, if I not only gave my pastor grace, but I willingly grieved the pain of his failed leadership. Maybe then I would be a broken leader, one that is moldable and open to the honest truth that taking that big step of leadership means pain.

What is it like for you to read her words? Perhaps they are difficult to hear given what is still expected from our leaders and the standards we've set for them. Perhaps it seems like wishful, idealistic thinking from someone too young to understand what real leadership requires. Perhaps. But there is something at once deeply hopeful about Sarah's reflections. She calls us to reckon with feelings each of us have felt in leadership—pain, brokenness, hurt, and loneliness—while showing us that these are the very qualities most needed in leadership today. Her call to reflect the brokenness we all feel is an invitation for each of us to breathe a little easier in our roles, to experience the freedom of leading from a genuine centeredness and allowing that to shape the very communities we seek to lead.

And yet Sarah's words also reflect a profound scriptural motif. Throughout both testaments—and most poignantly in the words of Christ—there is the paradoxical insistence that in order to find one's life one must be willing to lose it. On its worst days leadership can often feel like an exercise in self-preservation as you seek to prove to yourself and those around you that you are good enough and smart enough. But if we are to take this biblical call seriously, it becomes necessary to lay aside the pretensions of what "good leadership" requires and instead offer something deeply truthful of who we are and were created to be.

Ellen

"If you think you are a leader, turn around to see if anyone is following; if no one is, you're only taking a walk." The quote went something like that. I don't remember if the small, thin, square page of the outdated calendar included the name of the author of the quote. I was probably in my junior year of high school—and I thought these words gave an inspiring picture of what leadership is about. Since then I have led in various settings and, most prominently, within a local church. I have come to realize that followers are not a sole, valid indicator as to whether or not one is leading well.

I love to inspire. I simply do. It's fun, exciting, exhilarating, and I feel like I do it well! Taking the DiSC personal profile, I was thrilled to discover my results: I am an *I*, standing for influence, which is congruent with who I feel I am. My segment points in all three graphs are consistent; I am pleased. My classical pattern is inspirational! Yes! I knew that about myself prior to the test, and it feels good to be affirmed.

My pattern in the personal relations survey informs my work for personal therapy. I am growing in my awareness of people around me and in the engagement of drawing feedback from them. My tendency is to remain isolated and self-contained, and this creates a deficit in my ability to engage feedback and, in turn, my blind spot range intensifies. Not surprisingly, my blind spot is significantly larger in my relationships with superiors than in my relationships with employees and colleagues. This disparity reflects my mode of operation in relationship with authority. In a leadership and team setting, I tend to defer to authority in a way in which I lose my own sense of self. I fail to bring myself to the relationship—it's almost as if I forget how.

The leadership of a mainstream local church in the United States of America is generally comprised of white men. My paradigm places white men under the category of authority. This, combined with existing influence from my Korean culture in which women are inferior to men, creates an environment in which

54

I disappear and function from a place of fear; this causes me to disassociate, increasing my blind spot.

In my relationship with authority, the safest place for me to relate is from a place of idealization. When I idealize, I'm safe. When I place authority and white men in a stratum far beyond me and make myself small, they will know I respect them and I will not be a threat to them—or them to me. Here, I am often satisfied without too much attention; I'm happy to be allowed in the same space—to be given the privilege to participate, work, or just breathe.

This style of relating is obvious in my leader observation journal of a white male pastor. It's interesting to me how my assessment of him is disconnected from the way I relate with him. In my observations of him, I analyze him on two levels—one with a sense of honesty from what I see, and the other from a perspective in which I feel as though I need to idealize him to make myself safe. I'm learning to integrate myself—my fears and defenses with the helpful and perhaps harmful aspects of authority—I want to see and engage with authority where I do not relate to one part of them, but the whole of them.

In Romans 12 Paul addresses believers in regards to spiritual gifts. He exhorts people with the gift of leadership to lead with all diligence. People who are leaders must lead. The role of leaders in the body of Christ matters. As a follower of Jesus Christ, I am invited to grow what I have been entrusted.

As for myself, my personal God-given passion is found in the local church. Nothing in the world catches my breath or gets my heart beating faster than her—the Bride, the Bride of Christ. My dream is to serve as a pastor in one, again. I believe my personal narrative, my gifting, and my dreams find their flight on the wings (at times the broken wings) of the local church. I love her. That is where I want to be.

In 2003 I was 23 and idealistic. I thought all I needed was to love Jesus and love people. It was mid-August. My plane had recently landed in Los Angeles International Airport from Athens, Greece. Two days later, I was rummaging through my suitcases in northern California, preparing to preach on Saturday morning. It would be my first Sabbath in my new church, my first sermon from the pulpit where I was to serve as associate pastor . I was living out my wildest dreams. Lofty pictures of lonely people coming to find Jesus in the faces of people in our church filled my heart. I thought the whole world would be transformed through the ministry of our church community — why would it be any other way? After all, Acts 2 happened once, couldn't it happen again?

Two months later, I listened to a message on my answering machine at home, the voice was strained and angry; it was my senior pastor.

"If anyone is within hearing will you please turn this off, this is a confidential message . . ."

The message went on to tell me of his anger due to the exclusion of his junior high daughter from the high school student ministry. He ended the message snarling a quote from Luke 17:2, where Jesus tells his listeners, "It would be better for him to be thrown into the sea with a millstone tied around his neck than for him to cause one of these little ones to sin." I was stunned. I thought he and I had already talked about how we were going to separate junior high and high school student ministries. I took the message machine off the counter and slumped down on my kitchen floor and replayed the message, not once or twice, but maybe four or five times. I wanted to make sure I heard what he was saying.

Three months later, I was in a daze. The senior pastor's marriage was falling apart — according to the rumor going around — and now he was going to take a sabbatical. I had been in the role for five months, and now the eight hundred-member church would be under my five-month-old belt of experience for two months. *I could do this,* I thought. *This is all part of the process, I'll just give my best.* Church elders, the president of our conference at the denominational headquarters, and other members were pulling me aside to talk about the senior pastor of seventeen years being fired. Some told me that I would take his place. I had no idea what was really going on.

These two accounts barely touch the surface of my first two years of pastoring. The story only digresses to mark the most painful seasons of my life. Little did I know that the same people who talked of the deficiency and removal of my senior pastor would be the same people to foster false accusations against me or, worse yet, remain silent and watch my termination take place over a six-month mysterious and hushed process on the basis of something that could not be articulated by the powers at be. If I were in a healthier place in my personal life, I should have left my first two months in. I didn't.

Three years later, I'm still healing.

So what do I hope for? I hope for a place where I could integrate the pain and harm in my own story. I usually am overcome by the enormity of the harm I caused. I think by somehow grieving and acknowledging the events, the words, the pictures, and the stories of harm I accrued in my time in pastoral leadership, I will be able to recycle and reuse them for good—for myself and for the people I lead. It won't be easy. It will take time.

I hope to become a leader of a humble heart, who cares more for the people in my care than my own ego. I hope to be part of a leadership culture where people are urged and lovingly encouraged to be who they are—not because they must, but because we love to feel the glow and warmth of their glory

Nathan

In 2006 I managed a highly competitive political campaign pitting a political newcomer, my boss, against a highly entrenched congressman running for his thirteenth term. I was determined to work hard for this candidate and prove myself as a young political operative managing my first campaign after serving in lesser roles on campaigns the previous three election cycles. I had all of the institutional and strategic knowledge that someone my age could hold. I wrote a finance plan and budget, implemented hiring strategies, and set up grassroots political operations in the district's fourteen counties. I hired consultants and with them developed political strategies and plans of attack. Every facet of the campaign had been carefully developed months prior to Labor Day, and nearly all of our strategy played out to perfection.

The first of October, one month from Election Day, our opponent conducted a poll that showed my candidate closing on this "unbeatable" incumbent. Our fundraising was going relatively well and the national party entity involved in our campaign had just made a significant purchase of coveted broadcast television time to run political ads the final three weeks of the campaign. Then, the bombshell! On a beautiful October morning a local investigative reporter unexpectedly arrived at a closed press fundraiser featuring a national figure and nearly one hundred supporters of our campaign. I knew immediately why he was there. The previous week a reporter from the Charlotte Observer had come to my office to discuss the business practices of my candidate. She was investigating the possibility that he hired illegal immigrant workers at several of his development company's jobsites. The television reporter was undoubtedly linked to this bubbling story. Our campaign had chosen to take a hard-line stance against the use of illegal workers and outlined a platform to enforce tough penalties against businesses that did not comply. As the fundraising event ended the reporter rushed through a crowd of supporters and shoved a microphone into my candidates face and asked him point blank if his company hired illegal workers. Neither my candidate nor I was prepared for his tactics. We were both caught on camera looking confused and angry. The clip was later used in an attack ad against my candidate to highlight his apparent hypocrisy and lack of candor. The issue would define the remaining month of the campaign and we never recovered. A month later, on a rain-soaked Election Day, we lost by nearly fourteen percentage points.

So, where was the breakdown? How could we have allowed such a fatal mistake to cost us a chance at winning an election, or how could we have limited the damage to my candidate's personal reputation and political future?

The Monday morning quarterbacks blamed it on a host of technical and strategic flaws. We must not have done the necessary vulnerability studies on our candidate. We were too quick to take the advice of out-of-state and out-of-touch political consultants. The list goes on and on. And there is certainly truth within many of these criticisms. But the fatal flaw of our campaign was neither strategic nor institutional.

The fundamental breakdown was relational. Our campaign was not derailed on a beautiful October morning. Rather, our failure was the undesirable and natural effect of relational entropy that gradually eroded confidence, trust, and workability between multiple individuals over the course of a year. In other words, there was a leadership vacuum, and there was no greater suction force than my own narrow arena and desire to hoard power and maintain control; products, no doubt, woven deep within the fabric of my origin, and byproducts of an enterprise that pedestals personal ambition and gain over all else. These insights, however, were not immediate.

The most immediate effect of my personal/professional failure was a hopelessness and despair regarding my ability and desire to lead. I wanted nothing of leadership or responsibility. So, I walked away from a promising career and came to graduate school. For nearly two years, I intentionally dodged leadership roles and successfully avoided engaging my past experiences. But, the deep longings to discover new and better avenues of leadership persisted in the recessional depths of my mind. Therefore, I accepted the recent risk to participate in a class solely devoted to leadership. In this paper, I intend to communicate the insight gained into my personal leadership attributes, new paradigms and standards of leadership, hopes for a future generation of leaders, and the intricate connection of my Christian identity to each of these. The amalgamations of these categories formulate a personal theology of leadership that is to be the basis of continued personal transformation and hope for leadership in the future.

The possibility of redemption was going to necessitate transformation; the first being within the simple context of definition. What is the definition of leadership? My understanding of leadership operated through the paradigm of what position and how much power you hold. Therefore, being a leader meant you were in an elevated position within an organizational hierarchy. Leaders included pastors, chief executives, managers, and presidents as opposed to followers that included workers and laypeople.

These paradigms had to shift in order to transform my experience of leadership, and thankfully, the shift only required openness to this fact: we are all leaders. Leadership is all encompassing and entails the fullness of humanity. How you engage your own humanness and that of others is the basis of leadership. In other words, leadership is relational. Therefore, leading is not something you do to or for someone, rather, an action you engage with others. I had certainly been in charge of others for the benefit of someone (the candidate), but ultimately we failed to achieve our goals because of a breakdown in relationship. My feelings of superiority and privilege from being in a position of authority were a façade that led to closed-mindedness and fraction. However, leaders find avenues to release the full potential of every team member, and allow everyone to shine for the greater good of a common purpose.

The second avenue of transformation is neither expedient nor simple. The truth of transformation is that change begins with me. To live into the realization of a new paradigm compels us to examine the basic fabric of our leadership agency. But I had spent the previous two years trying to forget about being a leader. The last thing I desired was to once again soiree with painful memories. I would rather avoid any reflection on the past because I was fairly certain of the outcome.

60

Two psychological instruments served as the empirical basis of my reflection. The Johari Window was created in the 1950s to help individuals better understand their interpersonal competence tied directly to managerial achievement. The assessment evaluates your responses to a series of questions common to relational situations as a manager, colleague, and supervisee. Results are organized in graphical quadrants representing an individual's leadership arena (the total interpersonal space devoted to mutual understanding and shared information), blind spot (information known by others but unknown by the self), façade (information known by the self but unknown by others), and the unknown (areas unknown by the self and others).

I answered the questions with the 2006 campaign in mind because it represented the last season I viewed myself as a leader. The results were difficult to digest. All three sections revealed a limited arena and an enlarged unknown quadrant. I was not shocked, but the size of the unknown quadrant was silencing. The second psychological assessment would only confirm the Johari Window results and expound my despair.

In the second empirical tool, the DiSC Classic, individuals are asked to rank words that most and least describe their proclivities in twenty-eight word groups. The results are interpreted using three graphs to reveal leadership profile patterns based on self-perception, performance under stress, and the perceived expectations of others as well as a primary dimension of behavior based on the DiSC acronym (*D*-dominance, *I*-influence, *S*-steadiness, *C*-conscientiousness). In this study, like the Johari Window, my results were consistent through each category. My primary dimension of behavior was dominance with bottomed-out *I* and *S* scores and a relatively high level of conscientiousness. This showed an emphasis on shaping my environment by overcoming opposition to accomplish results coupled with a high level of perfection. My profile pattern was more revealing. Results placed me in the creative pattern category while both under pressure and as a perceived expectation. A creative pattern individual is broadly defined by the following:

Emotions: accepts aggression; restrains expression, **Goal**: dominance; unique accomplishments, **Judges others by**: personal standards; progressive ideas for accomplishing tasks, **Influences others by**: ability to pace development of systems and innovative approaches, **Value to the organization**: initiates or designs changes, **Overuses**: bluntness; critical or condescending attitude, **Under pressure**: becomes bored with routine work; sulks when restrained; acts independently, **Fears**: lack of influence; failure to achieve their standards, **Would increase effectiveness through**: warmth; tactful communication; effective team cooperation, recognition of existing sanctions.

Together the Johari Window and DiSC Classic helped birth an analysis of the 2006 campaign where my effectiveness as a strategic planner and implementer was overshadowed by a lack of interpersonal competence and fears of revealing my weaknesses and brokenness. I chose instead to rely on my own strength and remain hidden beneath a veneer of intellectual and strategic aptitude. In the end, the breakdown of relationship fatally poisoned my strengths. Failure was imminent well before October 2006.

Here is the paradox. Several weeks later, these revelations no longer leave me in despair. Instead, this season of my life serves as a confessional. I will unquestionably carry interpersonal patterns and traits into new leadership opportunities. But confessing my weaknesses makes it unlikely I will ever relive the story of the previous six years as a political operative. My large unknown Johari quadrant contains hope and opportunity as I allow my humanity and beauty to be revealed in relationship with others. Reflecting on the past reveals something that was, but not who I am. Of course, I am always capable of making similar and more egregious mistakes. But the call is now toward meaning and hope in leadership, and a shift toward a new paradigm for future leaders. And, as a follower of Jesus, it is centrally Christological.

The future of leadership holds relationship as primary. I recently tracked the actions and decisions of democratic presidential candidate Barack Obama. I do not identify myself as a supporter; however, one moment of relational leadership stood out in late March 2008. Obama's campaign came under intense scrutiny as portions of sermons surfaced containing fiery rhetoric from Obama's pastor and mentor, Jeremiah Wright, including the phrase, "God damn America." The subsequent attacks were filled with latent racial overtones and mischaracterizations of Wright. I expected Obama to react in a politically expedient manner and condemn Wright, and denounce individuals who identify with his ideology. However, Obama wrapped the controversy in narrative and meaning through an inspiring, nuanced personal story as the son of a black Muslim father and white mother, and held the relationship with his Christian mentor primary by appealing to Wright's humanity, rather than defending the fiery sermons that initiated the speech. The speech revealed a man deeply committed to bringing the country together without demonizing a mentor or dismissing a commonly misunderstood ideology within the African American community. He called the entire country to a more honest evaluation of race relations in the United States and showed fairness, strength, weakness, and honesty that reflected a model of leadership rarely seen. But leadership is not limited to positions of prominence and power. It is an embodiment of greater principles.

Therefore I cannot conclude this study without weaving the entirety of past experience and hope into a theological paradigm focusing on leadership as a spiritual discipline following the teachings of Jesus. I recently asked a coworker at Agros International, an international nonprofit based in Seattle, what it means for her to follow the teachings of Jesus. She said following Jesus meant living, and offering others to live, in dignity and gratitude without fear. To be fair, she and I were discussing our organization's mission statement in regards to our work with the poor. But as I reconsidered her words I began to see parallels between it and my hope for how leadership is defined and carried out in the future. In this context I propose that following Jesus releases the full human potential of those around you (dignity), increasing the opportunity for communal success (gratitude), without the fear of inferiority. Could this be a model of leadership for future generations to emulate? I do not wish to suggest that only Christians can lead, but I maintain a personal belief that Jesus provides an excellent example of relational leadership for future leaders to embody.

The epistle of James, a canonical text primarily focused on the teachings of Jesus rather than credos about him, contains great insight into the spiritual discipline of leadership. When feelings of despair and dejection undoubtedly creep into consciousness, James 1:2-4 counters, "Consider it pure joy whenever you face trials of many kinds, because you know that the testing of your faith develops perseverance. Perseverance must finish its work so that you may be mature and complete, not lacking anything." When thrust into a position of authority I overused condescension and judged by personal standards. James 2:12-13 reminds us to "speak and act as those who are going to be judged by the law that gives freedom . . . Mercy triumphs over judgment!" And, for the many times I attempted to increase productivity through malice or succeed by ambition alone, James 3:13-18 instructs, "Who is wise and understanding among you? Let him show it by deeds done in the humility that comes from wisdom . . . for where you have envy and selfish ambition, there you find disorder and every evil practice. But the wisdom that comes from heaven is first of all pure; then peace-loving, considerate, submissive, full of mercy and good fruit, impartial and sincere. Peacemakers who sow in peace raise a harvest of righteousness."

Perhaps no description of leadership could better conclude what could only be described as a beginning. My hopes for the immediate future are to gingerly begin leaning into a new paradigm of leadership that seeks relationship as its primary objective. It is necessary to keep in mind my interpersonal patterns and leadership past without being hamstrung by their many shortcomings. Rather, I constantly cling to the hope and example set forth through the teachings of Jesus, who offers freedom and mercy, fullness and dignity, and gratitude without fear.

Sarah

She has mousy brown hair, which doesn't really do anything but hang in a limp wave. She is sprightly and tiny although full of energy and an attitude that is asking you to dare her. She has a tiny face with chocolate brown eyes and dimples that hide a smile. She is running through the front doors of her church, which she knows as well as she knows her own backyard. She moves through the rooms like she owns them and shouts "hellos" to various adults, teens, and children. She runs up to the front of the sanctuary that is lined with stained glass windows without any pictures in them and a carpet of burnt orange. As she bounces up to the front she grabs her new best friend's hand and says, "Come on, let's go see the teens at the barn." Her best friend happens to be the pastor's daughter, and as she turns to tell her mom where she is going, the young, buoyant girl bounces up to the pastor and says, "Good job, Robert. Is it okay if I come over tonight?" The pastor's daughter, already having obtained permission to leave from her mom, is pulling the young girl's arm. "Come on," she says, "let's go." The pastor is being pulled away by a congregation member who wants to talk about the new music they have been singing and simply says, "Sure, see you tonight." With that, the two girls are off without any real accountability or worries, simply ready to create havoc on a group of teen boys.

Were you able to picture her? Did you know her? Maybe you were her? She was the child who was taught to think, to challenge, and to treat everyone equally. Sometimes that involved forgetting respect and courtesy. In fact, she never addressed adults by Mr. or Mrs., unless explicitly told she should. It wasn't until her friend mentioned that her dad did not really appreciate being called by his first name by a child in the congregation that she got a little bit wiser. But not that much. The story of this young girl growing up is interwoven with this pastor and his family. He was the key figure in recognizing the difficulty of leadership and the swift ability to fall, although he was always at the forefront of her mind and the one she will focus on in this essay as a prominent leader. That girl was me, and there have been many other people with stories that

have defined and shaped my view on leadership and my willingness to challenge it, but those stories are for another time.

I remember one time as a middle-schooler, I was on my way
home from the mall with my best friend, and I challenged her dad
(my pastor) about the music at the church. He explained the difficulties of pleasing everyone, and for the first time I understood
and sympathized with the difficulties of having old people in the
congregation. I also, somewhat defensively, told him that children
are capable of being given more responsibility. "Look at David,"
I said. "He was a shepherd all by himself!" He said it was a point
well taken. In high school, I told him flat out that he should go on
a sabbatical with his family, just them for the whole summer. He
simply stated that that was impossible. It was obviously a place of
contention, but that didn't stop me from saying what I thought. I
had eyes to see the strain of church in and out of the home, and I
cared.

As I was about to enter college, I was sitting in the car with my
mother at K-mart, of all unfortunate places, and my mother turned
to me and said, "I have news. Your best friend is pregnant. Robert
has admitted to a five-year affair and has been asked to step down
from the church he is currently pastoring. It was with someone
we know." I wasn't too surprised to learn of the pregnancy, and I
wasn't surprised very much by the affair. But I was heartbroken to
learn that they were true.

To this day I still love that family, and whenever we have
time to catch up and talk about life, we do, although when we get
together I still feel like the young girl in the back of the car that is
too young to drive but old enough to spout strong opinions. Over
the years my spirits have been tempered. I ended up living in a
foreign country that suppressed the vibrancy of my childhood but
strengthened my willpower and my ability to share what I believe.
As I went through college, a group of women encouraged that
vivaciousness back out of me. The ability to be goofy and silly
became a regular routine for me. I dropped the curtain of mature
control and let myself talk excessively when I wanted to, and that
often included talking about random things that I knew nothing
about. Often times talking too much would move into singing

made-up songs off-key and dancing offbeat to music I don't even like. The trust that was built during those moments of idiocy led to the slow breaking down of a few of the walls that I had built to protect me from weakness and embarrassment.

I could tell anyone anything and not reveal any emotion. Slowly, I was able to cry with one of my roommates. Over the past year I have been challenged by some peers to bring all of my raw pain and be vulnerable with it, to admit to those moments in my life where I was hurt by actions and words and yet never gave myself the room to feel the weightiness that accompanies the pain of betrayal, whether it was something big or small. It was huge to know that as I admit my weaknesses and my need, they may fail me, but sometimes sharing the pain and the burden is worth the risk.

With leaders such as my former pastor I was always able to look at the mistakes in their lives with an objective viewpoint. That did not mean I was not willing to speak out or speak up, but it kept me from allowing myself to feel hurt. It invalidated the pain that I was feeling and excused every mistake they made. Although the ability to be objective is valuable, there is also great strength in the ability to admit hurt and to sit with someone in that moment of their deepest pain and feel your own as well.

As I have thought and prayed about some key points to leadership, I am struck by the great need for grace and for leadership in my own life. I look at this story and see that I am not that different from my pastor. I have hidden my pain and hurt. I have taken other burdens upon myself without allowing myself the space to grieve or to even need. In fact, I fear needing others. I am scared that they will find me weak or, even worse, be turned away and off by my need and weakness. Imagine, though, if I not only gave my pastor grace, but I willingly grieved the pain of his failed leadership. Maybe then I would be a broken leader, one that is moldable and open to the honest truth that taking that big step of leadership means pain.

That pain involves hearing the things that have hurt and knowing that there is no way to fix the hurt; instead, I get to feel that gut wrenching ache in the pit of my stomach and then step into the truth of my part in causing it. It is the pain of being alone and knowing that it is completely unacceptable to journey alone, and it is necessary to risk by asking for company.

I am challenged to find accountability and to find someone to lead me and serve me. It is a frightening thing to be willing to be vulnerable with another leader and to let them take the reins, to need them more then they need me. But how comforting it is to know that they will fail me, and I have the ability to walk through that pain with them, just as I hope someone will have the grace to do with me. Perhaps one day I will be accompanied through the pain of my failure to the grace of forgiveness from those that I am suppose to guide and be the strength of. Would I have not then fulfilled my very goal of leading well?

Even as I put all these thoughts down on paper, I realize that they are not only thoughts but they are my hopes. Leading with grace, humility, and a willingness to be weak is something I continue to try to do. I regularly meet with a leader I trust to ask for guidance and to hear where I may be struggling. I try to hear what this person has to say and put value to it and spend time praying about it. It is laborious and often difficult to hear where I have failed. But it is accompanied by the encouragement of their visions of me for the future, and it is exciting to know I am not walking alone on a dark path where there is no one to point out the pot holes, but that there is someone holding a lamp for me and pointing to the beautiful clearing at the end.

For me, leading out of my weakness sometimes means something as small as those moments of impatience when I snap at a co-worker or friend, and I return to them and apologize to ask for their forgiveness and their help to hold me accountable. It is most certainly not something that I have mastered or even once done well. It is the utopia of leadership. It is the perfect image of a leader, which is actually impossible to attain, but it is an amazing vision and certainly worth trying for. I will continue to try to be the leader that I wish to see and experience, but I know that it will include entering that dark rough road and it will take a lot of courage and faith to even make the first step in the darkness.

My hope, even as I sit here, is that I will be able to go to this pastor and his family that I love so dearly and actually talk about the pain and hurt that has been hidden over the years. To be willing to sit in his pain of failure if he will let me, because sometimes that is even more difficult, but also to move into the glory of forgiveness and the hope for the future redemption that is possible.

Chapter Two Questions for Reflection

1) What feelings do some of these stories trigger for you?

2) If you were mentoring any one of these students, what words would you have for them based on their experiences?

3) How well do you think those you lead would accept your own brokenness? What prevents you from becoming more transparent in your leadership than you would like? Or more than you are willing?

4) In what ways can you encourage those around you to be more authentically human in the midst of their leadership?

Chapter 3

Stories of Self-Discovery:
Rude Awakenings

He lifted me out of the slimy pit,
out of the mud and mire;
he set my feet on a rock
and gave me a firm place to stand.
He put a new song in my mouth,
a hymn of praise to our God.
Many will see and fear
and put their trust in the Lord.
—Psalm 40:2-3

Epiphanies are moments when we discover something startlingly new, something that has usually been hidden in plain sight. The most provocative are usually those we have about ourselves. Sometimes they come in the form of pleasant surprises, a new gift or capacity we'd previously not seen or underestimated. And sometimes they come in the form of painful discoveries, the extent to which our fallibility and failure can lead to others' distress. Sometimes we learn of how the influence of others has shaped, for better or worse, the way we lead. Sometimes we learn of how our own influence is shaping how others lead, again, for better or worse.

The common denominator of most awakenings is a change of *sight*. What once appeared one way now appears a new way. And when that change of sight is self-directed, the moment can be off-balancing, even disorienting. Suddenly, navigational equipment we have long relied on seems faulty. Ways we'd hoped others would experience us turn out not to be the case.

In these stories you will find the refreshingly raw discoveries of self-insight of these four young leaders. What is strikingly impressive is the young age at which such self-awareness is emerging. This degree of self-honesty is rare among even the most seasoned and mature of leaders. To find it at this stage of life suggests an emerging generation of leaders far more capable of self-reflection and personal responsibility than has been the case in past generations. You will see the discovery of painful shortcomings, towering gifts, and the razor-thin line that separates the two. You will read courageous inner explorations of personal motivation, self-doubt, anger, fear, desire, and hope.

Most current theories of leadership would gladly espouse some degree of authenticity as an important element to building credibility. But when it comes right down to it, most of what is actually practiced in leadership is the proliferation of "looking good" as Phillip so aptly points out in the opening words of his paper. Looking strong, confident, and able feels far more gratifying than looking uncertain, weak, and incompetent. Or so we have long thought. Turns out that most people are reluctant to extend trust and credibility to leaders who appear to have it too much together. Tomorrow's leaders innately understand that things that look too good to be true usually are. The more human a leader appears to them, the more credible they are. That isn't to say that gross incompetence and excessive self-doubt are guaranteed attractors of loyal followers. Highly unlikely. But abandonment of the false binary split images of "effective" or "ineffective" will go a long way to building credible leadership presence with those we seek to lead.

Tyson puts it beautifully when he says,

It was revolutionary for me to associate the negative aspects of my leadership style with what I feel is my strongest gift or blessing. I think that we as human beings have a desire to see thing as black and white, either/or, all good or all bad. This is definitely how I had viewed my leadership style. When I realized that the personal characteristics that I despise (cool and aloof and cut off) are directly connected to the ones that I cherish (creativity and innovation), I had to abandon this binary view of myself and realize that people, myself included, are often more complicated than we would like them to be. These insights have helped me to realize that my work going forward is more complicated than simply learning new techniques to manage people. I need to change the way I view people. In plain English, I need to consider the interpersonal impact of both my relational style and my leadership style . . . to become a better leader it is first necessary to become a better human being.

May the way in which you view yourself in the world be reframed as you read these stories, which served as mirrors for their authors. And may God surprise you with the new reflection you see coming back your way.

Steve

The leader who has left the biggest mark on my life was my pastor of nearly twenty years. He was a control freak who taught me how to control situations better, and how to produce people that agreed with him or were too afraid of the judgment of God to dare question their pastor. One of my most vivid memories was of him telling us the story about how, in the very basement of the church in which we sat, he had gotten on his knees and prayed for God to kill him if he ever compromised the Word of God. Statements like that made it awfully hard to disagree with him. The Bible was given absolute authority in our church, and he carried the biggest one and quoted more of it than anyone else. Most of us sat in awe of his knowledge and lapped it up like dogs, feeling blessed to have someone hold the scriptures with such high regard. I have struggled with my own leadership style ever since, especially as I took over my first Sunday school class.

I remember my first Sunday teaching a class nearly a decade ago and looking out at only two other people. As the class grew week after week, I remember calling my pastor to share how we were doing. He was interested not so much in the spiritual growth of those involved, but he wanted to know how many were attending because God's blessing on our little Sunday school class was only going to be shown in the numbers. I can also see his influence in the way I conducted myself in front of the class, always making sure no one was whispering while I spoke from the Holy book. I went so far as to call people out in front of the class, in the middle of my lesson if there was too much talking. I would have made my pastor proud. Eventually I started to realize how detrimental his impact on my life had been. To this point I have only been in a few leadership positions, knowing how miserable I am at leading people. I have learned from my pastor that leadership is about blazing a trail, and everyone needs to follow.

I decided after a few years of fumbling around that I had to blaze my own trail. Like Ron Carucci said in class, many times leaders do not want to be leaders. I had decided to continue teaching Sunday school and take my hands off of the College and

Career ministry; they actually hired someone part time on church staff to run it. I had dreamed about being on staff for years, but I wanted nothing to do with being a leader anymore. A little while after that happened I was promoted at my DHL facility and became the p.m. manager with thirty-two people underneath me. I went about it the way I had all other leadership positions—I expected them to do the job right, and I was willing to make them look like jackasses if I needed to. Before long I was regularly yelling at my people and expecting perfect paperwork simply because that's what the job required. My management style was as difficult on me as it was on the people I led, and I had to do something about it. I had to do some personal inspection and eventually saw that the way I treated people in church and work was the way I saw myself: not good enough. I remember the day I actually put down my clipboard and helped someone unload their van at the end of a hard day, and I talked to them about their day and life outside of work. I knew that something had changed when the people that refused to do the paperwork right suddenly came in with perfect paperwork. At the very same time Sunday mornings started to become less about me standing in front of twenty people that needed the Word of God, and instead me sitting down and sharing my life and God's word. △ = true love

What provoked this dramatic change in my life was a counselor. She showed me what true love was all about, and even though I had accepted Christ many years before, I can truly say that she led me to Christ. People have always looked up to me, and I have always taken the leadership role. It frustrates me when I am surrounded by a group of people who want to talk more than work. I tend to be an action person. Indeed, my motto before this change in my life was "lead, follow, or get out of my way." I still have those moments, but because of this class and the last few years of my life, I have been able to see myself more clearly. There is still a part of me that wants desperately to run from leadership, but there is that other side of me that knows that this is what I was born to do, and I do it well.

As I entered our leadership class I did not know what to expect, and I wondered if we would be hearing lecture all day. I knew that I had enjoyed the books and that my leadership journal had already stirred a lot of memories inside of me. I had no idea that I would walk out of the classroom three days later with such a different view of myself. Now, let me stipulate that I did not leave a completely different person. I think the main point of this class is looking at oneself with different eyes, and my eyes are continually adjusting to a different view of myself.

One of the things that helped me immensely as I left the class were the two times we role played as pastor or parishioner. The first time I was the woman that was in a heated conversation with her pastor. I was thrown by the instructions that I could not get upset or show signs of being out of hand. I was dying on the inside because I felt like my strongest suit, my anger, had been taken away from me. I saw my inner world again much more clearly in the second role play. This time I chose to be the pastor, and I was much more comfortable in the role. I was dealing with a parishioner that wanted to make sweeping changes to our church. I started right out of the blocks getting into an argument with her, and when we had to break character, my pastoral counselor pointed out that our discussion should not be about doctrine. I cleared my head and went back in there and looked her in the eyes and disarmed every argument that I believed that she could make. One person said when we finished that it seemed like I talked over 75 percent more than she did. I did such a good job of disarming her that my friend who was playing the parishioner had to stop and ask for help because I had taken everything that she had been given. In that moment I heard the little voice in my head say "I won!" I heard that as clear as I have heard anything else that whole weekend. When we finished and talked about it, I told my whole group what had happened. It stunned me that there is a part of me that is willing to overlook a person and their feelings for a chance to win.

According to the DiSC my pattern is being a developer; I am mostly concerned with meeting my personal needs. The other term used in the personality assessment was "results-oriented." This was a hard pill to swallow. As I am read the results of this test I find that basically the DiSC agrees with much of the way I run my life.

Even with graduate school my goal is simply to accomplish every-thing that is required of me; just finish what is put before me, and I will win. This past semester I actually wrote down every assign-ment I had on a four-foot dry-erase board and put it up so that I had to look at it every night before I went to bed and every morning as I woke up. When I finished an assignment I crossed it off. This idea worked so well for me, I finished everything that was required of me, and I got the best grades of my life that semester. The DiSC is correct, and I am seeing it more clearly every day.

I took all of this news rather hard, and at the end of the second day, I approached Ron and asked him how I was supposed to see this information as positive. The way I saw it, my personality assessment told me that all I care about is winning, which felt sadly true. Ron looked at me and said, "I don't know you, but my guess is you are being hard on yourself. You do not look like a control freak who just wants to win. There is something good inside of you that is in there." That's when it hit me that I had to continue working on myself the way I have in the past. The last paragraph in the DiSC-developer pattern says that I "would increase effective-ness through: patience, empathy, participation and collaboration with others, follow through and attention to quality control."[1] What I realized is that this is what I have been working on for the last few years. As a manager at DHL I learned patience with drivers and tried to participate in people's lives. I told my new pastor just two weeks before this class started that I felt I could get past doctrinal differences, one of my main sticking points in the past, by looking into a person's eyes and seeing a real person, not simply a doctrine. And I eventually went back and fixed assignments last semester when I knew that I had done an assignment just to mark it off the board. There is so much hope in my life because I was forced to stop and assess my own personality traits and look at myself through a different light.

I am starting to see my theology differently because of this class. I went to Bible college to be a minister. I still see myself in church leadership in the future. I wrote in my journal about a man that I work with now that reminds me of my pastor. He is loud and slightly obnoxious, but there is something lovable about him.

I chose to journal about this man because he reminds me so much of my old pastor and they both remind me of myself. All three of us are about goals, and we are willing to shove other people out of our way if it means finishing the goal. There is little hope for either of the aforementioned men. They both have a steely resolve, and, truthfully, that's what I admire about them the most. But then I look at Moses in the Bible and clearly this man was a leader. But he screws up and runs away for forty years. When God calls Moses to lead His people out of Egypt, Moses comes up with every excuse, but reluctantly agrees to follow his life purpose. Then, with God's help, he sets God's people free and leads the whole nation for forty years into wilderness. My guess is at the end of his life Moses had to work on some things, and what amazes me most about his story is that Moses never gets it perfect. Like Moses, I want to keep working on things; I want to follow that part of me that is results oriented and develop all that God wants me to develop.

In the future I want to find myself being willing to put myself out there and fail in front of people. There is no doubt that I will be in the church for the rest of my life. I have seen God do too many things in my own life to go back on my own. I want to reach out to the people set into bondage, as I have worked so hard to set myself free from the bondage of my early Christian life. And I do not believe that my story with the pastor from my childhood is over. I believe that God can work in my relationship with him; I cannot leave that relationship behind because this pastor is also my father.

Pastor = Father !

James

Leadership is being intentional about how we affect and influence others. Every posture we assume, every decision we make or don't make, and every action we take or don't take alters relationships with others and with our own souls. We are leading whether we intend to or not. Accepting responsibility for how we affect others and purposefully moving toward healthier models is core to becoming more fully human, reflecting being made in the image of God.

If we are made in the image of God, then to be more truly ourselves is also to be more like Him. If we infer that God does not lie, pretend, manipulate, or force but rather is continually creating, shaping, bringing to life, caring for, and serving, then our model for leadership ought to be one of openness, relationality, redemption, and ultimately sacrifice. Having this ethos before us is helpful, and we also have to move from philosophical goal to daily practice, to ways of being that run through the depths of our souls and are not like a jacket we put on for a meeting.

The leader I chose to study prior to our course was my wife, Donna. She has been managing a substantial crisis related to the nonprofit pregnancy center at which she worked. Under Donna's direction the ministry has steadily moved away from baby saving and clinging to the Four Spiritual Laws to providing pregnant women a context of support within which they can make choices that ring true in their own souls instead of bending in the crisis to the will of others. The mission statement, ministry practices, and presentation to the public reflect postmodern, missional, inclusive thinking yet in a way that courts traditional evangelical support, so public perception is very important.

A thrift store had been opened to support the center with the understanding that its startup person would be self-sufficient and not add administrative load to the center, that Donna would handle all PR, and that volunteer staff would undergo orientation training so that they would model the center's vision as much as possible. It soon was evident that the startup person had no managing skills or common sense, took up hours of phone time with Donna over every decision, and proceeded to ignore or directly contradict every directive.

Eighteen months in and on the fourth manager, the store organizational structure was falling apart. Every volunteer and manager connected with the thrift store viewed the center's staff as being demanding, controlling, ungrateful overlords who only wanted the money and were too good to come down and help. The original startup manager, whose vision it had been to open the store, was divisive, rebellious, and passive/aggressive to the extreme, and insurrection was spreading like cancer throughout. Donna and her staff poured hundreds of hours of work into the store, diverting energy from women in more dire need of help in the center's ministry. Staff were asked to assist numerous times. Unfortunately, all of this was unseen, and the cancer was winning. After realizing the relational foundation was cracked and could not be repaired, they made the decision to close the store.

During closedown mode the community turned out in droves to protest the closing and report how much the thrift store meant to them. Some carried the accusations that the store staff had leaked out, but many just wanted to see the store stay open. No one volunteered to help. Still, in response to the cry of the community, the decision was made to reorganize and run the store.

In the DiSC assessment Donna is a high *C*, and in Myers-Briggs, an ENTJ bordering on ESTJ. As a leader she never stops thinking about how she can improve the ministry and empower her staff to empower their clients. Though she is a pleaser and a person for whom image is crucial, she uses diplomacy to create space for other voices and receptivity for her message, rather than as manipulation. Still, her Johari Window is small, not trusting that who she is can be good enough without first improving it for the public eye, leading to a defensive posture, which she skillfully never shows. I would have thought she was a *D*, at times thinking I was living under the tyranny of micromanagement. Learning that she is a *C*, with *I* second, and *D* a distant third causes me to realize that her motivation is not control but excellence.

Donna's desire to avoid conflict likely caused her to avoid early warning signs from the thrift store startup person and subsequent staff. In hindsight she could have been more assertive and risked hurting feelings earlier as no relationship was preserved anyway. With eyes looking forward she had done everything right in terms of communication, both in listening well and clearly articulating needed perspectives. The only thing lacking would have been communication with each volunteer at the mission to evaluate whether they were on board or needed to be relieved of duties—a difficult job. For her own sake I would like to see Donna become more open, and through greater acceptance of herself, she may find the strength for difficult confrontational tasks. Her expansive diplomatic skills are ways of connection rather than manipulation, and so she would handle the power with grace. I have learned through this leadership examination exercise to look to Donna as a model for effective leadership even within the areas in which we each need to grow.

My own Johari Window indicates a type *B* shape. I am not surprised by my openness to others on the feedback scale. What surprises me is the large size of my façade. I continue to think of myself as very open, transparent, and honest. The theme of posturing and posing came up for me in Practicum II, and I was shocked then. Ron Carucci has told us that type *B*s have desire for nearness but not closeness. That sounds so sad and does not reflect the desire of my heart. My desire to risk exposure, to expand my arena, and diminish my façade is stronger than my desire to be safe.

I am proud of my feedback percentiles hitting the "ideal" 80 percent with colleagues, but shamed by my exposure scores hitting 17 percent, 23 percent, and 13 percent with employees, colleagues, and superiors, respectively. This undermines my self-view of being open. I feel loyal, open, and committed to others and take it hard when the same is not returned, slipping easily into martyr mode. In the Christianity I have experienced, Christlike character is put on, and no effort to discover one's own uniqueness is encouraged. The word façade sounds like faking it, and that doesn't feel right either.

I was shocked to discover that in DiSC assessment I was a *D*. I loathe domination of others and hold autonomy as a supreme virtue. In my pre-class essay I waxed Nietzschean and said,

"Leadership is abuse," admittedly a dark comment. I thought my wife was a "dominant" profile, issuing dozens of directives per day, and that I was all about letting people be themselves. To discover she is a virtuous *C* and that I am the dastardly *D* is incredible, yet somehow I do not doubt the information. My *C* is very low, echoing my aversion to rules, which I see as dominance and robbing of autonomy and individual freedom. My ideas of integrity and ethics are to do the right thing in regard to God and neighbor. It puzzles me to think one would approach that through rules rather than living out of their heart. I think I am ethical, but not in a *C* way, and I have to get out of denial about my dominance.

The classical profile pattern of *inspirational* is mine, though *S* is much higher and *C* much lower than standard. The last sentence of the description reads, "Inspirational persons clearly prefer to accomplish goals through cooperation and persuasion instead of domination." I get to loathe domination. I even wince at persuasion. So then it is the opening sentence that is troubling, describing my type as a person who "consciously attempts to modify the thoughts and actions of others." That sounds pretty controlling. The description goes on to say that we only reveal what we want after we have "primed" the person, giving them what we sense they want. That almost feels slimy. Listed in the pattern's overuses is an attitude that "the ends justify the means," and under pressure the person can be manipulative. Through my own lens, as self-deceptive as it may be, I see myself as so valuing others that I could never operate out of the "ends justify the means," and yet I have. I sold Amway.

To dig myself a hole here, I see myself not as manipulative and controlling but driven by a profound sense of being right, coming to the aid of others as an expert problem-solver with a keen knack for having the right take in complex situations. Could this come from a dominance schema? Owning my dominance profile gives me a chance to see that we all have different abilities and we need all the perspectives our differences offer.

In the Cross Cultural Interactive Preferences (CCIP) profile recently completed by the MHGS community, my collectivist impulse was strong at 75, but individualistic instinct low at 36.

To me this indicates a person who deeply desires community, gets energy from being with people, but is conflicted about his own voice. I have not seen myself as shrinking back but rather as strong and confident, choosing to allow space for others. When we were commenting about the stories our groups wrote, I wanted to say something on at least half of them but have always operated by an ethic that says you don't interrupt another to speak. Every time I went to speak, someone got there first. To my ears it seemed that each person who spoke was cutting off the other.

I have a strong voice and can clearly articulate when given the chance but sometimes struggle with creating or maintaining the right context. I worry about taking up too much space, or crowding out another, and at the same time want big reactions to my words, as if they are insightful and maybe profound. These may be the conflicts of a dominant profile in culture informed by one model of Christlikeness.

I have valued and followed a servant-based leadership style for decades, based on Jesus's words that the Gentiles lord it over those under their charge but that we should serve one another. This has been very helpful and has led to a lot of collaboration and sharing of power. I think it would have been helpful to know about my dominance profile, as a way of bringing my gifts and submitting them to Christ, rather than the one-size-fits-all spirituality or there being one right Christlike way to be a servant. Mary's words in the magnificat also speak to the sharing of power: "He has brought down rulers from their thrones, and has exalted those who were humble. He has filled the hungry with good things; and sent away the rich empty handed" (Luke 1: 52-53). Humbling oneself, yielding power, and not lording it over others are serious kingdom themes. I wonder, though, if I have made intentionality equal to abusive will and power. In avoiding one-size-fits-all, there must be a way for us to take who we really are and present ourselves to God in service that doesn't always look humble in the same way. I see that I have avoided being intentional in leadership, running from domination, while getting mad when I don't have an effect on people. I'm looking for a new kind of humble.

Jesus said, "Come unto me, all who are weary and heavy laden, and I will give you rest. Take my yoke upon you, and learn from me, for I am gentle and humble in heart; and you shall find rest for your souls. For my yoke is easy, and my load is light" (Matt. 11:28-30). Looking through the lens that we are all leaders and we are always leading, we can imagine that taking up Jesus's load and putting on His yoke is accepting the mantle of leadership. In this He is calling us away from the leading we were doing apart from Him, which makes us weary and burdened. In his leadership he promises rest and uses words like easy and light, and all this from a man who is gentle and humble in heart. I have always pictured the hard-charging fortune 500 leader as the polar opposite of this. While Jesus and His kingdom are legitimately different, subverting the world's ways, we don't have to shrink from leadership because what is modeled for us is the gentile domination model. We can be intentional and humble. We can shape and influence others and be gentle and not controlling. As one made in God's image, I will value being the creator and shaper that he is and not shrink from the call. To God be the glory.

Philip

humanity
integrity

Ground Breaking

"It's about looking good." These are the words that ran through my mind when I first was introduced to leadership. It was something about the way the person speaking in front of the room carried themselves. They looked intelligent, they looked powerful, and they looked good. My hope was always that one day I would be in front of the room. It has taken a number of unfortunate experiences, formative events, and difficult realizations to come to the understanding of leadership I have now. And it is simply this: humanity and integrity win. Together they paint what it means to actually "look good" and allow there to be a new way of leadership, a way of leadership of which I want to be a part.

Early on in my life I had multiple encounters with youth leaders, teachers, babysitters, and various types of authority. While I can't remember an exact event or person, I can remember a distinct theme. Throughout those years I had the belief and understanding that those in leadership or authority didn't know how to speak to me, didn't know how to relate to me, and, most of all, didn't know how to be with me. So, the theme became, "you don't how to understand me." The majority of this came from their inability to be themselves in their role of leadership. In other words, humanity was lost within those individuals as they negated their true self for a fabricated version. As a result their humanity is unseen in the individuals they lead, and therefore no one really feels heard, understood, or safe.

A large part of becoming aware of my humanity has been my work with children. Presently, I work in a hospital psych unit with children who have various emotional, psychological, and behavioral challenges. Unlike myself at their age, these kids are comfortable saying that they're different and that, as an adult, you don't understand them. They are in a psych unit, removed from their peers and placed with other peers like themselves who are struggling with similar problems. Normally, in an element of teaching the teacher takes on a role mimicking what is to be expected, and then the students respond accordingly. My work with my kids is the exact opposite due to the extreme contrast of challenges these children face. I am constantly mimicking a lesson plan of how I believe it ought to be presented, and then I as the teacher am adjusting to the several learning styles of the kids. This obvious imbalanced power differentiation means I am often awkward, nervous, frustrated, and confused. The imbalance occurs from the realization that conforming for these kids has never worked, and so they will simply not conform. As a teacher I must come down to their level to play, and each one has his or her own level.

As I teach and facilitate interactions with these kids, my awkwardness is anything but unnoticeable. Most kids I work with are socially sensitive and aware of their surroundings (and socially blunt enough) that they are quick to call out that something is uncomfortable. Early on while working with them I would attempt to cover it up and play off the accusation with humor or misdirection of conversation. This would often lead to more challenges from the kids, more behavioral problems, and ultimately more testing of my authority. On days I would admit my awkwardness, sadness, frustration, or confusion, I had more kids respect my honesty and listen to what I had to say. Something about them knowing that I don't believe myself to be "normal" allows them to also know that with the challenges they face, they don't need to fit into some categorical set of rules.

Whether we realize it or not, we humans cannot live in uniformed structure; we're simply not good at it. We need to be different and we need it to be ok. As a leader I believe that the first step in growing as a leader is learning to be ok with myself and allowing myself to not be uniformed. I need to accept my failures and my success, unrated by any standard other than what I set individually for myself. Being ok with who I am has been such a hard journey in the last several years. I believe that learning to lead myself is the first step, and leading myself means creating room to flex, to bend, and be able to be both softened and hardened. Humanity in this form allows a starting ground for leadership beyond myself, for if I cannot lead or sit with myself, how can I ultimately lead or sit with someone else. So, in leadership I dream of relational leadership that promotes minimal hierarchal

relational

structure and a more even playing field of relational creativity and acceptance.

New Lenses

Through my time in evaluation and self-reflection (and DiSC assessment), I have been deemed as someone who acts as a "people mover," who initiates, demands, and contemplates. The feedback continues to say that I desire to be in control of my environment and knowingly act in benefit of inspirational thought and manipulative tendency. Upon hearing this, I am struck by an interesting realization. I do indeed desire to control my surroundings, and because of this I do not wish to be a leader. Being a leader in this postmodern society with the integrity and humanity I desire means that you must lose the control of your surroundings. To be rigid and concrete means to become brittle and stiff. In order for organizations, people, and systems to flex and bend, a leader must give up his need for control in every aspect. He must not manipulate, and he must accept that an opposing idea or majority of thoughts can be a good thing.

One of the suggestions I received in my feedback was to wonder how to increase effectiveness as I attempt to not control. It was suggested that I should have a willing heart to help others succeed in their own personal development. Instantly, I was taken to my recent job offer to coach the junior varsity football team at a local high school. What better way than coaching to aid someone in achieving personal growth. However, in my first camp with my team, I learned that I have equal opportunity in coaching to experience growth in both myself and young men.

At a recent football camp I had the exciting experience of coaching a team to win the championship game. The week of the camp began with me as a new coach to a dozen sophomore boys, who knew very little about me. In our first games we were successful as a result of pure talent and luck. As the week continued we began to solidify as a team, and the players began to ask questions about me as we played more. Soon, we became very consistent and the intensity in our play increased, as did the players comfort with me. Toward the semifinal games I was finally asked if I was going to be returning in the fall as their new head coach. At the time I didn't actually know and could only answer that they would need to wait and see.

Because of the uncertainty about my coaching future, the relationships I had with my team chilled considerably over the next couple of games, and they didn't talk to me as much. Prior to the championship, however, I was offered the head JV coaching position and decided to wait until we won the game to announce to my players that I was going to be their coach in the fall. When I revealed my plans after the game, their reaction was great. They cheered, and later that night they once again became more curious about who I was and asked many questions.

I believe this story shows that my players wanted to attach to me, they wanted to know that, above all else, there was going to be consistency. They wanted to know they weren't investing into something for only a week. I like to think that part of leadership is this ability to stay consistently committed to individuals within a setting, creating the ability for them to feel safe and comfortable with you. As a leader you cannot create a close bond with those you lead, it has to form organically. Being a leader in the future requires that you be attune with the needs of those around you, reading what they need from you and at other times simply asking them.

It is this dynamic that makes the issue of control in leadership difficult. A leader will not lead a group he or she forces to be in relationship with or fails to pursue. A leader must stay humble and consistently be ready to show both success and failure until those around them are comfortable enough to attach. Within that attachment a leader must then strive for the success of that group's growth. That growth may come at a price of their own, and with a great deal of patience and consistency.

The Gridiron

My recent experiences of having multiple arenas to play in have been both beneficial and extremely hard. The arenas of a psych unit, the football field, and graduate school hold so much diversity that I have started to feel them push against each other.

As a leader the arenas I choose will eventually call for me to be able to step into different shoes, and ultimately become a master of strength and tenderness.

Within the world of mental health the conduct of care is heavy in cognitive behavioral technique and medication. This creates an arena with little therapeutic opportunity but great relational consistency. As a football coach the arena shrinks, as my humanity is somewhat lost amongst the battle for pride and dominance. In this arena I often battle those original voices that say leadership is about "looking good," as many players and coaches do nothing more than cheer when successful and yell and argue when they fail. The opportunity for introspective challenge and growth is rarely available. But again, consistency is the most important. The arena of coaching requires sacrifice for the sake of others through the strength to not back down but to fire forward. Surely, this arena is as much about integrity as it is our humanity. Graduate school has proven to be an arena of tenderness and introspective contemplation of self and story. While challenging at times, the general sense is that tenderness reigns amidst the difficult times.

Strength and tenderness are aspects that a leader must have. I have struggled to know how each arena can benefit from the next, and how to be a consistent leader in all three. Blending these three arenas is stressful, and it is much easier to fall back on my façade and allow integrity to slip by. Various places of leadership create the ability for diversity in a leader. However, I struggle with what it looks like to lead with strength in the arenas that are lacking in it, and how to lead with tenderness in places that are only strength.

The colliding of arenas creates great opportunity and a large amount of responsibility. Leading with either strength or tenderness in the wrong arena of leadership can have consequences. My hope to is pull from all my arenas present and future, and remember that my formative years are now. I am moving in the direction of the man and leader I was meant to be and can only grow and learn from here. I no longer desire to "look good"; rather, I desire to exude integrity and humanity, unashamed for who I am and who I am becoming.

Tyson

My first job after college was running the adventure program at a Lutheran summer camp in Washington State. I was part of a small staff that worked at the camp full time. The site manager who was charged with maintaining the site and facilities was older than me and had great life experiences that I envied and respected. He had been a canoe guide in the Boundary Waters, a wild land firefighter with the forest service, and he was the hardest worker I had ever seen. He was strong and capable, and I wanted to have those qualities as well. We worked together for about a year, and I learned from him about how to plan and organize projects and supervise groups. A couple of months before the beginning of my second summer season at the camp, the site manager quit. I was sad to see him go; he had been both a mentor and a friend to me. With the summer rapidly approaching, our executive director was unable to replace the site manger, and his duties were spread amongst the remaining full-time staff members. I was given the task of planning and supervising the series of work parties in which the summer staff cleans and prepares the camp for the summer season. I made list after list and planned out everything. I was going to do everything differently and better than it had ever been done before. The organization was relying on me, and I wasn't going to let them down, and I resented every moment that the community was not working to help me get my very important jobs done. My blood boiled every time someone asked me if we could stop early or take a longer lunch break. I stood on the front steps of the office with my glasses off, massaging the bridge of my nose, as I thought about everything that was wrong with the people whom I had been given to work with. I spent more and more time alone at my desk or doing projects that I could "do better on my own." I couldn't understand why everybody else couldn't or wouldn't work as hard as I did, and I hated them for it.

As I have passed through different leadership positions, it has felt like the leaders, mentors, and people I have worked with have been slowly pulling at the loose threads of the sweater of self-deception I use to keep warm in my isolation. I lost a big chunk of that sweater recently when I read through my results from the DiSC Classic. The accuracy of this simple pencil-and-paper evaluation based on my responses to twenty-eight groups of words made the hairs on the back of my neck stand up. I was surprised that the DiSC identified my "profile pattern" as "creative." While I have always considered myself to be a creative person, I would never have considered creativity to be one of my primary or defining characteristics. Before taking the DiSC I had never really considered how my creative drive impacts the way I behave in relation to other people. A couple of statements from the profile description really stood out for me.

> Persons with a creative pattern display opposing forces in their behavior. Their desire for tangible results is counterbalanced by an equally strong drive for perfection, and their aggressiveness is tempered by sensitivity . . . Creative persons exhibit foresight when focusing on projects, and they bring about change. Since individuals with a creative pattern have a drive for perfection and demonstrate considerable planning ability, the changes they make are likely to be sound, but the method they choose may lack attention to interpersonal relationships . . . In their drive for results and perfection, creative persons may not be concerned about social poise. As a result they may be cool, aloof or blunt.[1]

It was revolutionary for me to associate the negative aspects of my leadership style with what I feel is my strongest gift or blessing. I think that we as human beings have a desire to see things as black and white, either/or, all good or all bad. This is definitely how I had viewed my leadership style. When I realized that the personal characteristics that I despise (cool, aloof, and cut off) are directly connected to the ones that I cherish (creativity and innovation), I had to abandon this binary view of myself and realize that people, myself included, are often more complicated than we would like them to be. These insights have helped me to realize that my work going forward is more complicated than simply learning new techniques to manage people. I need to change the way I view people. In plain English, I need to consider the interpersonal impact of both my relational style and my leadership style.

Coming to Mars Hill Graduate School (MHGS) to study the intersection of text, soul, and culture has helped me to understand myself better, particularly myself in relation to others. One of the first classes that students at MHGS take regardless of their degree program is entitled Interpersonal Foundations: Presence and Dialogue. The following course description appears in the syllabus: "This course considers the incarnational relationship and what it means to be present in the face of the other. It seeks to develop a paradigm of listening and relating that is dialogical in its intent." Through the lectures, readings, and discussions that were a part of this course and others in the MHGS curriculum, I was exposed to a wide variety of theological and psychological perspectives on the fundamental nature of interpersonal relationships. Through this process I developed a theology of interpersonal relationships that is influenced by Trinitarian theology and Christ's incarnation.

The adoption of a Trinitarian concept of God eliminates a doctrine of existence based on domination and replaces it with one based on interaction and interdependence. Everything that is exists in relationship with everything else. Countries, cities, neighborhoods, families, and individuals are seen properly as unique webs of relationship.[2] This understanding of existence based on interconnection and interdependence makes it possible for humanity to interact both with one another and with the divine. God's continuing revelation of God's self to humanity through the Spirit and the Son consistently demonstrates the relational nature of the God. Leadership informed by this theology embraces the relational nature of existence and seeks to recognize the unique image of God that resides within each human being.

When Christ became an actual flesh-and-blood human being, Christ surrendered his divine otherness and became human. In doing this Christ surrendered everything that was separating himself from humanity. Because of his surrender of this aspect of his divine nature (kenosis), Christ was able to enter into authentic relationship with humanity.[3] Christ incarnate does not seek to

92

dominate or submit to humanity but instead seeks to establish a transformative relationship with humanity through the cross. There are two primary aspects to Christ's work through the cross: the crucifixion and the resurrection. The crucifixion shows humanity how we are to live in relation to one another, and the resurrection directs humanity toward a future reunion with the divine. The crucifixion makes two things clear about human relationships, 1) true relationship (genuine encounter) requires surrender to the will of God, and 2) what must be surrendered is separation from the Other. Christ's infinite divine nature separated him from finite humanity. In surrendering to death on the cross, Christ shattered the separation between man and God. Leadership that is informed by the Incarnation recognizes the danger of separation and isolation and puts the good of the Other before the good of the self.

To become a better leader it is first necessary to become a better human being.[4] In both good ways and bad ways, this is the work of a lifetime. The question then becomes what can I do today, tomorrow, next week, next month, next year to be a better human being and therefore a better leader? The most obvious, and I feel most important, answer is that I can relate to others in a way that values them as a unique expression of the incredible creative power of God, and not simply as a means to an end or an obstacle in my path to be pushed aside or ignored. To do this I will need to take a close and honest look at my behavior and have the courage to embrace the change even though to do that will cost me both comfort and stability. I will need to be honest about my shortcomings and accepting of feedback. As I commit to these changes, I am excited to see what this new course will bring over the horizon.

Chapter Three Questions for Reflection

1) What self-perceptions have typically undergirded your leadership? When have these self-perceptions been challenged? What has shaped these perceptions?

2) What justifications have you used to minimize the severity of your leadership shortfalls? How honest and balanced an assessment do you feel you have done of your leadership strengths and development needs?

3) Which self-perceptions were challenged as a result of reading these stories? In what way were they challenged?

4) Who or what serves as a reliable mirror in which to view yourself and the impact of your leadership on others? How do you calibrate the way others experience you?

Chapter 4

Stories of Want: Almost There

But Moses said to God, 'Who am I, that I should go to Pharaoh and bring the Israelites out of Egypt?' And God said, 'I will be with you.'
—Exodus 3:11-12

Ambivalence. Do you know the word? I mean, do you *know* the word, as in that ancient Hebraic way of knowing, which is born from an intimate, lived experience? Have you truly felt the weight and utter bind of what this word carries? Have you yearned for intimate connections with those around you to blunt the isolation and loneliness of leadership, only to pull away for fear of it being too great a risk? For fear of it costing too much?

Indeed, there is a push-and-pull tension in all of us: we deeply desire to be known by others but are also desperately afraid of actually *being* known by others. We want intimacy and community but not if it means we are exposed for who we truly are at our core. The hard work of our lives has been to cultivate a self acceptable to others and acceptable to one's self. Being truly and deeply known shatters our fragilely constructed worlds and leaves us to reckon with who each of us truly is. Does that really sound appealing?

If you feel the ambivalence of most leaders, you're response is most likely, "Well, kind of!" And, indeed, it's a familiar dilemma for many leaders today regardless of their position, rank, or age, or whether they are pastors, city council representatives, or business owners. Each of us desires the intimacy of close friendships and confidants, those people to whom we can turn when the demands of our job rough us up or feel too heavy to carry on our own. And yet we're also constricted from intimacy for fear of what revealing our weaknesses says about us, for fear of being seen as too weak in our leadership or not tough enough to handle the demands of the job.

Whether we realize it or not, we expect a certain level of impersonal drive and dispassionate, superficial relationship from those who lead us. We expect that they'll keep their distance in order to make the "objective, tough decisions" that leaders must ultimately be asked to make. And we reinforce this behavior in our leaders by invoking mantras like, "It's not personal, it's business," or by implicitly demanding a level of perfection they'll never attain. But those who lead us are humans with real emotions and real struggles. Our idealization of what leaders ought to be only serve to further isolate, depersonalize, and distance those people from what they truly need: the voices of a supporting community.

The folks you'll meet in this next section of essays deeply understand the ambivalence of being a leader. They are good people and good leaders who, despite their admitted weaknesses, are in desperate need of a model of leadership where they can lead with integrity, without needing to sacrifice a portion of who they are in service to an arbitrary model of what leadership ought to look like. Jeff gets to the heart of this tension (and his own ambivalence) when he writes,

> The reality of my own stubbornness and flawed ideal of leadership did not come to me until after the campaign was over. As I look back I see a fundamentally cockeyed approach to my position as campaign manager. I kept pushing competent and gifted people away who could have helped me in remarkable ways. Had I admitted my feelings of inadequacy, I could have stopped hiding and running and received help and assistance. But the more I tried to bury those thoughts and feelings, the more I moved away from

those who wanted to help. I led them away from me, not toward areas in need of help.

Like Jeff, emerging leaders are at war with their own ambivalence and know their ambivalence all too well. They have been taught and mentored into traditional models of leadership and have tried desperately to make those models work. Yet the weight of leader-as-ultimate-decision-maker has very real costs. These stories reveal good people who suffer under the weight of a leadership model that ultimately isolates, demonizes, and burdens these individuals.

Beth adds insight by calling herself (and others) toward a way of leading that finds humility and comfort at its core, "As I commit to hold people accountable, I must be willing to allow others to make me accountable and surpass others' expectations of me, all the while learning to rest. As I become more comfortable in my skin and who I am as I leader, I believe that I will be able to take comfort in the unique beauty of God that is reflected through me."

The ambivalence of wanting to be known, yet not wanting to be known, is common to each of us. When we assume leadership roles, however, that bind is intensified as we are given a unique and powerful platform for speech and influence. As you read these essays, consider the ways in which you, too, are craving the intimacy of those around you but simultaneously pushing them away. Our hunch is that as you begin to invite more trusted voices of companionship into your leadership, it may make your journey a little more comforting.

Beth

When I was walking to the first day of our course on Thursday, I was thrilled to be attending a class at Mars Hill Graduate School about leadership. Having transitioned into a leadership role at my workplace a few months earlier, I was desperately in need of guidance and of what I believed this class was going to offer me to become a better leader. One week prior to class starting, one of my most inspirational mentors from work had left the company. So walking into class I was excited and enthusiastic about the leader that I would learn to be during the three days to follow.

Unfortunately, when I walked out of our final class on Saturday evening, I felt saddened. The three days had been inspirational and yet incredibly challenging. It was a time of reflection on who I am as a leader, and the reflection I saw of myself wasn't what I was anticipating nor hoping for. I did not leave class with new leadership tools to improve my leadership with my direct reports as I had anticipated. However, I did leave with a better understanding of who I am and how that affects my leadership.

One of the measurement tools that I found helpful was the Johari Window. Through this tool I learned that I operate with a large "façade." My fear and lack of trust drives this protective front, which results in a lack of trust from those I interact with and can breed anxiety and hostility. A moment of insight for me was Ron's analysis that when the "arena" (what is known by self and known by others) gets larger with colleagues and superiors, "one is comfortable being influenced by others but not by influencing others." Recently, my manager encouraged me to be more confident and comfortable with what I have to offer. She said that I often have a deep knowledge and understanding, yet I look to others for their voice instead of being confident in my own voice. Ron's insight helped me to understand what my manager was saying, and it allowed me to examine how I can operate differently than I have.

One of the most influential moments of the weekend was when Ron said that those having a large façade desired nearness, not closeness. I struggle to get close to others and reveal who I am, yet

I love to be near others. When inquiring of Ron how I might shift in this area, he talked about allowing someone I trust to get close to me. That very day I began to drop my façade and allow a college friend into an area of vulnerability. And yet the following day I played my familiar part of being near those when I wrote a narrative without investing too much of myself or allowing myself to be vulnerable. This is how I "showed up" in my team of four, putting my voice out and then retracting, allowing the *I*s (influencers) to direct the story we would present. Since our leadership class, I daily reflect back on the concept of allowing people in and am trying to lower my guard and trust people.

A second tool that was useful in understanding more about myself was the DiSC. When I used this tool years ago I was a *D* (dominance), and this time I was definitely an *S* (steadiness). I could relate to demonstrating patience, helping others, being a good listener, showing loyalty, and creating a harmonious work environment. I definitely feel a desire to receive sincere appreciation and credit for work accomplished. I also get physically ill with conflict and desire for it to be nonexistent. According to this tool, I perceive myself as a practitioner (confidence in ability to master new skills and sensitivity to criticism) and yet under stress and to others I respond as a perfectionist (give attention to detail, accuracy, and diplomacy). I believe the perfectionist pattern comes from a desire to perform and to please others. As I reflected on how I might transition from being a *D* to an *S*, I realized that I have spent many years allowing my "voice" to be quieted. When I am intimated or feel a lack of acceptance, I become quiet so as to not escalate conflict. This fear-driven response results in taking the easy way out; the path of least resistance.

In spite of fear and insecurity I believe leadership has pursued me and I have an opportunity to shape the future. Dan Allender states, "When the body can no longer bear the weight, God begins to woo the leader's heart to a new way."[1] It is now evident to me that I can't do leadership on my own; I am tired and long to have God lead me into a new way of leadership. During the leadership class I journaled, "The gospel is what I have said that I would die for and give my life to, not brown water." Yet, a move to Seattle to pursue graduate school unexpectedly led me to a company where I have an opportunity to reach, influence, and reveal God to people who most likely would never enter a church building. In a corporation that "embraces diversity" alternative lifestyles are the norm and spiritual beliefs are mostly kept to oneself. Yet, the prevailing hope that I can influence and make a kingdom difference gets me out of bed in the morning. I walk into work daily praying for those with whom I work and lead, asking God to make a difference in their lives and longing to be a part of the transformation. As names cross my computer screen of people of influence and power, I ask God to do a new work. But I believe as Christian leaders we have more to do to influence and shape our world than to simply pray. So I attend a leadership class and have my foundation shaken and begin to contemplate how I can be a different kind of leader who impacts her world.

Through reading, discussing, and reflecting on *Leadership and Self-Deception*, I am made aware of my frailties in leadership and my daily struggle to be "out of the box" toward my co-workers. I struggle to not objectify others and to see those who wound me and ostracize me as people. Yet, to lead with influence, it is essential to change my view of others and attempt to lead humbly and with compassion. Even today I was able to step out of my box and publicly offer a peer genuine appreciation for what she has provided for me and our team since January. Though I continue to struggle with the pain and disillusionment that I have experienced in the last few months in my new position, I realize that if I change and begin to respond to my co-workers from outside my box there is hope that I can establish a safer, more trusting relationship with my team and peers.

As I look to the future and hope to be a different kind of leader, I reflect on the amazing leaders who have influenced me over the last few years. I appreciate the multiple leaders who have chosen to focus on my potential rather than my shortcomings, choosing to draw out my strengths. They are leaders who have exemplified what it means to "assume positive intent" and genuinely believe in the good of those with whom they work and lead. These are the leaders I want to follow and emulate. I have been blessed to have had two years worth of managers and other superiors that have encouraged me and slowly helped me to lower my guard and release my fear of being shamed into change. I desire to provide this same kindness and care to those who report to me. As I commit to hold people accountable, I must be willing to allow others to make me accountable and surpass others' expectations of me, all while learning to rest. As I become more comfortable in my skin and who I am as I leader, I believe that I will be able to take comfort in the unique beauty of God that is reflected through me.[2]

Like Allender, I want to recognize the reality that as a leader I will disappoint and be disappointed by those whom I follow. Yet, I experienced an unexplainably sweet presence of God when Ron and Dan talked about their relationship as leaders of Mars Hill Graduate School and as friends. I long to allow someone to care for me and sharpen me similarly. I recognize that at Dan and Ron's level of leadership, they have suffered grave harm and hurt from people they have led and loved, and yet they open their hearts up to one another demonstrating the choice to trust and be shaped by another. I believe this to be a true model of leadership, and what I dream future leadership can look like.

Choice to trust + be Shaped

true model of leadership

CARE/SHARPEN

move into problems — not away from them

Jeff

When operations and organizations are moving along, it is the joy of success that propels and celebrates, but hope is needed when things are broken, problems are looming, and growth is desired. In this regard, with leadership tested and hope needed, we move into problems, not away from them.

Here's a hopeful saying: leaders can count on failure. As humans we are a flawed and imperfect race; we are bound to mistakes. That can be a relief, and the sooner a leader embraces such aspects of themselves and others, the better failures will be. The question is, and here hope resides, how will you fail well? What will your reaction to failure be? How will you hide and when will you fight, how will you blame others and minimize your own mistakes? These are good areas to note and can be indicators of when you're off the leadership path.

Failing well requires an openness to those around us and an acceptance of our ourselves as failures. It requires we stop hiding, blaming, and pretending that everything is happening precisely as planned.

Failures catch us off guard; we don't want it to happen, and when it arrives, we don't want it to surface. We can be moving along in good stride, helping those around us, and progressing toward mission and goals. Then, suddenly, something surfaces—it could be disaster striking or a simple bump in the road. And depending on our reaction as leaders, we can move into these times in health or in illness. It takes a skilled leader to move in stride with a failure, and most of us simply haven't had the lifetime of experience and refinement necessary to hone these skills. And skilled leaders would say the learning never stops.

The difference of leadership in the midst of failure depends on the manner in which we respond. Here, we will move into or out of leadership. The courage that is necessary to accept not only our own failures but also how our failures breed failure is no small feat. Leaders are asked not only to own their own failures but also the failures of those surrounding them. Leaders are the owners of failures. And it is in these moments of leading into failure when our fears will appear monumental, greater than life with the cost seemingly too great to bear. In these moments courage will always ask for a price to be paid, and as leaders it is our role to pay. Often, the cost will be our self-image and the manner in which we appear before others. Courage will move us into our fear and beyond the futility of our own image for the sake of the larger body's success. If a leader isn't willing for failure to be a catalyst for growth, then neither he nor those surrounding him can learn from their mistakes. Failures are sure to happen, allowing those failures to be known will be the learning ground for the leader and those surrounding him.

And here we will need strength—the ability to shoulder the weight of failure. Strength then is admitting our weaknesses and mistakes. Strength coupled with courage will move us into fearful situations, allowing us to stand under accusations and own our role humbly and with dignity.

Hope, then, comes in the strangest of places. It comes in our ability to enter into our failures, not to be without them, for it is the embracing of ourselves as flawed that will free us to stand for others as leaders. It is as we enter, not avoid, areas of suffering that we will find hope. *Self deception*

Yet, how can we be honest with one another if we struggle to be honest with ourselves? Self-deception is a fundamental stumbling block within leadership. Here, the inflation of our ego trumps the importance of others' thoughts and feelings. Our propensity is to shift blame and look at others as the problem and seek little to no responsibility. There are multiple problems with this approach.

First, it deceives the leader into blaming rather than owning and admitting. This approach doesn't encourage growth in another person; it burdens them with the weight of their failure as well as the weight of the leader's failure. To move in the other direction, to see first our own failings and how we contribute to the problem, is to relieve the burden of the other and carry the weight leadership requires. As Uncle Ben said, "With great power comes great responsibility." Leadership understood in this way moves the leader into a realm of primarily supporting those around him or her.

103

A Campaign Narrative

The metal gates rolled up into the awning and the start of a new day began. Each morning drew closer to election day, but months of work lay ahead. The campaign had good momentum: an inspiring candidate with a grassroots approach, a city ready for change, a message of hope, and more people joining every day. The local press had treated us well and continued to spotlight the inspiration and brilliance exuding from our candidate's platform. Our website was far superior to the other candidates', we were raising funds faster and in better numbers than others, and the diversity of people we were attracting was stunning.

And I was buried underneath it all. As much as I tried to delegate, I couldn't assign tasks fast enough. My systems of management were elementary, and I always felt like I was doing three times the amount of work necessary for the task. I was unsure of myself, scared, and under a remarkable amount of pressure.

Our top advisors were nationally renowned political players, including a former mayor of the city, a prestigious lawyer, and me, a college student.

The expectations I put on myself were unreal. I had never operated in the political arena before, yet I excepted myself to understand how to navigate in these circles. I had never operated in a management position before with hundreds of volunteers reporting to me, but I expected myself to know how to direct. I thought to be a leader meant to be in control without a need for help. I shouldn't have questions, I should have answers. I should be able to handle this—if I need help it's a sign of weakness.

When people asked me how I was doing, my response was a quick "fine," a smile, and a transition toward something busy. But I was drowning and in need of help.

Our campaign did well on election day, but I never thrived. My work produced, but I believe I could have done so much more. My inability to admit my own shortcomings isolated both others and myself from problems that could have been resolved corporately. Additionally, I worked myself into the ground when I had willing volunteers available.

My unwillingness to ask for help blinded me from being able to see opportunities where others could help. I didn't think in ways and realms leading to teamwork and therefore couldn't see ways in which others could be of help. Because I thought I needed to do everything myself when it came time to recruit help, the opportunities I offered others were limited by my own narrowed sight. In doing so I limited both my ability to delegate and the ability of others to participate and enjoy the feeling of contributing.; a lose-lose situation.

The reality of my own stubbornness and flawed ideal of leadership did not come to me until after the campaign was over. As I look back I see a fundamentally cockeyed approach to my position as campaign manager. I kept pushing competent and gifted people away who could have helped me in remarkable ways. Had I admitted my feelings of inadequacy, I could have stopped hiding and running and received help and assistance. But the more I tried to bury those thoughts and feelings, the more I moved away from those who wanted to help. I led them away from me, not toward areas in need of help.

The course instrumentation reiterated this when it revealed that in the relationship with colleagues I am known and know myself well. As a promoter I'm skilled with people and language, I'm optimistic and enthusiastic. However, the areas that hinder my leadership ability are entwined within these gifts. In the midst of engaging people, speaking clearly, and inspiring movement, there is a self-serving element feeding my desire to be adored and revered. In my belly dwells a fear that I am not enough, that I'm a phony, and that I'll be left alone. This propels me to prove myself to the ends of the earth in order to conceal my fear.

One of the exercises in class was to write a narrative together in a group, and it helped me see an area hindering my own leadership: my tendency to hide. Our story was filtered through my writing as our group complied thoughts. Later, in the larger class setting, we read the story aloud to our colleagues, inviting feedback. Comments were spoken directly to the style of writing and its illusive nature, disconnected feel, and distanced stance. The character in the story moved throughout her crisis alone and isolated and almost separate from herself; the world around her passed by as if she were only a witness. She didn't reach out for help but removed herself from the situation by retreating into her office with fantasies of resignation.

While our story called for similar themes, it was particularly the style in which I wrote her perspective that emphasized isolation and in that way mirrored the manner in which I related. This has been my story and continues to be my struggle. How will I invite others into my own story and struggles? How will I open myself to others in a way that allows them to help? Where and when will I hide?

Leadership Tomorrow

I do not learn what leadership is through a book, a class, or a movie, but through the life and breath of a leader before me. Today and tomorrow I want leaders to live what all the chapters and lectures and scenes can only reflect.

I want leadership to scare me to the bone. I want leaders to call me into the most challenging areas of my life and evoke the most costly dreams. I want to see these leaders bear the cost of their dreams, then turn and entrust me to carry forward the work that has gone before me. I want the blessings of my leaders upon me to create new and relevant work for today. And I want to thrive, and then, as a leader, pass the torch.

I want leadership to model for me what failing well looks like. I want leaders to embrace their failures in ways that I cannot see because of my limited years. I want leaders to go before me, see my potential, and offer their understanding through modeling. I want leaders to be transparent and available.

Bible Intersects Leadership

I see two biblical passages that apply. First, Luke 6:42 states, "How can you think of saying, 'Friend, let me help you get rid of that speck in your eye,' when you can't see past the log in your own eye? Hypocrite! First get rid of the log in your own eye; then you will see well enough to deal with the speck in your friend's eye." How quick we are to point out the speck in another as we

Out-of-the Box thinking

foolishly miss the log sticking out of our eye. If we approach another looking primarily for the ways we have failed, we will see first the ways in which we can change and the manner in which we contributed to the problem. This frees the other person to look at their own eye with the weight of blame to carry. This is out-of-the-box thinking.

The second passage that applies is John 12:25, "Those who love their life in this world will lose it. Those who care nothing for their life in this world will keep it for eternity." If all we have to hold onto is our image, the need to be right, and a place of power over others, then we will never taste the sweetness and freedom of giving life to others through the sacrifice of our agenda. More than the taste of such leadership is the creation and life that it inspires in others and within organizations.

Shannon

Coming into the class I was in crisis. Quite a few successive family, relational, and work-related issues were piling up to the point where I felt like I could barely function. Sitting in class I was physically in the room but not really able to be present. I found that I was having a hard time breathing under the weight all of the things being asked of me. One of these crises was one of leadership. At the end of May, the pastor of the church I attended prior to moving to Seattle handed in his resignation amidst accusations and mass betrayals. That particular pastor and community had spoon-fed me hope when I had none. I usually showed up, walked through the doors, and began crying immediately. They entered into my heartbreak and held me without pushing. I learned how to take communion with them and accept the broken body of Christ into my own rampant brokenness. They inspired me, challenged me, had coffee with me, made awkward puns of delight, and helped to create a community that did not shoot their wounded. They were a community that welcomed and nurtured me into a sense of safety and home. I feel not only betrayed by what has happened, but it also leads me to deeply question what my own calling will look like. How am I to love people without having it come at the expense of myself or having to shut myself off? How do I acknowledge the mess that I am and still invite others to relationships and growth? Is a safe and honest community of Christ even really possible?

I loved hearing Ron Carucci's certainty in class that we can change the world and, in the process, be transformed and transformative. I don't entirely know that I believe it anymore, but I felt stirred by his passion. I learned from my leadership journal that there are just some crappy, difficult managers and leaders out there who cannot make their public image line up with their internal or private selves. I would hope that I could be different, but I don't know how.

I am a female in the master of divinity program with a vague and undefined calling. I am, and will be, bi-vocational at the end of my term at Mars Hill Graduate School. I work professionally as a speech-language pathologist and am as equally passionate about giving voice to the voiceless as I am to following the call of Christ and finding my own voice. I just wish I wasn't so terrified of that calling.

The results that I had from the instrumentation were both troubling and not surprising. I have known for some time that I am resistant to leadership roles and to receiving feedback of any kind. Much of this stems from an overwhelmingly negative experience I had when I was a student intern with a supervisor. My supervisor was oppressively unkind and, in many cases, cruel. She used her influence and power to harm me both personally and academically. After continuous negative feedback about every detail of my therapeutic style, I broke down and told her that if there was nothing positive about me then I would leave the field. She told me, "Well, I like your hair."

I continued to attempt to make adjustments in my sessions that would please her but ended up losing my own style by being crushed into hers. After that it was unlikely I'd want to ask for feedback or receive it without overt hostility. So in that way, my Personnel Relations Survey results of having small arenas was not new information to me.[1] I feel like knowing myself and my limitations is perhaps not so helpful at this point, since I already feel so stuck. My unknown is so vast because I'm sick of hearing negativity. I don't really want to know or be known in my work environment. The words DiSC used to describe me were horrifyingly accurate: *stubborn, arbitrary, rebellious, defiant, obstinate, mobile, discontented, fidgety, impulsive, emotional, enthusiastic, adventuresome, risk-taker, decisive, forceful,* and *demanding.* The only ones that I did not see reflected in me were *self-promoting, trusting,* and *outgoing.* I wonder if I would have been that way had other events occurred. I had a general highlight of "influence" and a classical profile pattern of "inspirational." In reading the overall descriptions of the patterns, I found myself wondering how much of who I am is the result of my psychopathologies and how much is in the deep root of who I really am. I guess that is to be revealed as I journey.

It's hard for me to dream of the future as I am firmly committed to being and feeling the present right now. I feel like I have kept bumping my head on the ceilings of theology, community, and relationships. I feel bound and constrained. I don't really know where to go anymore. The path I truly want to find myself on is wild, overgrown, a bit scary, and shrouded with mystery. I have a dam inside of me and I've been holding back and holding on so tightly that when it breaks, the landscape is going to look totally different for all of us.

My future is bi-vocational. I want to both co-create Christian community and further the cause of those who have no voice. I'm not quite sure how the two work together at all yet. I feel so separate and split. I have an amazing career, and I have an amazing community of faith, and whenever I try to make the two meet somewhere in my middle, I feel a force of resistance that makes me push them back into their opposite corners again.

My dream for the future is a community of faith that actively invites children and teens with special emotional, physical, or cognitive needs into our homes and our churches. I dream that those children who have been abandoned or rejected here in the state of Washington would find safe and knowledgeable harbor. I sincerely hope that some of that harbor will be with me in my home. I hope that others will be called or challenged to follow suit. There is something of Christ to be lived out in the embrace of the ones who are orphaned and/or difficult.

Right now I work in the homes of these children. Every week I hear stories of the failure of the system, the intense need for basics like formula or toys for development, and the isolation that is often felt. I wonder what it would look like to have a community of faith that can step in voluntarily. I don't think what is needed is another nonprofit or agency. What is needed is a community that is aware, responsive, and resourceful. A community that has faith investing in the development of a child and a family can change the world. My current co-workers and agency are amazing. However, we are stretched thin, limited by resources, and often unable to enter aggressively into situations that require more intensive support.

to lead is more vulnerable than to resist

The needs are so great, is it reasonable to ask for anyone to do or give more? I don't know.

I want to be a part of a community that is not so idealistic that failure is oppressed. This concept was enhanced by reading *Leading with a Limp* and the role-playing exercises we performed. I want to be able to give voice to my own failings. The more freedom I have to speak when I make a mistake, the more likely I am to grow. A community that always has a fix (spiritual or behavioral) or an answer stifles me. My dream is a community that invites failure and conflict. As we grow, we will be awkward and desperate. That is where I believe glory will be found. As I have failed, I have come to know that I am truly loved. *truly loved*

I want to use my voice to encourage dignity, honor, and beauty. That statement is vague, but true. My voice is raspy with misuse and soft in fear, but put me in a position of encouraging a child to speak, and my voice is as loud as a lion's roar. I am not exactly sure when my voice became so very quiet on my own behalf. I frequently do not speak for myself when it is appropriate. I want to use my voice not only for honoring others, but for honoring God reflected in me. I have taught children how to say "no" and how to, metaphorically, push back. I have begun to tiptoe into those areas myself and have seen how much more my community can hold than I thought they could. I may often search for areas in walls that can be flexed, and I'm learning that there is a sense of give or movement in many areas I had previously seen as solid, impenetrable fortresses.

I'm sick to my soul of having a theology of negation. I know firmly what I am against at this point, but I don't, as of yet, know what I'm for. I'm more comfortable being against injustice, hate, and oppression than I am being for justice, love, and mercy. To be for something is more personal and less institutional. It's safer for me to stand against and push back in resistance than it is to lead the way with a cry of hope. To lead is more vulnerable than to resist, and I have less than 1 degree of exposure on the PRS. I know firmly where others fail, and I'm more than willing to put them "in the box." I'd rather focus on what is being done wrong than I am to admit my part in that or my role in not stopping or changing my own behavior. The call to leadership is personal. It's easier to look at following a system or a way of conversing than it is to be willing to expose my failures and myself.

What I believe and what I want to believe are not adjacent on the spectrum of faith. I think about Jesus's comment about faith and the mustard seed in Matthew 17:20 and Luke 17:6:

> He replied, "Because you have so little faith. I tell you the truth, if you have faith as small as a mustard seed, you can say to this mountain, 'Move from here to there' and it will move. Nothing will be impossible for you."
> He replied, "If you have faith as small as a mustard seed, you can say to this mulberry tree, 'Be uprooted and planted in the sea,' and it will obey you.

The faith I actually have that something good will come out of my mess is tiny and inconsequential. What I want to believe is that my tiny grain will change the landscape of the world. That trees will grow in the oceans and that mountains will move out of the way in response. As many Mars Hill Graduate School students do, I live in the middle of great tension and ambivalence. It's easier to stay in known places than it is to suffer the agony of hope for change.

My current leadership theology is one of muted, off-key hope, meandering dreams, and tiny faith. I'm glad we have two more classes.

Chapter Four Questions for Reflection

1) Scripture is laced with stories of good friends. Moses needed the assistance of Aaron and Hur to hold his arms so the Israelites could win a battle, and of course Jesus had his disciples. Who stands with you during battles? Who are your Aaron and Hur?

2) What are some ways you can invite others into your struggles as a leader?

3) Some modern notions of leadership have sketched a paradigm where personal issues should be left at the door. How will you forge a space where leaders' weaknesses are welcome and their strengths are celebrated?

Chapter 5

Stories of Truth-Telling:
From Deception to Honesty

❧

Surely you desire truth in the inner parts,
you teach me wisdom in the inner place.
Cleanse me with hyssop, and I will be clean;
wash me, and I will be whiter than snow.
—Psalm 51:6-7

The fundamental character trait of integrity as a pillar of effective leadership is so universally accepted it is almost cliché. So, too, is the increasingly widespread cynical belief that it is a rare trait. Moral, financial, socio-political, and legal failures have mounted to such a degree that most of tomorrow's leaders have simply come to expect that telling the truth isn't something they will experience from the vast majority of leaders they encounter. At best, information will be spun, and at worst, out-and-out scandal and deceit will be standard fare. *dismantling our facades*

In these stories, you will see the traditional definitions of truth and honesty broadened to include far more than just how accurately information or opinion is expressed. For tomorrow's leaders, truth and honesty are about "dismantling our façades" as Jeanette suggests. Being honest with ourselves is equally important as being honest with others and, in fact, are inseparable. One cannot be self-deceptive, cover it up, and appear honest to others for very long.

.

Eventually, our self-deceit will find us out, and our integrity with others will be compromised.

No doubt you have your own well-grooved perspectives on integrity, honesty, and truth and your own experiences of both having integrity breeched as well as breeching your own. Pay close attention to the standards of integrity you have shaped as a leader as you read the pages ahead. When do you have the courage to call the tough questions regardless of political risk or relational tension? What circumstances call you most to "spin" information, withhold it, or out-and-out lie about it, and what have been your justifications for doing so? Your capacity and opportunity to influence tomorrow's leaders and be influenced by them will directly hinge on the degree to which you are seen as a leader of deep integrity, humility, and courageous truth telling. To the degree that your harsh life experiences tempt you to dismiss the high standards you read about as naively idealistic, may we challenge you to momentarily abandon that thought for the slightest possible hope that the gospel indeed does suggest something more than settling for what has always been true—though truth may be a rarity, it indeed does set us free.

Listen to Greg's stand on the vital importance of telling the truth.

We have been disappointed by leaders who live two opposing lives—saying one thing, but living out another behind closed doors . . . [Tomorrow's leaders] will need a new level of honesty and integrity, which is not widespread in our society. It is through this telling of the truth that I believe that the new generation of leaders will stand out the most. We live in a culture that often hides and controls through deceit and deception. However, true leaders must be able to take a stand by telling the truth. The challenge of this approach to leadership through honesty is that many around us do not place a high value on the truth. Instead, power and influence—that are gained through any means necessary—are what are often seen as paramount. Even when we are close to someone and they can be trusted,

116

we often still struggle to admit our failures or mistakes to them. Instead, we make excuses and offer weak defenses in an attempt to make sure that no one notices that we are not perfect. The Emperor has no clothes, yet he is unwilling to admit it . . . One specific type of honesty that is especially countercultural is telling the truth in tough situations, especially when the leader does not have all the answers.

To him, telling the truth and living the truth are equally as important. The double standards to which many of tomorrow's leaders have become accustomed have left a wake of disillusionment in their path.

May the stories ahead reveal to you the kind of truth you have long desired to set you free. And may the standards of integrity to which you have lived be both strengthened and challenged as you read the stories of these leaders whose aspirations for truth are as high as the gospel has called us.

Angela

Let me start out with the confession that I'm a pastor's kid. And, frankly, where I'm from, I'm a *preacher's* kid . . . a *preacher's daughter*. This will fill in the blanks for many of you, and others of you will likely find yourselves somewhere in these pages regardless of your familiarity with church, pastors, preachers, or even Christians, for that matter.

I grew up in an environment where the unspoken but golden rule was that perfection was the ultimate goal. It was not really expected that any one person would attain perfection, but any nugget or illusion of it was simultaneously praised and subtly despised. I hungered so desperately for approval and praise that I presented at all costs my best version of perfection. I was happy and nice and strong. I was pure in the Christian sense of the word. I was influential. I rejected no one and befriended anyone. I was wise with poetic words. I had scripture verses for every ailment. I was smart and articulate. I did not waiver to peer pressure but stood out as a role model and leader. I was fearless and confident. I was the illusion of perfection. I was precisely what everyone wanted me to be. *But . . .*

. . . and I stress this as what is coming is my whole point . . .

It was all a lie. All I was really great at was pretending. Role playing. Acting. My entire life was a stage.

It was lonely and desolate. And it was painfully comfortable. I knew what was expected and I never let the audience down. I was a success. For nearly twenty something years, I was a success. I was a miserable, lonely, aching, dreary success.

This sort of success was difficult to let go of because it was my identity. False or not, it was all I knew myself to be. I had sacrificed what was true of me for the sake of the witnesses, and the process of welcoming the truth back into my life has been with great risk: The great risk of losing everyone else's approval, praise, and applause. Who am I without them?

This was the question that I began pondering several years ago when something within called me out of character and off the stage and into the body and the mind and the heart that is my own. I was dying inside. So much lying was too hard to bear. I wanted to be kind, not just nice. I wanted to have joy, not just plastered smiles. I wanted to have the integrity of one who is truly authentic simply because she is worth it. And because she believes the world around her is worthy too.

The answers to this question have brought me to where I am today. Today, I am still struggling to make the choice in any given moment to honor others and myself with my own authenticity. I am tempted often to take what sometimes feels to be the easy way out and plead innocence or nod in agreement or smile with a false satisfaction. The trickery of silence is that it whispers the allure of innocence, all the while sucking us into a dark hole of compliance and guilt. The moment for me is right now. As I have struggled to write this paper, I have faced two doors. Behind one door is the eloquent and articulate character, ready to write whatever the selected audience wants to hear. And the other door? Behind the other door is me. Me as me. Me with my fears, my hopes, and my truths. I fear that what I say will fall on deaf ears or, worse yet, the critical ears of cynics. I fear that you will see me as too young, too immature, too . . . less than you. I hope that you will hear me and that you will be impacted by what you hear. I hope that in this I am not alone but that others too will find themselves somewhere in these pages. My truth is that I am ready to be heard. I am ready to risk deaf ears, cynics, loss, and rejection simply because I believe it is all worth it. With all of these fears and questions and doubts and hopes, in this very moment, I am choosing door number two. I am choosing door number two because I believe that is what makes me a truer person, a stronger woman, and an even greater leader.

I do not write from a fancy chair and a giant desk with a computer and important work papers and my own business cards and a giant phone with a secretary on my speed dial. I do not write with many titles and credentials after my name. I do not have important projects and accounts and clients to attend to. I write from my couch. A computer on my lap and books strewn about.

Not yet do I have business cards or a fancy phone. Maybe never will I have a secretary. Today I am a student. This is my title. And today, on the couch, without the fancy chair or giant desk, I am also a leader.

The fact that I am able to make this declaration is quite impactful, as I was hesitant to take the leadership class for which this paper is the final assignment. I was hesitant because I was caught in suspension between believing whether or not I am still a leader. The person behind door number one was always seen as the leader. The person behind door number two . . . well, she's a lot more vulnerable. She's less sure. She's afraid. Nevertheless, I took the class and remained true to myself in the midst. I was reminded that there is a leader in me . . . there always has been and there always will be. It is not because I was born with a certain super power or because I am just that special or perhaps that cursed. But it is because of who I strive to be. The most important idea that I gained from this class (and much was gained, mind you), but what I treasure most is the realization that leadership is not a position. Leadership is a posture. Real leadership is not simply about doing but is about being. Before one can *do* for the greater good, one must *be* for the greater good.

We all could probably name the faces of the executives and pastors and managers and bosses that hardly belong in their own role. Perhaps they get their jobs done, but often it is without any hint or skill or posture of true leadership. They exist, but you hardly know them. They know your name and shake your hand and give you praise when it matters, but in the aisle at Wal-Mart, you're just another stranger in the way of their grocery shopping. Leadership is not about using people around you to accomplish your goals. Leadership is about serving others. A leader will make the effort and sacrifice to cultivate relationships with those whom she serves. She does not pretend and perform from a distance. She is honest and real and true, and she encourages and expects others to be the same.

I learned in this leadership class that I am an *I* in the DiSC. This means that I bring influence. I also scored high in the *D* column, which stands for dominance. The other two, steadiness and conscientiousness, were rather low on my test. By being an *I*, it means that I place emphasis on shaping the environment by influencing or persuading others. I am a motivator and entertainer. I am generally optimistic and playful.

Having that said, I also learned that I have a small window on the Johari Window Model of Interpersonal and Team Processes. It was not a surprise to me that in all three contexts my biggest window was that of a façade. Though I am naturally influential, I do not allow myself to be in a posture of the kind of vulnerability and truth that begets influence. At least I didn't then. Though I am proactively changing now, given my life-long commitment to perfectionism and the stage, this test could not have been more right-on in deciphering my code! So, though I am an entertainer, I am optimistic, and I am persuasive. I also hide. I hide from revealing my thoughts and feelings and tend not to be receptive to the feedback of others. It is no wonder I felt so comfortable on that stage.

Learning all of these things of myself are definitely helpful in terms of deciphering why I work the way I do, why I react the way I do, and how to pursue my potential. I also learned that despite the flaws and imperfections, there is a function and a purpose for people like me. I find that these instruments can be both comforting and dangerous at the same time. It is always encouraging, I believe, to realize that there is a category that we "fit in." Despite our flaws and secrets and idiosyncrasies, there is a much larger diagram that, for the most part, we fit into . . . with all the other people very similar to ourselves. We are not alien to this planet . . . we actually belong . . . even if it is in a very small box on a diagram.

The danger of these instruments is that we sometimes figure out what box we belong in, and we pack up all our stuff, and we move in. We paint, we decorate, and we nest. We make our home, and we plan to stay there for a long, long time. The trouble with this is that no human being is exactly alike. So in order to fit perfectly into a very small box on a diagram, something of us as individuals has to be sacrificed.

I think this is where the hard work of integration is necessary. I mentioned earlier that I am a preacher's daughter. I was raised in the church and reared in a Christian home. Though growing up the way that I did led to moments of difficulty and heartache, I have never wanted to walk away from my faith. The hard work of integrating what we learn to be true of ourselves through personality testing and self-evaluation and what we learn to be true of ourselves through the eyes of God and for God's greater purpose, I believe, is the necessary work for any great leader. A great leader knows that she is not the point but believes that she is part of a much larger process. To me, the larger process is God's purpose and God's kingdom. Though I have many, many moments of doubt and fear, I have faith that God's purpose outweighs all the others. God to me is not a dictator contracting our every move but God is a God who will use all of the *D*'s and *I*'s and *S*'s and *C*'s, those with big windows and small windows, those with fancy chairs and big desks and those with couches and strewn books, in a way that fosters ultimate redemption. We are not alone, and we do not do this work alone. However, until we learn what it means to live in humility and truth, we often are unable to see the bigger picture for all the spotlights and shadows hovering over us on our black stage. I believe that as leaders, we are tired people. We are tired of striving for perfection and never reaching it. We are tired of countless performances, one right after the next, where the applause is deafening and the crowds never stay. There is never enough time or power or support. We are hardly appreciated for what we do and rarely appreciated for who we are. However, I believe that this can change. I believe that it already is.

My hope for leadership is that it will become a welcoming environment for people to be authentic. I hope that leadership will not only welcome authenticity but also perpetuate it, require it, demand it. I hope that leadership *is* authenticity. I hope that leaders find themselves humbled on a daily basis. At the same time, I hope that leaders are supported and encouraged and appreciated both for what they do and who they are. When I get to the future, or honestly, as I sit here on my couch, with my computer in my lap, in this very present moment, I choose to bring authenticity to leadership. I bring a respect for the past, encouragement and excitement for the present, and hope for the future. When I get to the future, with whatever title I acquire next, I will lead by being a person of integrity and truth. I will use my gifts and skills and my personality to encourage and support and to create. I will not just be nice, but I will be kind. I will not plaster smiles to my face, but I will both ache and laugh with joy. I will voice my opinions and beliefs. I will not nod and smile innocently, but I will speak. I will also expect you to do the same. I will expect you, as a leader in your own right, to both teach me and learn from me. I will expect you to honor me as I honor you. Lastly, I will expect you to come out of the character and off of the stage and into the body and the mind and the heart that is your own. I will expect you to do that for yourself as well as for me and for the others whose lives you will impact. You deserve it. And so do we.

Greg

For many generations of young adults the main goal in becoming parents has been to make fewer mistakes than their parents did. Likewise, many young people entering leadership roles have approached the role with a similar mindset. "If only I can lead better than so-and so," they say. However, a new generation of leaders has arrived and these leaders of tomorrow are ready to turn the concept of leadership on its head. We are not satisfied with the status quo or leaders who seek only power and control. We have been disappointed by leaders who live two opposing lives—saying one thing but living out another behind closed doors. The time has come for my generation to stand up and boldly state what we will be as leaders and lay out our plans for what we hope to achieve. In the following pages I will explore three key values that I believe the new generation should hold tightly and I will explore my personal thoughts on those in light of the insights that I've gained from the Personnel Relations Survey and the DiSC Personal Profile System. Finally, throughout the discussion I will attempt to connect these key areas to my theological beliefs and to my personal leadership aspirations.

If the new generation of leaders can be honest with ourselves, we must recognize the arrogance and self-deception that we carry with us into this task of becoming a different kind of leader. We oftentimes struggle to name great leaders, as we see any blemish a sign of great weakness and we fail to see the same struggles in ourselves. A lack of humility could be this generation's downfall if we are not careful. Granted, the generation of leaders that we grew up watching sometimes did not live up to expectations. One president had an affair in the Oval Office while another started a war without solid evidence of a threat. Our congressmen are better known for tapping their toes in a public stall and blaming it on a "wide stance" than for the bills that they passed and the pains of the country that they eased. And some of us have personally witnessed the painful downfall of pastors who have failed gravely by harming children. These types of leaders are not role models, and they leave us large shoes to fill. However, aspiring leaders in the upcoming generation must be humble enough to know that we are all broken individuals and that we are not superheroes rushing to the scene.

Our world needs fewer heroes and saviors, but far more leaders. Many of us are young, passionate, and energetic as we head into these roles of leadership—and that is a great asset. With these strengths, though, we carry with us the arrogance that we will be the answer, and that can be harmful. Humility will allow us to take a step back and recognize our own humanity, the humanity of those that have been leaders ahead of us as well as those that we will someday lead. The pastor who sees herself as more signifi-cant than the members of the flock she leads will surely have lost perspective on how Christ sees the church. And the political leader who thinks he is above the law is surely headed for trouble. In the Gospel of Mark, Jesus reminded his disciples that humility and servanthood would be necessary in order to be the greatest. "If anyone wants to be first, he must be the very last, and the servant of all," he states.[1] Humility that allows us to serve others, to be watercarriers, as Max DePree refers to it, is necessary for us if we are to be successful leaders and human beings.[2]

Personally, this area of humility is a challenge as I contemplate current and future leadership roles. As an individual who does not expose my true being to many, my façade carries with it the risk of hiding behind a mask and withdrawing from others. In doing that I can tend to devalue those around me, and I find myself often being hostile to those who don't see things the way I do. Combine that with my personality profile of "conscientiousness," and you get a leader who is easily disgusted with people who don't measure up to perfectionist standards. Recognizing my own and others' personal worth as much as our accomplishments will be an aspect of leadership that I will need to improve upon and that will require humility.

In looking at the leader who I most admire, I have become aware that I look up to this person because I know very little about him and that what helps me think of this leader so highly is naiveté. It seems as though once I get to know a leader person-ally I diminish their value in my mind, likely because I see them as just as human as me. This tendency is one area in which I need to have grace and humility. For me, it is easy to identify humility as a strength that I have come to admire in the leaders who I look up to. There is something magnetic about leaders who recognizes that they are not the stars of the show, something magnetic about someone who steps out of the way in order for the mission and purpose of the organization to shine through. However, I recognize that the ability to remain humble when you are in a position of power is one that takes much focus. Much like Lou in *Leadership and Self-Deception*, good leaders will need to be humble enough to admit their mistakes and allow others to see them as they are, broken and still trying to do the best they can.[3]

Another aspect of leadership that the next generation will need is a new level of honesty and integrity, which is not widespread in our society. It is through this telling of the truth that I believe that the new generation of leaders will stand out the most. We live in a culture that often hides and controls through deceit and deception. However, true leaders must be able to take a stand by telling the truth. The challenge of this approach to leadership through honesty is that many around us do not place a high value on the truth. Instead, power and influence—that are gained through any means necessary—are what are often seen as paramount. Even when we are close to someone and they can be trusted, we often still struggle to admit our failures or mistakes to them. Instead, we make excuses and offer weak defenses in an attempt to make sure that no one notices that we are imperfect. The emperor has no clothes, yet he is unwilling to admit it.

One specific type of honesty that is especially countercultural is telling the truth in tough situations, especially when the leader does not have all the answers. We have come to expect our leaders to have all the answers and to be able to direct us in the way we should go. This is easy to see as we consider the arena of politics. The likelihood that a politician who was been fully honest and expressed their fears and doubts would be elected is minimal. Instead, we are drawn to confident leaders who boldly lead, even if their decisions are flawed or their sense of direction is off. As Americans, we clamor for leaders who seem to have their act together and can tell us which way our country should head. Being honest, especially in the face of fear and uncertainty, is the daunting task that we face as leaders. We will need to be able to help change the views of our culture, as well as take the personal step to be honest with those around us, in order for our impact to be felt in this area.

How we live out our lives in private as well as in public is yet another type of honesty and integrity that will be required of us as leaders. Many of us live with the mindset that we can hide behind a mask in our leadership roles. The truth is, however, that living two lives—one public and one private—is not a path that an effective leader can choose. As I noted previously, our generation knows far too well the need to reconcile our public and private lives and the need to live with integrity. When I was in high school I was approached by my youth pastor (who I'll call John) and asked if I'd be joining his wife and him for an early-morning Bible study, something that was developed specifically for the leaders of our church youth group. I declined the invitation and offered that my schedule already included three early mornings per week for jazz choir and I couldn't add another. In response to that John replied, "Do you think Jesus worried about what time he had to get up the day he went to the cross for you?" The guilt in that response only made me more resolved in my decision. However, months later, John and his wife packed up in the middle of the night and disappeared. No explanation offered, no goodbyes. Eventually, it came to light that John not only had an internet pornography addiction, but that he had been soliciting prostitutes while on youth group trips out of town. To this day the lack of integrity on John's part devastates me. On the one hand he criticized me for my lack of effort to make a Bible study, yet was secretly a very broken and troubled leader in his private life.

To live with honesty and integrity means that a great leader's façade needs to be minimal and their arena (their willingness to know others and be known by them) needs to be large. This requirement will be one of the toughest for me, as I have discovered that I have a very large façade based on the Personnel Relations Survey. As a leader, I often do my best to hide and to present a face that is confident and unaffected by what is going on around me. My ability to rid myself of that mask will be central to my growth in becoming a strong leader. I need to be able to recognize that I am valued as a person, not based on my accomplishments, and that I can feel comfortable showing my true self with others and being honest about my feelings.

Finally, I believe that the next generation of leaders needs to have passion and concern for others in a way that radiates in the work that they do. Let me share an example from my career as an example. Nine years ago I started my career in fundraising at a company in Seattle, helping to raise money for nonprofit clients. Although it was a small company that experienced a lot of financial ups and downs (especially in the months after 9/11 and the anthrax scare), we were a tight-knit group of employees who were dedicated to the mission of our organization. We worked long weekends if needed, and we fought like the underdogs we were. The two owners of the company weren't in this work only for the money, and the tough financial situations in which we found ourselves at times reflected that. The employees were scrappy, client-focused, and passionate about the work we did.

Years later we were acquired by a large corporation that focused on marketing for both for-profit and nonprofit organizations. With over a thousand employees, they were seen as an industry leader, and we suddenly went from being the underdog to the leader of the pack. Over two years have passed since we were bought, and some things remain, including many of the original co-workers and leaders that I began my career with. However, it seems that we are less focused on client results and relationships, and our focus is now more centered on the profit margins from each client and how we can sell additional projects to our clients. During a meeting last year, one of the client contacts that I worked with stated, "I don't know if you guys are recommending that tactic because it's the right thing to do or if you're just trying to make more money of us." That comment stung, but it sticks with me because I wasn't sure if even I could trust our motivations. It feels like we are a narcissistic company that is mostly focused on ourselves and that is worried more about how many millions of dollars of profit we can make for the owner than the clients' results. I feel like we are less passionate about our work now, and I sense that throughout the office. Our level of passion and concern has dropped, and it radiates throughout the company.

The same can be seen in leaders that are in top roles for the wrong reasons. As discussed in *Leadership Jazz,* great leaders must be focused on the right things and see their followers as people.[4] It is only through care and concern for others that we as leaders will be able to succeed. As stated in Philippians 2:3-4, "Do nothing out of selfish ambition or vain conceit, but in humility consider others better than yourselves. Each of you should look not only to your own interests, but also to the interests of others." When we see employees and followers as necessary annoyances and clients as profit-drivers, we have reached a critical point in our roles as leaders. When we climb the organizational or political ladder solely for the feeling of power that it generates within us, we are truly unfit for leadership. Instead, when we find ourselves as reluctant leaders who are passionate about the mission of the work we do, we have found our true selves in leadership. God has a history of choosing people to lead who may not seem the most suited for the task. He asked Moses, a man who struggled in speech, to ask the Pharaoh to free the Israelites. And Paul, a man who murdered Christians, was chosen to present the message of grace and redemption to Jews and Gentiles. I believe God still works in the same way today. When I think I am the best suited and most qualified for a leadership role, I may be in the wrong spot. As Dan Allender notes in *Leading With a Limp*, it is often through our weaknesses that God shows up the most in us as leaders.[5]

What drives leaders to the greatness that they eventually achieve? Undoubtedly, it is the passion and concern for the efforts they work on behalf of that leads them to reach such great heights. Martin Luther King Jr.'s story spoke tragically to the need for civil rights for blacks. The drive in Mother Teresa, derived from the calling that she heard from God to serve the lowest of the low, led her to live in squalid conditions most of her life. And it was Gandhi's passion to lead the Indian people to independence that led him to the slow, painful work of nonviolent civil disobedience.

driven by

All of these great leaders were driven by compassion and concern for those who they worked on the behalf of, and I believe that the same will be seen in the most successful leaders of the coming generation. Our goals need to be focused on people and missions instead of power and position in order for us to truly change the face of leadership.

The time is now for the next generation of leaders to step up and lead with honesty, humility, passion, and care for others. Not only will we need leaders with these values in the White House and in the halls of Congress; these types of leaders will be needed in the corner office, the classroom, and the pulpit. Achieving success in these three areas of leadership will not be easy. But, with help from God and the hope that our generation can lead the way into a whole new vision of leadership, we can strive for greatness. As a current political figure states, "Yes, we can!"

Jeanette

Is there hope for the brokenness of leadership to be changed and transformed? Based on what dominates our culture, so much of me wants to say no, it cannot be done, and it is too complex. Where could I possibly begin to make a difference? The task of this paper, in true Mars Hill Graduate School fashion, is calling me to quickly and concisely jot down what feels like a life's worth of wandering, wondering, and discovery with only a few days worth of searching under my belt. And, as usual, the task feels overwhelming. But what I like about these assignments is that they force me to actually start the journey in the first place, to pick something that stands out to me and sit with it for awhile. Without challenges like this, it is so easy for me to become bogged down and paralyzed under the grandiosity of something that I would otherwise never approach out of fear that it will be too big to ever finish or change. That said, if I had to choose which tip of the leadership iceberg to begin chipping at today, it would be in the arena of character development. A person's character is the building block that great leadership is founded on. In particular, I have been struck by the need to develop a climate of honesty as part of the expectation of a leader's character. I don't mean only honesty with others, but also the foundational necessity to seek honesty within and toward one's self. My hope is that leaders could work toward creating environments where honesty is the norm and is rewarded, where the protection that hiding and lying offers will no longer be necessary.

Recently, in a class about the nature of leadership, I participated in several simulated leadership role plays and various personality tests. As I participated in each one, I unwittingly operated under the assumption that there was something that needed to remain hidden for the sake of myself or other people. By the end of the three-day class, I saw that each activity screamed a common theme to me: everybody puts a lot of energy into hiding from one another, and we do it without batting an eyelash. What are we protecting? I know that in some of my own real-life experiences, my incentive to withhold the truth or to lie has been mostly about personal protection. I used to work in a very interpersonally divided company, and as a middle manager I ended up having the favor of the upper management, but they did not like the person who worked under me at all. I was afraid to lose the favor of those in power, so at times it was just easier to collude with their attacks on the bottom-rung manager instead of seeking to shed light on the tribelike camps that were forming at the company. I could see exactly what was happening, but I didn't know how I could possibly make a difference (and I wanted to keep my job), so I mostly remained silent and just tried to work amidst the alliances as best I could. Even today, as I think back to my time with that company, I am unsure how I could have acted any differently considering the level of relational toxicity that was present there.

It seems to be the norm to find ourselves stuck in a quandary about how much to say and what to reveal. This happens whether we are in the boardroom with our boss or in the car with our children. Deep down we wonder: Will it be safe? How will they react? We spend our lives hiding behind façades of strength, control, self-righteousness, and perfection in order to avoid being blamed, disliked, deemed a failure, exposed as foolish or incompetent . . . the list goes on. What if, as leaders, we made a commitment to start seeking out the truth and dismantling the façades? What if we could make a place safe for truth? What if we had to guts to say, "Hey, everybody, game over. Let's admit that we have all been lying to ourselves and to one another, and start to be honest about what's really going on." This is dangerous business, to be sure. Dan Allender, in *Leading with a Limp*, cautions us that "only the foolish invite honesty without being honest with themselves about its danger."[1] He also reminds us that seeking more honesty will require "stepping into the morass of hurt, accusation, and defenses in order to hear and see the real issues."[2] Allender has touched on a key issue about the cost of honesty: if we want more of it, we have to be ready to enter into a level of complexity and interpersonal pain that has been boiling beneath our carefully laid façades.

A decision to pursue more honesty and authenticity within a community of people will not be easy, and it is important to note that, as leaders, we can only ask people to go as far as we are willing to go ourselves. Therefore, here's the kicker: we must first be honest with ourselves about who we are and what makes us tick before we can expect those in our care to do the same. We must take to heart the ancient Greek aphorism to "know thyself" and seek to understand our behavior, our reactions, why we do the things we do, how and why we make decisions, and what controls us. Deciding to be honest with yourself about who you really are can be very freeing; can you imagine the gift of fostering this kind of self-discovery and honesty within your given organization or community? Can you imagine a place where honesty begets more honesty, instead of cover ups inducing more cover ups?

Take, for example, the story of Jesus and the woman at the well in the Gospel of John. I am not a biblical scholar by any means, and therefore cannot claim that what I see in this story has any true scholarly footing, but it seems that there is something valuable to be seen about Jesus's interaction with this woman in the realm of honesty. In the story Jesus says that he can offer her abundant life. The woman says that she wants this life and asks Jesus to give it to her, but Jesus says that she must do something first. She must go and get her husband. Jesus, of course, already knows that she doesn't have a husband, so what is his point in asking her to do this? Interestingly, the woman responds with a sort of half truth by saying only, "I have no husband" (John 4:17). While this is true, there is obviously more to the story (common interpretations of this passage of scripture indicate that the woman had a less than honorable history with men). It seems to me that Jesus is calling her to a life of deep-cutting honesty before he can gift her with this abundant life. He is asking her to "know thyself," to break down the façade that she has been using to protect herself from her own painful story. Allender offers insight into our tendency to avoid facing ourselves, saying that "we only know—or let ourselves know—part of our story . . . we flee from the parts of our story that most deeply expose and unnerve us."[3] I think that Jesus is asking this woman to come to terms with who she is, to be honest about it with him, and only then can she be ever be truly open to receiving and experiencing the abundant life.

133

What happens next in this story is amazing. Jesus agrees with the woman in that she is telling the truth about not having a husband, but he then calls her to a deeper confession by naming the painful reality about her relationships with men. What would you do if someone named your secrets, your sins, in this way? Somehow Jesus was able to name the hard-hitting truth in a way that was freeing instead of condemning. And, ironically, he is naming a secret that is really no secret at all—it's like Jesus is finally pointing out the elephant in the room. What is so amazing here is that, at that moment, when Jesus names her secret, he transforms this woman into a devoted follower. Having her secrets bared, she returns to her community to tell everyone about what happened, and for some crazy reason, the people decide they want to meet this man who is a truth-teller, a sin-revealer. Pause here for a minute to think about this. Imagine what it would be like to have someone come to you and say "Hey, this guy just told me every-thing I ever did. Wanna meet him?" Would you be running out to greet him, the way these people apparently did? I think I would be the one who made an excuse to stay home and tend the fire, not wanting to risk public exposure of my secrets. But, somehow, Jesus's acknowledgment of this woman's sin had just the opposite effect—she was drawn to him, and her story drew others to him, too.

What would it be like to be a truth-teller the way that Jesus was? What would it be like to find freedom amidst painful truths, as the woman in this story did? What would it be like to seek to discover and bear not only our own personal humanity and the fail-ures that lie therein, but to bear it for others, too? In leadership we have the opportunity to be the healing hands of Christ to someone, to offer them a place to be open and honest without getting burned or scorned. Max DePree, author of *Leadership Jazz*, brings this idea home in a very tangible way. He writes:

> We need to commit ourselves to individual authenticity
> with openness and expectation, with grace and humor. We
> need to drop our guards . . . in a society and a world that
> have serious problems and suffer all too often and far too

painfully from heartbreak, each of us needs a haven. Part of the touch of leadership is to create such a haven. A good family, a good institution, or a good corporation can be a place of healing. It can be a place where work becomes redemptive, where every person is included on her own terms. We know in our hearts that to be included is both beautiful and right. Leaders have to find a way to work that out, to contribute toward that vision.[4]

DePree's point is clear: leaders can be, and need to be, models through which authenticity is encouraged and expected. First, however, we must be willing to discover and hold the truth about ourselves, and be okay with the brokenness that we find. Only when we are comfortable with our whole selves can we bring that comfort to others.

I won't lie. Everything I have said feels idealistic and almost entirely unattainable given the kind of world in which we live. I have no idea how this could possibly work in a society where it seems that so often the bottom line of greed and getting ahead wins out over people and relationships. I think that, given the current state of our culture, taking steps into the world of honesty will need to be done carefully and thoughtfully. We will need to be good judges of whether the people we are currently in community with can handle honesty, and at times it will be in our best interest to continue living within the web of façade. But, if we are willing to look for the opportunities, I do believe there will be moments when we can risk exposure, and will be rewarded with greater freedom to move about within both the beauty and depravity of our humanity.

Laura

People tend to have an unbalanced view of leadership. On the one hand, there are those who are suspicious of leaders and question their motivation, and who see leaders as power mongering, exploitative, and egotistical. On the other end of the spectrum are those who place leaders on a pedestal, seeing them as noble servants to be awed and revered and rarely capable of doing wrong. Unfortunately, both of these views paint a false picture of leadership. First, we must begin with the premise that all leaders are human. As such, they possess both the glory of God and the depravity of the Fall. Leaders are capable of accomplishing astounding good, and they are also capable of doing enormous harm, and most leaders will fall somewhere in between. It is impossible for any of us to be perfect, but we must strive to accomplish much more good than harm.

A common misconception is that leadership is a position of authority. This is sometimes true; however it is also quite possible that someone in a position of leadership is not really a leader—at least not a good one. You can likewise be a leader without carrying any sort of leadership title. Leadership is much more a state of being than it is a title. If people have grown to respect you and trust you enough to follow you, then you are indeed a leader.

Integrity is essential for leadership. Only 57 percent of Americans trust leaders to be honest.[1] There is good reason for the skepticism. We have seen too many leaders who believe that they are above the rules. Any leader who does not possess integrity will quickly lose respect from those they lead. And if someone is in a position of authority but is not respected by those they are leading, then their capabilities as a leader have drastically dwindled. Instead, a leader must be an example to their followers. Parents are known for saying, "Do as I say, not as I do." We all know that the children will inevitably mimic the actions of their parents much more than they will take their words to heart. The same principal applies to leadership. If the actions are not matching the message, the followers will take notice, and respect for the leader will be lost. However, it is also important to note that while actions do speak louder than words, they do not always speak for themselves. Actions accompanied by no voice can seem random and purposeless. It is not safe to assume that your followers will understand the point you are trying to make. It is also possible they won't even notice the action unless it is pointed out to them with explanation.

Along the same lines, the leader must be willing to get their hands dirty. A leader should never ask a follower to do something that they themselves are not willing to do. It is inevitable that a leader cannot do everything, and must focus the majority of their energies on their specific leadership responsibilities. However they must not have the attitude that they are above doing the duties of those who are under their leadership. They must train their followers likewise. Larry, the owner of a small paving company, did this well. One day one of his senior employees came to him and complained that he had gotten stuck spending all day doing manual labor while another employee who had less seniority had been able to spend the day doing the technical work. The employee did not think this was fair. Larry usually spent a majority of his time in the office making sales calls, making bids, and taking care of the business end of things. But the next day Larry went out to the jobsite, picked up a shovel, and began doing the manual labor. Not knowing what to make of this, his employees offered again and again to let them take over for him, but he refused. Larry spent the entire day doing manual labor because he wanted his employees to know that no job was beneath any of them. He, as their leader, was willing to do the most menial and dirty work; therefore, the same would be expected of everyone else. It was a lesson the employees never forgot.

Leadership is always about people. If there are not people involved, then it is not leadership, because a leader needs followers. But the people must always be treated like people, not objects. In our society we have a tendency to objectify people. We look at them through the lens of how they can be beneficial to us, or how they are a hindrance to us.[2] This takes a toll on the human soul, and will not go unrecognized. When we look at a person, do we only see how they can help us on a project or how they are holding us back? Or do we also see them in their complete humanity—someone who has a family who loves them, someone who has hopes and dreams and fears, someone who is not unlike ourselves? These are questions we must constantly be asking ourselves. We must also ask them of others, as we can easily deceive ourselves.

Communication is essential for leadership. This is something I had always known to be true; however, it became exceptionally apparent when I spent a month observing the actions of my boss as an experiment in leadership. I noticed that in circumstances where there was a lack of clear communication from my boss, I tended to draw my own conclusions based upon the silence. The conclusions I drew were usually negative, although my imagined negative scenarios were usually much worse than the reality. I noticed that lack of communication can cause followers to live in fear and uncertainty. This in turn will hinder their communication with their leader. This is a recipe for a downward spiral.

Communication is also important in casting and moving toward a vision. One of the duties of a leader is to inspire followers to be on board with their vision. This is not likely to happen without intentional communication of why the vision is worth pursuing. Communication is also essential to let the followers know what the vision is in the first place. Often it is assumed that people must already know this; but it is often not the case. In a poll conducted by Harris Interactive, it was found that just over one third of people said they have a clear understanding of their organizations' purposes and goals.[3] This leaves one to wonder what the other two thirds are working toward! Proverbs states that where there is no vision, the people perish.[4] It could also be said that with no vision, an organization will perish.

It is vital for a leader to be passionate about what they are doing. If a leader is passionate, the followers cannot help but to catch some of the enthusiasm. Passion is contagious. At the same time, if a leader is not passionate, even the zeal of the most passionate follower can quickly be snuffed out. I have seen this happen. I was once under the leadership of a woman who was asked to lead a project for which she did not have passion. Her lack of passion about the project was quickly apparent to both her direct staff and those whom they were leading. Staff who had come on board exuberant about the project gradually had the life sucked out of them until the work became drudgery. Good ideas were shot down simply because the leader did not have the energy or enthusiasm to bother with letting them be carried through. While some good still did come out of the project, the majority of people finished disappointed. Almost everyone left with the sense that it could have been so much more. A leader who is not passionate cannot inspire passion in her followers, and will stifle the passion that might already be present.

Another important aspect of leadership is developing followers. One key failure of leaders has been when they do not understand that the power of a leader is not meant to be hoarded and lorded over their followers. A leader, instead, is to use their power to empower others. The best leaders are those who have more faith in their followers than the followers have in themselves. This faith is ripe soil for growth. A striking example of this can be seen in Luke 10, when Jesus sends out the seventy-two. There is no mention of where these seventy-two people came from or how they were chosen. What is almost certain is that they never could have been prepared for the task Jesus was about to give them. His instructions were to go on ahead of him to all of the towns and villages he was about to visit, heal the sick, and tell them that the Kingdom of God is near. Heal the sick? These instructions are mentioned so nonchalantly in the text that it is almost comical. But that is exactly what Jesus tells them to do. Undoubtedly these seventy-two must have questioned their capabilities of carrying out these instructions. But they returned from their task exuberant, exclaiming, "Lord, even the demons submit to us in your name."[5] Jesus's response is filled with wisdom. "I have given you authority to trample on snakes and scorpions and to overcome all the power of the enemy; nothing will harm you. However, do not rejoice that the spirits submit to you, but rejoice that your names are written in heaven."[6] His words encourage the seventy-two to continue acting out the gifts he has given them, yet he also cautions them from becoming too excited about the authority he has given them. A leader must not become drunk with their own power.

In his book *Leadership Jazz*, Max Depree writes that we should view most people as volunteers. No one *has* to follow you. If they do not like the way you are leading or the mission that they are being led toward, they have the option of moving along to somewhere else.[7] This is especially pertinent in today's society where the average length of stay in a single job is nineteen months, and on average a person will work six to seven different jobs during their career.[8] This is not only a corporate phenomenon; ministries are also not immune to this trend. Missions organizations report that the length of time people serve in the same field or with the same organization has drastically declined.[9] With this in mind, it is necessary for leaders to earn the respect and trust of their followers rather than rely on their position of authority. Authority does not carry the weight it once did in the minds of younger generations.

Leadership can be a complicated and burdensome task. It also has the potential for accomplishing great good. Much of the outcome depends on the character and integrity of the leader. While no one is perfect, it is important that the leader have the wisdom and humility to seek out the areas in which they are weak, and recruit help in those places.

The world has a desperate need for good leaders, leaders who will serve with integrity and passion and leaders who will speak the truth boldly and lovingly. The world needs leaders who will cultivate the gifts and voices of their followers. What type of leader will you be?

Tamara

I have been a reluctant leader because I have taken the responsibility so seriously. I've begun to evaluate my own perceptions of leaders as I have been deliberately stepping into this role, and it wasn't until Dan Allender said that "our parents are our first leaders" that I was able to understand that I was struggling with my parents' style of leadership.[1] Of course I'm a leader for my own children, but I had never applied the label to myself as a parent. It seems so simple now; parents are a human's first leaders. I've also been evaluating other leaders in my past: elementary and high school teachers, pastors, managers, and employers. I can now see that there have been many other people who spoke valuable words into my life that led to my growth, people who, at the time, I would not have considered leaders. They were women who took an interest in me, and men who called me to more responsibility than I thought I was ready for. Perhaps this word "leader" has a more ambiguous meaning than I have allowed it to have.

For me as a leader truth is very important. I will follow leaders who have proven to be trustworthy by their integrity. I don't want to follow blindly after a leader just because I'm told to, and I don't want that for those I lead. The scriptures encourage us to seek after truth ourselves. We do not adhere to a passive faith. Jesus said that for those who are to follow Him, they must first deny themselves and take up their crosses.[2] This is a hard statement to understand during any era, but nevertheless the whole statement is one of action. To lead requires seeking after the truth, thinking critically, and acting.

As a leader, I want to value each individual whom I come in contact with. This is difficult to do based on my family of origin's perception of those who are different than them, and all my unnamed biases of those who may resemble someone with whom I have had a negative experience. I want to see "people as they [are]–as people".[3] My goal is to get to know myself more. I want to put myself in situations where my assumptions of others are revealed and challenged.

I believe that God has made each person in His image. As I press into what this means, to be made in the image of God, I see a sea of multicolored faces that each reveal a part of God to me. I want to know those parts. I want to focus on the beauty that God sees in each of us. So much of life is painful, especially as we try to bear that pain alone, but being alone is not God's design for His people. I want to be an agent of community and to be in community.

Because I've already made this commitment to be an active participant, I have the responsibility to be a leader worth following. If they are looking to me for "wisdom, direction, perspective, or a decision" and thus am in a position to influence them for an "opportunity for good," then I have the responsibility to be held accountable for what I believe and how I act.[4] So, if I say, "God is love," and yet by my actions I don't show that I live this out, then why would they believe what I say about who God is?[5]

I think that followers have a right to question leaders, especially when their actions seem different than what they profess to believe. For example, the word "Christian" has lost its credibility, especially in the eyes of the mainstream media. And there is good reason for this. Look at how Christians have publicly and privately pursued their own agendas for wealth, power, lust, and hate over the past twenty years. The labels "American" and "United States" have also suffered this same fate for the same reasons. We have had presidents who did not tell the truth to the people of this country, we have had presidents who did not keep their marriage "vows," and we have U.S. companies who have abused their employees working for them on foreign soil, as well as companies who have refused to look into the future and change for the common good of all and this earth.

We have to encourage creativity from whatever source that it may come.[6] We want growth and healing for our nation from war, homelessness, poverty, drug addiction, and abuse, and yet if we don't step into leadership for these causes, nothing will change. We need to get back in the game. We have been trained to blame others for our problems: blame the president, the government, the economy, global warming, our neighbors, parents, and children.

142

By blaming we are disempowered from what we can do to change the very things that cause our blame. Because I am a leader, I must hold myself accountable and expect, if not insist, that I be held accountable to live up to and into these very labels that I represent.

Therefore, I must make a commitment to all who follow me to listen to them for the purpose of understanding them. I must value their diversity. I must speak truth to them and surrender myself to the truth whatever voice that truth may come from. I want to grow their confidence in their value to God, to themselves, and to me. I want to show that I value them and that we are a team by delegating to them and letting them carry out the job their way and by empowering them to believe in their own abilities and gifts.[7]

I think that this is a critical time in our world's history. Now, more than ever, we need to grow individuals to be critical thinkers. This is the vision that I think that leaders of today need to develop for leaders of tomorrow.

Christianity is a religion that has Truth embodied in a person, Christ Jesus, at its core. Many of the first citizens of United States of America were Christians; they believed that all people were created equally. The United States of America was founded and won by individuals who were willing to stand up for what they believed was right. Many who came to this land were running from religious and economic oppression. Free speech, the right to bear arms, and the pursuit of happiness are granted to every citizen within our country's constitution. However, we are at a critical point where we can no longer take these freedoms for granted. We must ask ourselves, "What do we want for ourselves, our children, our country, and our world?"

Chapter Five Questions for Reflection

1) What has been the most painful experience of breeched integrity you have experienced as a leader—both yours and someone else's?

2) What has been your experience of telling the truth in a difficult situation? What did it cost you?

3) How has your definition of integrity and honesty been challenged or broadened as a result of reading these stories?

4) As a leader, what relationships are currently struggling as a result of too little honesty? What aspect of honesty or integrity would need to be adjusted for this relationship to become stronger?

Chapter 6

Stories of New Voices:
Moving Toward Something Beautiful

*As long as Moses held up his hands, the Israelites
were winning, but whenever he lowered his hands, the
Amalekites were winning. When Moses' hands grew tired,
they took a stone and put it under him and he sat on it.
Aaron and Hur held his hands up—one on one side, one on
the other—so that his hands remained steady till sunset. So
Joshua overcame the Amalekite army with the sword.*
—Exodus 17:12-13

Ask any parent and they'll tell you that each milestone their
young child reaches is filled with excitement. A child's first
words or his ability to sit up on his own (among many others) often
fills parents with joy as they witness the next stage in their child's
development. And perhaps no stage is more exciting—and simultaneously filled with as much terror—as when their child begins to
take his first steps. For the child, walking represents a newfound
autonomy as he's able to transport himself around without an utter
dependence on mom or dad. And yet while the parents are likely
filled with delight, they are also filled with the terror of knowing
the child can move (and disappear!) in the blink of an eye. Indeed,
after growing accustomed to a year or more of leaving a child in
one spot and knowing he'll stay, a child learning to walk unsettles

these expectations. Spend enough time around a curious toddler and you recognize that if you're not careful, he will inevitably empty your lower kitchen cabinets, or worse, wander off without you even noticing!

In many ways the toddler's adventurous spirit is captivating, and she looks to explore the world more broadly in this stage of life. Yet despite her growing freedom and autonomy, learning to walk can be a painful event. The toddler doesn't quite understand her surroundings, and she isn't fully aware of the power of her legs. She has a sense for what walking is like, but in her earnest efforts to move, she stumbles and falls, waddles, "toddles", and struggles to remain balanced. She lacks the stamina for the type of walking older children are used to and will often look to mom and dad to carry her when she's exhausted, or when she simply has had enough. It takes time, practice, and years for children to fully grow into walking comfortably. And parents are eager to see them do it successfully.

In this next collection of essays, you will meet emerging leaders who find themselves in a similar developmental stage. They understand they have a powerful voice of leadership to use in a litany of ways but struggle to fully live into that voice. They've stumbled and waddled their way through leading—sometimes failing miserably—often choosing to dismiss their leadership gifts and potential altogether. While they glimpse the effect they may have on others, they often choose to prohibit themselves from gaining the balance and the confidence needed to really strive in their leadership. Ultimately, these are leaders who, through their own cascades of self-doubt, get in the way of themselves, and along the way, gain glimpses of themselves as potentially dynamic leaders whose influence can shape the trajectory of lives and communities. And just like the toddler who suddenly gains momentum in his gait and, upon realizing his newly discovered speed, snaps from elation to terror, so too must these forming leaders continually rediscover the thrill and terror of their burgeoning voices.

Jeremy captures the imbalance of this growth very well when he writes, "Even with [my] promising future as a child, I have found myself disenchanted and untrusting of leaders and staring at the bottom of the bottle of Apathy, curious now about how I will ever get back home. It now seems like a long way from any kind of hope, but as I encounter more leaders who have held hope, I am sobering up and beginning to feel the sting of how far I have to go, and what kind of spiritual act of repentance must occur to get me out of this place." His words are both a recognition of the cost of his cynicism and a concerted desire to move beyond it for the sake of hope.

Throughout this book you've heard stories of people being harmed by leadership, having deep-seeded contempt for leadership, or simply being dismissive of current leadership. What sets these next essays apart, however, is their surprising and often ironic optimism for leading others earnestly and thoughtfully. Despite their struggle to embrace their voices, they present honest and good visions for a new way of leadership, and simply need those ideas culled from the depths of their own fear.

And yet we can't help but wonder how these students would flourish if they had someone alongside them, mentoring each of them, calling out their brilliance, and encouraging them to speak. Like a toddler who needs to hold her parent's hand for balance, sometimes emerging leaders need to be invited to speak, to be reminded their voices matter and they have something important to say. We would wager that of the emerging leaders you likely know in your own contexts, the bulk of them lie in this camp—good people with good visions but simply unable to find a welcoming ear to hear what they have to say with the patience to let their ideas form along the way. If emerging leaders are going to make a difference in this world, it will be, in part, because incumbent leaders have chosen to engage, mentor, delight in, and make a space for their voices to matter. We invite you to consider those people around you who need space for their ideas to breathe, who need you to be the hospitable host for their flourishing influence.

Jeremy so eloquently continues, "It is hopeful to envision a generation of leaders who recognize that their role is only as strong as their followers make it and are able to more fully utilize the

147

community's strength. Curiosity will give way to dialogue and help us work together rather than quietly submit."

As you'll come to see, the world desperately needs these voices. They are talented leaders and thinkers who simply need a shot of confidence and trust, a hand to hold as they find their balance. And once provided, we will benefit greatly from the unleashed brilliance awaiting such an invitation.

Caroline

Most of us know what good leaders are supposed to do: form visions, develop strategies and plans, oversee the execution of the plans, measure successes, et cetera. MBA graduates come away well equipped to be great doers. I propose that a matter of greater importance is the character within the leader. A party of hikers may set out following a leader who relies on his compass and map to guide the way. But if the compass is broken, or the map proves unreliable, the trek is going to take longer and be more difficult and dangerous than the leader and his followers ever imagined.

A leader's "map" is his beliefs about leadership and his "compass" is his moral strength. Both of these are malleable qualities that can be changed and strengthened. Thus, preparation for the leadership journey begins inside, and adjustments are made along the journey. Wherever we are as leaders, still at base camp or lost in a swamp, it's always wise to re-check the map and compass.

A good way to begin identifying what leadership map you are following is to think about the metaphors you use to describe leading. Leadership is about words as well as action because "a leader's voice is the expression of one's belief."[1] What we say about ourselves and others tends to become self-fulfilling prophecy. Do you fight daily "battles," "hit home runs," and calculate your "next move?" If the military, sports, and games inspire the metaphors you apply to leadership, you will likely lead in a way that produces winners and losers, adversaries and not collaborators. The easiest way to change the map is to change the metaphors.[2] Metaphors are the common language of fellowships, people devoted to making things "as they are not now but should be."[3]

Let me suggest Dan Allender's metaphors of prophet, priest, and king as an alternative. Dr. Allender proposes that these are the three critical offices that leadership of an organization must provide. Kings build infrastructure and govern societies. In this capacity they make decisions, allocate resources, and develop others. The king's primary objective is the survival and growth of his subjects. He is the one who plans the route, pairs inexperienced hikers with more experienced hikers, and ensures that everyone has the necessary provisions for the trek. A priest creates a common narrative that bonds and inspires those she represents. She defines mission and guidelines for living peacefully and prosperously, with each other and with the king. She suggests breaks when weaker hikers are lagging and stops the group to point out mountain sheep grazing nearby. The prophet disrupts the status quo when complacency replaces discipline or when deceivers infiltrate the kingdom. They are the one who will stop the hiking party, declare that they are lost, and point out the likely results if action isn't taken promptly.

Every leader is called to act in all of these capacities, but the reality is that our abilities and talents usually make one role a more comfortable fit than the others. So, a good place to begin examining our character would be to assess which of these roles we would most comfortably fill. The second question we must ask ourselves is "Am I willing and capable of performing the other roles? If not, am I willing to share power with those who can?" Generally, this requires orienting yourself on the map of your life. How has your life brought you to the place where you are in a position to lead? What has helped you succeed? Where have you known failure? What is your motivation for leading?

Of course, the minute we begin asking ourselves these questions, we have to guard against the possibility of self-deception and self-betrayal. There is a spiritual discipline known as an "examination of conscience" that provides a useful model. A series of questions, based on beliefs about how one should live, is used as a guided prayer. The person in prayer asks that her spirit would be moved to repentance regarding any failure to live in accordance with her core beliefs. A process of confession, reconciliation, and restoration follow, if needed. When words and actions don't have congruity, self-betrayal is in play (and possibly betrayal of the other).[4]

Characteristics of self-betrayal include inflating others' faults or virtues, inflating the value of the things that justify self-betrayal, and blame.[5] When we first deceive ourselves about our behavior, our conscious usually prods us, and we lack peace about our chosen action. However, the pressures of our life and the norms of our culture often lead us to self-betray about the same things over and over.

I shudder when I hear some businessperson say, "It's just business," because that usually means something is being done in the name of business that would not be done if that person were doing it in the name of himself or herself.[6] We become adept at finding plausible reasons why we couldn't have done anything other than what we did. Over time we become desensitized to the issue, and our bad behavior becomes habitual. A good rule of thumb would be to always question when others become "the problem." That's a sure sign that you are no longer relating but are objectifying. Genuine care and openness are no longer present.

This is when we most need other people to help us see reality. However, others are also carrying around their own self-betrayal baggage, so there needs to be some agreements, some principals followed, that open up our defensive wall (even if it's only a crack). I have always found I gain a better perspective when I reconsider the situation while choosing to believe that everyone involved has the best intentions toward everyone else. I believe that this is usually true. Few people truly desire harm toward others. Thus, if there is conflict, it is likely a communication failure, or a failure to fully understand the needs and desires of the other. I find it helpful to enter potentially conflictual conversations with the goal to, "Seek first to understand, then to be understood."[7] Doing so allows me to see myself and my actions through the other's eyes. I may not agree with their conclusions, but at least I'm sure of what I'm disagreeing about.

I turn my attention now to the compass, the leader's moral strength. Our assessment about our character is as prone to self-deception as was defining our beliefs. So, everything said above is equally relevant here. Character is such a broad term that it feels overwhelming to even name what we should be looking at. As a starting point, I suggest considering the attributes that Max Depree considers essential for leaders: integrity, vulnerability, discernment, awareness of the human spirit, courage in relationships, a sense of humor, intellectual energy and curiosity, predictability, breadth, comfort with ambiguity, and presence.[8]

cover/hide or Choosing Change (handwritten)

It's probably incorrect to say that we can simply choose to grow these attributes on our own. However, we can place ourselves in situations that provide the opportunity for God to grow them in us. These are almost always relational contexts: marriage, parenthood, leadership, et cetera. And I'm comforted by the thought that God seems to pick leaders who are flawed. He puts them in the crucible of leadership and slowly, carefully turns up the heat so that our "dross" rises to the top and is revealed. It is our choice from there. We can choose to cover and hide, or we can ask Him to show us how to skim the crud off the top. Choosing to change requires effort and courage to be exposed, to take risks, and to do things in ways that we've never done them before.

choice (handwritten)

Leadership is both a privilege and a daunting responsibility. The skills to take the actions required of a leader can be taught in classes and lectures. The development of a leader's character, the well from which all her actions will spring forth, is the act of sanctification. This is a holy endeavor, meant to be done in the community of the Holy Trinity and human companions. If you find yourself lost or struggling, may you remember to return to your map and compass. And may you turn toward and not away from those you know who diligently maintain their own maps and compasses. Most importantly, may you turn to the One who called you to the challenge before you.

Jen

How often—even before we began—have we declared a task "impossible"? And how often have we construed a picture of ourselves as being inadequate? . . . A great deal depends upon the thought patterns we choose and on the persistence with which we affirm them.
—Piero Ferrucci

Framing it

Once upon a time there was a girl who translated the world as she experienced it into shapes, colors, lines, and space on a canvas. The convergence of intellect, emotions, laughter, and tears paralleled the interactions of brushstrokes, color, charcoal smudges, and water drips. She observed, absorbed, and then poured out reflections of the most ordinary moments of life and of the most extraordinary. Her own life could not be removed from the process of painting the lives and stories of others that drew her, which brought interesting tensions, balance, wear, texture, and form to her paintings. Each one did not go without struggle. None were completely smooth to the touch.

Now, this painter did not live in isolation from the world, but the way she engaged her work in the studio, she also sought to engage her work of regular life and work in the ministry. Her personality was not naturally of a forceful kind—persistent and pursuing, yes, but not forceful. Dominating was not a word to characterize her either. Akin to the painting process, she operated more from intuition and listening than from long bouts of reasoning. Oddly, though, she was a bit of a perfectionist and loved when things were well done in her art and in her life. She had a mind to do the right thing and follow the rules, while also having a mind to test everything and live with some air of defiance. Her paintings would not go far if she did not continuously test and find the freedom to begin a work anew for the second, third, or fourth time. Yet neither would a painting go anywhere if she did not listen and develop a mind for when to concede and let it speak more to her than her to it.

153

In life (and in painting) this did not always lead to the most appropriate or timely decision making. She could listen for quite awhile and contain much before speaking. It was not a fool-proof way of keeping herself, others, or a work of art from harm or dissonance, but it was her way of being. Often, she had voices inside that told her she needed to be different if she were to be a leader. Being an artist was already a bit of an odd thing, especially in ministry circles, so she felt she must take on a different kind of identity when she walked out of the studio and put on the minister's hat. How that hat looked, she wasn't sure. She just had this feeling that it didn't have paint splotches on it. This felt untruthful, though, and as she came to know herself more, she strove to live well with who she was—in fullness—in her life with others.

However, before coming to learn some of these things about herself, she had an encounter in her ministry work that became something of a crippling force in her life, echoing many of the thoughts already plaguing her. One day this painter approached a pastor who she had been working with. She had key involvement in that specific ministry for a few years, he was new, and he was in a position of authority above her. His entrance into this position came at a fragile time when the former leader she served under moved elsewhere. High school students were the focus of this ministry, and there was quite a large community of them. Over her few years of involvement, the painter had come to know and love the students. They consumed a significant number of hours of her weeks to which she voluntarily gave her time. Though it was not always a joyous endeavor, it became a labor of love, and she imagined she would do this work, or something like it, for the rest of her life. That said, it was harmful when the pastor seemed to be keeping her out of the loop of his intentions over the direction of the ministry (which was obviously different than what it had been). Functioning as a bridge between this new leader and the high school students (who did not like the direction things were going), she sought some information on what was going on. So, she approached him to request better communication to better engage the students, while also hoping she would be validated in the process for the position she had been in the past few years.

In very bold and straight forward words, the pastor responded by saying that the painter had to prove herself to be a leader before he would let her on his team. The conversation felt final, and she did not know what to say. Words had never been her strongest suit, and here she felt shocked by his words.

"Prove myself to be a leader?" she wondered.

And, "Before he lets me on *his* team?" she continued tossing around.

"What have I been doing the last few years? Has he no awareness or respect for what has been?" the thoughts continued.

Now, much of the painter's story has been left unwritten here, but it may be too obvious to say that the pastor's words cut like a knife. In retrospect, the painter could see more of where the pastor was coming from and what he may really have been getting at. But the truth was that that one sentence cut deep and clung to the other voices from her life that had already told her this same thing, only on other terms. As the pastor took this new position, he never sought to know what and who had been before, and in his process of trying to change directions, he silenced those who had invested in the students within the ministry. Being a little more than wounded, the painter tried to continue working with the pastor and tried to navigate around the work he was doing, but rapidly she found herself disappearing into a growing confusion of what he thought a leader was, and what she obviously was not. Her image of the pastor was that of a controlling, dominating, smooth-talking, put-together man. Is this how the painter needed to be in order to be a leader in the ministry? It seemed so. She hoped for more conversation, but he seemed to always close the doors to conversation before they ever started. Behind his suaveness, he maintained great distance, and she grew in distrust.

Fast forward slightly, and the painter did not stay within this ministry much longer. She held on for longer than many other leaders because she was quite loyal, and of course wanted to "prove" the pastor wrong. Yet it became abusive for her to stay, and eventually she left after weighing her feelings of abandoning the high school students. A few years later she moved away to attend seminary and continue making art. However, before moving away, it had become increasingly difficult for her to see herself as an artist. Though it was a struggle, she began to find her identity as a painter easier than she did herself as a minister. After her interactions with the pastor, she began shutting down her desire to lead others from any place more visible than from behind a canvas. Anything that required her spoken voice was too costly, and she was convinced that was just not meant to be for her.

As mentioned earlier, this one interaction is not the only one that had shaped her view of leadership or of what she "needed" to be, but every time she recalled the words of that pastor, they came back sharp and strong like a potent drug ready for the kill. Unknowingly, she let the pastor's words hold the desires of her heart in captivity. They furthered the ill-conceived thoughts in her head that the way the painter paints is not how she must engage the rest of the world. The way the painter paints is fine work for the studio, but if she were to engage the rest of life this way, and especially the ministry this way, she would be at fault. There is no space for a painter like her leading people, not with words. Her way of being is not wanted, understood, or accepted in any position other than the studio.

It took years before the painter received enough understanding of the interaction between the pastor and herself that she could see they had fundamentally different ways of being, and their different ways of being naturally brought them to different ways of leading, and therefore to some conflict. The circumstances surrounding the interaction were not simple. They were hard times in the ministry, yet even so the pastor portrayed an unawareness of the years of time, labor, and energy she had invested. He seemed to want to just move on, see a certain type of behavior, and then check it off as success. The painter wonders what both could have done for the story to be written differently.

This is a true story of my life, a true interaction that certainly has left its impression me. It is always difficult to reflect back on an interaction and see that I was not merely a victim in the larger circumstances of the ministry and Michael's new position. It is hard to hold where I felt deeply wounded, knowing that in the larger context of our time in ministry together, the job was an awful position for him to be placed in. However, it has proven a helpful experience for seeing how I can be in places of leadership, and what it would be helpful for me to own as my way of being. Michael, as well as the ministry context we served, had a very clear image of what it meant to be a leader. To Michael's credit, he perpetuated what he knew and how he was trained. Unfortunately, that view was quite limited and pushed many people out of the picture for leadership, including myself.

As I sit with my feedback from the DiSC, I am surprised by the accuracy this profile system offers. Though I struggled to accept the classification because of its title, the "perfectionist" pattern that arises in stress situations and is seemingly the way the world sees me, makes quite a bit of sense, and so does my high *S*. My perception of myself as the "agent" also resonates, and there are elements overlapping between the two that make a great deal of sense to me. As for the *S*, those who carry this as the highest letter from the scale have been said to be incredibly loyal, team players, good listeners, and the "glue" that can hold organizations and systems together. All of these words have been spoken to me on numerous occasions, and I have seen places where my presence has affected the group like "glue," where after leaving the group there had been struggle for the group to stay together.

Though now I can read this profile and see great resonance with me in it, I had no framework to understand the complexities of personalities in leadership when Michael spoke those words to me. We were incredibly different, and he seemed to really want me to act like him before he would consider me a "real" leader. Even if my strengths were recognized, they were not recognized as leadership qualities to be nourished. Rather, they were seen as elements of my personality, but leadership was a different hat that one put on, and it looked more like a corporate business *man* than an artist. Because my strong points do not come out through a dominating presence, they feel harder to be seen—by myself and by others. Especially considering that a lower view of self-worth is often tied up in both the "perfectionist" and "agent" styles, for me the result is a quieter voice and conceding presence through a notion that my presence, whatever style it may be, doesn't really matter anyway.

This is one area the test says I would do well to increase in. If only it were as easy to grow in as recognizing the importance of realistic deadlines.

As I have remembered and written this story and sat with the DiSC responses, there is an image of a woman who has continually come to mind—a woman whom I have resonated with a great deal in my coming to read and reread her story over the past years. It is hard for this to not just feel like an afterthought or addendum, but her face and posture as I have come to imagine her have been with me throughout this writing. In the Gospel according to Matthew (26:1-13), a woman comes to the home where Jesus is dining with religious leaders and falls to the floor behind him, weeping. She comes bearing a large flask of perfume, and she pours it on his feet, wiping both the perfume and her tears away from his feet with her hair. She is vulnerable in her position before him and does not try to hide the fullness of her emotion, even in the presence of others. This is a holy moment, and surely one that doesn't seem the most controllable. Likely, it looked to the disciples who were nearby that this woman was a nuisance, and in her gratitude and worship, a mess. The disciples berate her actions by saying that what she has done is a waste—something more practical could have been done with the amount of money the perfume cost. However, Jesus responds by saying that "she has done a beautiful thing to me" (26:10, ESV), and another translation says "she has just done something wonderfully significant for me" (MSG). As I remember this woman's story through the lens of leadership, there is a part of me that does not want to see her bowing down, her tears, and her "waste" of perfume as leadership. And yet, how can it not be? Jesus says that "wherever the gospel is proclaimed in the whole world, what she has done will also be told in memory of her" (26:13). Those final words linger so powerfully. Really? *This woman* will be remembered *wherever* the gospel is told—*in the whole world?* This woman's outpouring to Jesus carried influence, and it was an influence that in this moment Jesus wanted to forever be associated with the gospel.

As I remember this woman's presence and the interaction between myself and Michael, I am beckoned to believe that though my way of being may be different than the loudest examples of leadership I have seen in my life, it does not mean that my way of being is invalid as leadership. It does mean that I need to do some work reconsidering and trusting what others see within me, especially that which I struggle to see myself. It does not mean that an artist cannot or does not influence in ways other than behind her canvas or other work of art. And should an artist also be a pastor, it does not mean that she has to take on a completely different identity to fill a certain role. Rather, she most beautifully, truly, and effectively will pastor in the places where her artistry converges with ministry; and will most beautifully paint in the places where her shepherding touches the canvas. If leadership does not emerge from within a person's soul but is simply something ascribed as a job description might be, then it is empty and the alabaster flask does not carry perfume, but only still water.

Johnny

Upon completing our Leadership 1 course, I find myself asking several questions because so much has been stirred. This class has drawn my attention to what a good leader is and what a good leader is not. Having a better understanding of the difference between the two, I am finding myself in the place of being a leader in the process of being sculpted into a great leader. And in order to become a great leader, I must be willing to engage the difficult issues that surround me, including those issues within me.

As I begin this journey I am grappling with who I am. I am a Latino who is becoming more aware of what it is like to live in this world as a minority, while not allowing this to hold me back from who I am and to what I'm called. I am also discovering that my very own story plays a crucial role in becoming this great leader. As I continue to encounter my own story and how it plays into what I bring and how I bring it, this will directly affect how I am as a leader. This is just the start of my journey. There is so much to be learned about myself, about where I will fit in beyond my time here at Mars Hill Graduate School, and about leadership.

As a Latino, I'm usually in a place where my voice is not heard. Often I am not even acknowledged because people think that I have nothing to offer. But I know that I bring a different perspective to the table; a different set of views and visions. And there is much to be gained from this experience. I am able to bring a view of perseverance that ties directly to my own story of growing up. My upbringing was not the norm; I did not grow up with all the privileges of the typical American. My parents often struggled to put food on the table. What was instilled in me was how to persevere through difficult times, knowing that after some time, things would become better.

Another thing that I am able to bring is my courage. Life has had its fair share of struggles. I have found myself in places where it would have been easy to give up my search for that "something deeper." But I have battled through this and made it further than many people thought I could. Knowing that there was opposition from a young age, I did not want to settle for something mediocre.

I had a drive within me to reach for that great "something." To this day I have that drive for something deeper, for something greater. It is my hope and prayer that I will not lose this drive and desire.

Knowing that I have much to bring when I am in the role of a leader, I have to look at how my past sheds light into the present. Upon taking the DiSC personality profile test, I have come to learn that I am an *I-S*. This means that I have a tendency to emphasize the shaping of the environment by influencing others. I like to create a space that is comfortable and enjoyable. I want the working conditions to be favorable. I want to take the logical approach, and when it comes to appraising others, I tend to be realistic.

Being an *I-S* has shed a great deal of light on my own story. Initially, I was very skeptical of taking any types of these tests because of some bad experiences. There was one time, while employed for a church, the senior pastor and the board decided that we would take a couple of days and do a staff retreat. One of the focuses of this retreat was to build community among the staff. I thought it would be fun and exciting. We took this same DiSC personality profile test, and it was quite interesting. Of the six people who took it, I was the only one who "scored" differently than the other five people. They were all the same personality type! From that point forward, they used it against me in very mean ways.

This time I noticed something different. This test was not actually designed to out me from an organization, but it was created to help me understand myself better as a person. It made a lot more sense as I have begun the process of understanding myself in the leadership role. Using it for this purpose has shed more light in how I do when I am under stress. Knowing that I like to make a place comfortable and like to make people comfortable, I know that I have a tendency to be overly flexible and overly trusting with people when I am in a stressful situation. I have the tendency to begin to shut down.

This was beautifully illustrated with another test, the Johari Window, which illustrates how well I know myself and how well others know me. The assessment is done in three parts: it asks me to answer according to when I am working with others, when I am working under supervision, and while supervising. When stress arises and I have the tendency to shut down, as I mentioned before, my arena starts to become smaller. I become less known by others, and I tend not to see my own idiosyncrasies in stressful situations. The area that is not known by others and by myself becomes greater. This can be a place that is not the best as I pursue to be a leader that is open and honest with myself and with others.

Thinking back on these tests, they have helped me make much more sense of how I work. It feels like the puzzle pieces have started to fall into place and I'm seeing the greater picture. I'm starting to enjoy it for the beauty that lies within that picture. I am becoming more aware of what I have to offer as a leader and how I am able to bring it in light of the past and the present.

So where do I want to go with this information? Where do I want it to take me? How do I use it for the good of the people I am working with, and how do I not get carried away with it? These are questions that I need to continually wrestle with. I know that I would like to use my gifts to reach people who work with youth. I feel as though this could be a good way to use the leadership qualities that I possess. I love being engrossed in the culture that we live in. I love the creativity of the world around me. People are quite gifted when they are using their talents. Whether through movies, music, art, or written words, I know that youth of today are very much involved in what is going on today. They are very much in tune with what is going on in the world. Unfortunately, most youth workers are not in tune with what is going on. Also, most of the churches that they work for are out of tune with what is going on in the culture.

I strongly feel that we could use what is going on in the world to make an impact on the lives of these youth. I would love to create a space in which I can become that bridge between the youth workers and the culture. Because my tendency is to create a space where everyone is comfortable, I think that I will be able to present the culture in a light that will be appealing to the youth workers. This could be done through the means of creating my own organization or working with an existing organization that works with youth workers.

However, I do have to be realistic and approach this idea with my head screwed on straight. In presenting the culture, I could face situations that could be stressful. This stress could come from people who are very set in their ways and who think that the culture is not helpful. I am hoping to continue to work on understanding myself, the culture, and the church community, and how to present this in a manner that is not offensive to those who are hearing it. It is my hope that I could be able to maintain my arena from the Johari Window and not have the usual tendency of having it become smaller when I am in stressful situations.

Also, another thing that I have to be realistic about is the people that I am presenting to. Some of these church communities could be older and very set in their ways. These types of churches tend to have issue with, and do not often listen to, those who are younger. In 1 Timothy 4:12, Paul tells Timothy not to worry about his age, but to go out and be an example. He is to be an example for believers through speech, and in conduct, love, faith, and purity. All of these are attributes of a good leader.

I desire to be a leader that conducts myself through love, through faith, and through purity. It is my goal to be ever evolving as a person and as a leader. The journey of becoming a leader has just begun. I have so much to learn and so much to look forward to. It will not be an easy process but one that will be gut wrenching at times. There will be times when I want to give up, but it will be worth the hard work and the wrestling. Pursuing my dream of becoming a leader will demand much work on my end, but with courage and perseverance, I will be able to work through what I need to in order to be this great leader that I have been called to be.

Through my own story and being a Latino, I will be able to bring a very different perspective to culture. I will also be able to bring a different perspective to youth workers. I have been in youth ministry before and have experienced what they are going through. Understanding this dynamic of what is needed in the youth ministry world, I will be able to bring this fresh perspective to this world. I am very excited to see where this all leads.

Jeremy

Drunk from a Liter of Apathetic Culture

How did I get here? As I think back on my childhood, I really was a happy and mischievous little kid. I was the oldest of five and told from the beginning that I was the cutest little entertainer that would grow up to be "president of the United States or just the greatest actor since Gene Kelly." I went through a brief stint of interest in both careers by the age of ten, but as my family became more involved in the local church, I found my future career as bright as day: I wanted to be a preacher. I remember asking for any video of Billy Graham, reading his biographies, and doing book reports and research papers all through middle school and junior high on him. I was told that I had the charm and charisma to mesmerize a crowd and a preacher certainly needed those to move a congregation. As I continued in this pursuit and more opportunities became available to help in the church, it became more evident to me that a preacher also had to lead. By high school, I was a paid youth intern, teaching Sunday school and organizing events, and I became aware of one more quality of leadership that would be necessary to pastor: I needed to know my Bible better than the parishioners. If I was going to lead a church, I needed to be able to teach the objective Truth to help my congregation grow in their faith. Faith comes with more knowledge and the pastor has to know it if he is going to lead others to it.

So with the two beautiful sisters Charm and Charisma by my side, I marched in pursuit of this objective Truth. As I learned from my own pastor and other mentors in my life during high school, the pursuit of objective Truth in the scriptures requires a literal reading of the text. Late into high school, as I climbed the ranks of ministry into junior high leadership, Sunday school teaching, and youth intern, I began to study the text more on my own. As I continued to study, though, I started finding different ideas about the scriptures than what I was learning from the rest of the church. With the abundance of information at my fingertips in my generation, for every response that the pastor had to a text, I could find 2,787 other ideas about the same text (and all in .05 seconds with the beautiful world of Google). The interpretation of texts became increasingly difficult as I read others' ideas. I continued in this pursuit of objective Truth with a biblical education at a conservative Bible college, only to find that my professors, in their own literal readings of the text, had different interpretations as well. How can there be different interpretations if we are all reading the same text literally? I came to the end of a four-year degree in biblical studies with less certainty about anything than when I had arrived. I was certain of one thing, however: charisma, charm, and objectivity now looked like nothing more than cheap cover-ups for others who really had no clue. My cynicism drained any hope of ministry leadership, because no one was going to follow a cynic whose primary aim is to disprove the validity of everyone else's interpretations and never arrive anywhere. Upon graduation, I found that it was far easier to use my charm and charisma to sell, and avoided job offers and ministry opportunities within the church, instead working with coffee and beer.

Though my story is one of particular grief, I am finding common beliefs among peers and writers of my generation. There is a growing discontent with leaders who give us pat answers and tell us how to make meaning out of something. It makes sense why most of us receive our politics from Jon Stewart and Stephen Colbert. In solidarity with us, they mock those who claim to know and get a good laugh out of it. My generation has enough information to know that anyone who claims that they have the answer is a fool, because it is never the full answer. In the end, with this fatalistic frame of mind, the culture can worship and follow no king, but only laugh with the court jester. Even with that promising future as a child, I have found myself disenchanted and untrusting of leaders and staring at the bottom of the bottle of Apathy, curious now about how I will ever get back home. It now seems like a long way from any kind of hope, but as I encounter more leaders who have held hope, I am sobering up and beginning to feel the sting of how far I have to go, and what kind of spiritual act of repentance must occur to get me out of this place.

As I observed one particular leader, Sarah, in preparation for this course, I found that she could easily find herself in a similar place of fatalism and cynicism. Sarah currently holds a position in a company run by men and has worked hard to prove herself in her own position. There is conversation about gender and diversity within the company, but it is long work to fight against the old norms of culture. The company has worked hard to listen and adapt, but Sarah could easily become cynical, as others have within the company, or quit and find a job with another company that is further along in the process. I found that her ability to hold hope on behalf of the company, however, is part of what has enabled her to be such a strong voice and leader in her position. Like Sarah, if I desire to be an agent of change, I must learn to hold hope in the midst of adversity, and begin to dream of what could be rather than wallow in what is not. To engage, arouse, and enliven the next generation to a re-visioning of what could be, a leader must enter into this story of our generation's disappointment with the leaders of our past, and she must begin to find places to hope.

Hungover but Hopeful

Though it is a crass way to say it, I have certainly imbibed religiously of the delicious nectar of my own culture's apathy. I am only just beginning to awaken from my cynical stupor, and I am still feeling the effects. As you can tell as you read, I still stink of cynicism, but as I keep bumping into more and more people who are hoping on my behalf, it is waking me up. My vision of the gospel is growing, for my own life and for the potential for redemption of a culture. I wonder if those Israelites wandering in the desert found the manna to be good for their hangovers as well. I think that some of the qualities that I have found in others that I respect in leadership have also given me a vision for who I could be and where my story has the opportunity to be redeemed. Rather than dogmatism and narcissism that seemed to be norms for leadership, I am finding that honesty and curiosity offer much more and give more room for God to be bigger than we have allowed in the church lately.

As a culture, we are moving from the pursuit of objective Truth that had held so much security for the previous generation. We now view objectivity as naivety to complexity, and instead seek honesty and mystery in our spirituality. We begin as skeptics with anyone who leads, but we desperately want someone to help us find some kind of meaning in this mess. We listen to those who are willing to listen to us, and it will take a leader who is willing to remain curious to help us move. These qualities of honesty and curiosity will change the way a leader looks in front of others. Charisma and charm might be present, and even some objective ideas, but to follow, we must trust that our leaders are here for us, with a willingness to be transparent and sit with us in the unknown rather than explain it away.

I hope to become a leader who encourages honesty by example. As I interact with others and have even subjected myself to a few different profile tests, I am learning that honesty is part of my blood, that my attempts to edit (I work hard to articulate exactly what I mean before I say anything) do not work well, and that I cannot hide as well as I thought. I am learning to find my voice, believing that I have something to offer, and that my intonations and demeanor can be disarming. I am beginning to move past some of the shame of my past in leadership, when I stood before others and claimed to know, using those beautiful sisters Charm and Charisma to distract from my ignorance. Dan Allender says it eloquently as he explains why he believes that admitting your failures even publicly is a way to lead well, for "doing so invites others—by the Spirit's prompting—to look more honestly at their own need for forgiveness, freedom, and courage. It also removes the dividing wall of hierarchy and false assumptions about people in power and gives the leader who humbles himself the opportunity to be lifted up by God."[1] This honesty disarms, invites dialogue and community (which includes you rather than worships you), and gives humanity to a leader who is often otherwise glorified as a god.

I hope to become a leader who believes more in the community than my own ability. As Max Depree writes, "A group dominated by a leader will never exceed the talents of the leader."[2] If I truly believe that my community has more to offer than I do, I will approach others with curiosity rather than authority. Roy Barsness, in an article on the place of surrender and transcen-

surrender

therapeutic encounter, speaks of curiosity that ensues a willingness to surrender and does not neglect the power of either participant. A leader does stand for a cause and yet remains willing to hear and be changed by the other. As Barsness says in comparing surrender and submission, "The willingness of surrender is not submission to the domination of the other, which submission connotes, but a willingness to be open to the surprise of what more can be revealed and what new meaning can be achieved."[3] It is hopeful to envision a generation of leaders who recognize that their roles are only as strong as their followers make them and are able to more fully utilize community strength. Curiosity will give way to dialogue and help us work together rather than quietly submit.

As a leader who does believe in the gospel, I must stand for something (while culture remains in ambivalence about everything), but I want to exhibit an inviting strength that provokes action and gives voice to the other. An inviting strength is one that emanates from a located voice, one who articulates a certain stance and purpose, ultimately on behalf of the other. Strength that invites will beckon the other's located voice and necessarily needs other voices to receive and respond. I think about the cicadas near my house growing up. Lying down in bed, as I slowly attuned my ears to the silence, I would often hear one solitary cicada that directed my ears to the other noises beyond the silence. Almost immediately, other cicadas would come into my purview, creating a symphony of mating calls. Obviously, I did not lay down to the first cicada call of the evening. There were others before, but my hearing was piqued with one cicada, which directed my ears to the calls of others. I hope for leadership to be the same way, that although one voice might pique the interest of one or even many others, ultimately, that voice will resonate with others who will respond. I hope to be a voice that brings freedom to others, rather than one that sings into corners only to hear the beauty of my solo.

As it pertains to the church, my generation does not want a leader with all of the answers to why things are the way they are. We want to follow someone who helps us, by example, wade through the mystery of a great God. We desire leaders who are

168

willing to show us who they really are and expose their own struggles with the pat answers and the reality of pain in this life. We want someone to help us find our own voices, to free us toward sober usefulness for a gospel that is actually as big as Jesus claims it is. We want to know the works we will do are greater than His, and how we can learn to do that together (see John 14:12). Most will continue to mock and jeer at any attempt to find purpose, but hold hope for us. We have been told that we will be presidents and agents of change, and there is a quiet voice that continues to whisper that we were meant for more than a court jester. As leaders, help us turn up the volume on that whisper. The volume will certainly be disruptive, as any good headache from a hang-over is, but I am beginning to believe that the gospel that provided freedom for the captives might be connected with that whisper.

Jessi

You do not lead by hitting someone over the head—that's
assault, not leadership.
—Dwight Eisenhower

If your actions inspire others to dream more, learn more,
do more, and become more, you are a leader.
—John Quincy Adams

I don't care if they eat me alive 'cause I have better things
to do than survive.
—Ani DiFranco

Over the last few years, the question has arisen about whether artists constitute leaders, and if so, what the parameters of their leadership happen to be. This has been especially true over the last eight years, since the elections of 2000 and the inauguration of George W. Bush's presidency. During this election and the 2004 election, as well as the upcoming 2008 election, the promotion of candidates by artists has become the norm. Suddenly, we are no longer voting for John Kerry or George Bush, John McCain or Barack Obama, but for Harvey Danger, Pearl Jam, or John Mellencamp.

On the night before Election Day in 2000, I saw Pearl Jam at Key Arena in Seattle. I think it was probably one of the first times I was keenly aware of the strife of politics in this country. Even before we entered the arena, the powerful emotions and opinions involved were striking fires and assaults. Standing in line we encountered people from both sides of the political spectrum, including both a conservative Christian wearing a sandwich board promoting the damnation of all and those who were hurling back insults and damnations. I couldn't help but feel caught in the middle of these two opposite sides, and tears welled up in my eyes because of the hatred that existed. During the concert, that hatred was amplified as Eddie Vedder made several comments about voting, specifically voting against Bush. At one point someone jokingly held up a sign saying "Vote for Bush" and Vedder, more serious than I would have wanted to think, told the crowd to kick him out of here or he was going to do something that he might get arrested for. Later on during the show, Vedder made the statement that everyone should go out and vote the next day because if not he might do something he could get arrested for. The crowd reacted with a response similar to a Baptist church choir to their charismatic preacher. No one was hurt that night, but I was keenly aware that had Vedder said "jump," 90 percent of the room would have jumped. I realized that there was a room full of people willing to move with the statement of one man. That is a lot of power for one person to have, and is a powerful form of leadership.

The second experience I had was at a moveon.org concert in the fall of 2004.[1] I was there to see the group Harvey Danger with a friend. During the concert everyone was once again raging against George W. Bush and the fresh horror of a preemptive strike in Iraq. The atmosphere was charged with anger and frustration, both of which were valid given the state of the country at that moment. Yet what struck both my friend and me was that while most of the statements centered around the war and president, there were also statements about people who possessed religious backgrounds. Religious people were critiqued just as heavily as those with dissenting political views. Yet what some of these leaders failed to understand was that within the room were people who held similar political leanings, but held them *because* of their understanding of faith. As I sat there thinking and praying, I was once again struck by the power of the artist, similar to when I was at the Pearl Jam show four years earlier. There was something desperately missing from artistic leadership during these times. Whatever was happening culturally and politically, it forced artistic leadership to become something that it shouldn't be—blatant and cruel.

The nature of all art is, to some extent, political. Art is a subversive form of cultural prophecy. Through the use of metaphor and images, it offers a back-door critique of the world. Historically, artists have lived in cultures that are dominated by powerful leadership which can and will seek to silence and destroy those who speak out against it. Therefore, artists are forced to be creative in

how they couch the prophecy they offer. The whole concept of the
"fool" or "jester" character in historic royal courts (and in artistic
expressions) is a specific archetype created to be the wise character
whose wisdom is often guised in a trickster mentality.[2] In the midst
of the biblical narrative, we are given an artistic vision of this
character type. The prophet Nathan, standing before King David,
weaved a story of the King's sin that affects and changes the heart
of the King. It is effective because while it is his story, it is not his
story. Through the use of story the prophet (artist) tells of David's
adultery and subsequent cover-up by using the tale of a poor family
who loved their single lamb and the rich neighbor who takes the
lamb, instead of one of his many animals, to feed a guest.[3] What,
then, does this have to do with the author and her understanding
and experience of leadership?

Theatre and film are the fields to which I feel called, both as
a leader and vocationally. Since art is the lens through which I
encounter the rest of the world, a discussion of leadership for me,
much like a discussion of anything else, centers on the role of the
artist. The image of the cultural prophet is the best way to explain
what I envision artistic leadership to look like. It is a fusion of
both my artistic outlook as well as my faith. Like the prophets of
the Old Testament, I believe that the artist as prophet is called to
creatively engage the issues and abuses (as well as the glory and
beauty) that they encounter in their culture. This happens when the
artist offers the chance for their audience to "wrestle with Truth."[4]
Wrestling with Truth is what the prophets offered to the people
of God, the chance to encounter God through creative means
and expression. Aren't the stories of Hosea being commanded to
marry a prostitute or Jonah being eaten by a large fish anything
but wild creativity? Yet in spite of the very diverse and creative
ways in which God reveals God's self throughout the biblical text,
the expectations of creative Christian leadership is sometimes the
cruel expression of what is subtle, creative, and dynamic Truth.
Professor Thom Parham of Azusa Pacific University, in an article
entitled "Why do Heathens Make the Best Christian Films?,"
writes about the fact that many Christian films have become more

propaganda than invitations to sit and wrestle with the questions of life, faith, and God.

To quote Dan Allender once again, "One cannot lead where they have not been."[5] This means that I must continually choose to enter into spaces where I am invited to sit and wrestle with God. Currently, this means two things that are connected for me: first, I must begin to trust my own voice and the manner in which God uniquely speaks to me (i.e. artistically); second, I must step out into the call to gain more experience as an artist. While I have been involved in the arts for years, I have always lived with one foot out the door, never fully committing to my passion and desire to work in this field. I often battled the fear that I wasn't good enough to do art and the voices of those who didn't think it was my calling, and they stood as walls inhibiting my ability to fully embrace this passion. Through the course of my time here at Mars Hill Graduate School, I have been encouraged and challenged to step completely into that desire and passion. Over the last three years I have been with people who see leadership specifically in the context of artistry. One of my profound encounters recently was when I met with a spiritual director during a prayer retreat. Within the first five minutes she was saying, "Girl, I've only known you for something like five minutes, but just sitting with you here, I can see that art is where you are called. You go girl." In gaining more education through working in film or by pursuing a second master's program, I will receive training that will help me create more diverse and crafty ways of storytelling, both as an actor and a writer.

What is the role of artist as leader? I have come to see it as one of creative story and truth telling. Taking on the guise of a trickster and cultural prophet, I hope to lead as one who stands before the king offering a story that is the king's story, told in a manner that asks him to wrestle with Truth so that he can wrestle with himself. I also hope that I will be one who continues to choose mystery and brokenness over the need to influence others through the abuse of the power.

Kevin

Mine is not a sad story.

Therefore, the hope I carry into the future for leadership is not a hope laden with disappointment from the past. It is an easy hope, carried by experiences rich with encouragement and a tradition of leadership done well.

Don't get me wrong, there have been some very hard times. I am sure no one had a map to leadership paved in a direct line, but through the twists and turns that have come my way, I have learned much about what my own voice sounds like and have learned to treasure hearing the voices of others. There have been several times when people in positions above me have identified a skill within me, or my potential to develop a skill, and put trust in my voice even before I did. As I carry my goals for leadership into the future, my hope would be that I can continue developing these skills myself, and that they would inspire similar growth in others.

Leaders need to use both their voices and their ears.

When I was younger my family called me "The Mouth." We were a family who loved to tease, and this was one of the many nicknames applied at one point or another throughout my childhood. When I was young I talked all of the time. Whether it was incessant chatter in the backseat of the car or having the last word in an argument, my mouth was always moving. There was a period in my life when all that talking drove everyone crazy, and I became scared of my voice. Eventually, I stopped using it altogether.

A teacher first helped me find and refine my voice in high school. Vance Jennings, the local high school English and Drama teacher, asked me to head up a school project. I never ran for class office or served on the associated student body, and I was never very popular. I certainly never wanted to put myself in a situation where others could vote to prove my low self-worth accurate. We had received a grant to write a musical about making choices and tour it around to area high schools. None of us had any idea what we were getting ourselves into, and I had no faith that people cared about what I had to say.

It was my first big project bringing together people with various artistic skills, managing our progress, and seeing it through to completion. The next year Vance asked me to direct our production as we performed the show at home and toured Washington and Portland. I didn't believe anyone cared what I had to say, neither my collaborators nor our audiences, but Vance believed that I could lead our small group through the process and come out the other end with a quality product.

Over the two-year process Vance nurtured my voice out of me, but he did more than just nurture my voice. He taught me how to listen well to my collaborators. I am not musically inclined, so if the entire thing had been left to me, it would not have made for a very enjoyable viewing experience. Instead, I was able to pull together a great group of students to write music, lyrics, and dialogue, to plot out our story, build portable sets, run the light and sound boards. Because of the thoroughly collaborative nature of this project, I also learned very early on the importance of listening.

A leader must have accountability in roles of responsibility.

When I first started driving, I was horrible. My siblings took to the road like naturals, but I struggled immensely. In fact, I remember the first time I got behind the wheel after getting my permit, my mother made me pull over about a half mile down the road so she could drive. You see, I was the third of four children, and we lived out in the country. My older siblings grew up driving vehicles on the farm or, at the very least, driving the car up the driveway after getting the mail. I never got that opportunity because they were getting their licenses and they did all the driving. Needless to say I didn't get to practice much, and driving is an awesome responsibility with the highest level of accountability to others on the road. Like me as a growing driver, a leader needs to be given increased levels of responsibility and be held accountable to their performance.

My next distinct leadership opportunity came when Jim Lortz, a professor at Western Washington University, asked me to stage manage the musical *Sweeney Todd*. Once again, I had no idea what

I was getting myself into, I had no idea the amount of responsibility this role would entail, or the level of accountability for every action taken and decision made. But this experience helped me grow my leadership skills to another level.

For anyone who hasn't seen a staged production of *Sweeney Todd,* it is impressive. The cast includes nine principals, a chorus of at least twenty, a full orchestra, and two-story set pieces that move on and off the stage on castors. For a first time stage manager, it was intimidating, and I had no idea if I could do it. And yet having had the equivalent of driving in the driveway in high school, college was my chance to go on the open road. There were a trials as I learned to facilitate meetings between choreographers, designers, and the director, as well as working as a liaison between the actors, the grunt labor, and the visionaries.

I was accountable not only to the people above me, but also to those under me. The responsibility for things running smoothly, from auditions through curtain call, fell on my shoulders. Every step along the way, I was held to the highest level of accountability for how I interacted with individuals and the flow of the show. I believe that my experience as stage manager for this show set me on the road for being selected as the Theatre Department's outstanding senior when I graduated in 2005.

A leader must be given the opportunity to succeed as well as fail.

I moved to New York City after college graduation. As a theatre and dance major, I thought I should go to a big city and spend some time auditioning, but I soon found how difficult, and expensive, the Big Apple can be. As I was interviewing for jobs to help me stay afloat, I met with a girl who was starting a new boutique in Brooklyn's Williamsburg district. I went into the interview looking for a position as a sales clerk and left with much more. Hannah was currently working as a production manager for emerging fashion designers doing some technical design, and then seeing a few lines through production. She decided that she would open an atelier to feature some of the designers she was working with as well as other new and emerging designers. But Hannah also had a business opportunity in San Francisco she wanted to take.

Hannah was giving me an amazing opportunity; an opportunity to succeed or fail. It seems often times in leadership positions there is such infrastructure and support in place that true failure is not going to happen, and true success is hard to pinpoint. All I was looking for during that interview with Hannah was a position as a sales clerk, but instead she handed over the reins to a new venture as well as her clients on the production management side. I worked for Hannah for six months before she decided to close the doors on the boutique, and I decided to return to Alaska. During that six months I worked hard, long hours, was on the phone with my bi-coastal boss daily, and learned more skills than in any college course. And in the end, the business failed.

The importance of those lessons learned through the opportunity to succeed or fail have stayed with me. I am much more likely to try new and innovative ideas, to look outside the box for options others may not have thought of, and to rework and tinker with the status quo. I have participated in a venture in the very fickle fashion industry that didn't quite make it off the ground, but it gave me the opportunity to work hard, learn to collaborate, and ask for help often.

A leader must commit to their passions.

And now I look to my future. These leadership experiences have helped mold my passions and my expertise. Through people in positions of power believing in my abilities or potential before I even did, I have been able to rise to the occasion. Along every step of the way I have found myself in highly collaborative situations where I acted as a link and coordinator to help a group of people realize their dreams. Sometimes those dreams worked well together, and sometimes it took a lot of work to make them line up, but across the board I was able to learn about myself and how I work with others.

As I look forward, I am more aware of my strengths and weaknesses. I know that my voice can be very powerful, but only when paired with my reliance on listening to those around me. I know that I like responsibility, but the importance of having others to hold me accountable to actions taken, even if there is no one in a position over me, is something everyone in the organization should have the right to expect. I know what it feels like to have rousing and unexpected successes, and what it feels like to fail. And I know I can live through either. Beyond all of these things I know that I work best with collaborating on artistic endeavors with others. I know that my passions lie in the arts, and we are most successful when connected with our passions.

That leads me to my last point. Though I have a full class schedule and work full time, I know I cannot lose touch with my passions, and so room must be made. Over the next year I will work with Sacred Spaces at Mars Hill Graduate School a few hours a week to bring art and dialogue about art to our community. Whether it is finding time to dance when my schedule is tight or facilitating collaborations with old college friends, by committing time to those things about which I am passionate, I will continue to grow as a leader and as an individual.

Zach

As I consider leading in the future, I face a pivotal question: will I choose to lead in the manner in which I've been trained, or will I choose to lead in a new way—utilizing both my strengths and my weaknesses? My experience thus far in leading (and being led) has left me weary, cynical, and disillusioned. For my future participation in leadership to be redeemed, I must choose to hope. Dan Allender writes, "Disillusionment births true hope in the same way that death is the context for resurrection."[1] Over the last seven years, I've experienced plenty of "death" in leadership. Will I hope for life to arise from the ashes of that experience? I'm aware of an acute resistance to any hope. Cynicism appears to be the easier option; yet, I'm also aware that the path of cynicism only leads to a different kind of death that would shackle me to the mistakes of the past. So, I will choose to hope, in spite of circumstances that seem to indicate the foolishness of such an exercise. I will learn from my experiences and envision a way of leading that breathes life into myself and those around me.

The Breakdown

The story repeated itself with such precise regularity that it was nearly comical in its predictability. My wife could see it coming. My employees could see it coming. My leaders could see it coming. But despite their best efforts, it happened *every single year.*

The nonprofit I worked for operated on a typical school-year schedule. We had students working with us from September through May. In the summer our staff was involved in preparations for a new group of students to arrive in September. I was the director of the program, and the entirety of the program came under my purview. Throughout the early parts of the summer, I would delegate tasks that needed to be accomplished. Most of the things I assigned people to do were menial, simple tasks that were easily achieved. The major tasks I kept back for myself, fearing that without my direct involvement these tasks would fail.

Around August of every year I would tighten things up to an even greater extent, keeping more and more of the tasks under my direct supervision. My employees were constantly asking me for more to do. Meanwhile, I was drowning under a sea of duties that were keeping me from doing my most important task—caring for my employees and hearing from them. All the while I was becoming more exhausted, angry, and self-righteous. Why was I the only one qualified to carry out these tasks? Why did I have to work so long while everyone else was able to enjoy themselves doing whatever they pleased? Clearly it was my style of leading that led to the situation.

So every year around the end of August, I would have a break-down. Sometimes it would be obvious, and other times it would be subtle. The starkest example took place one year at a co-worker's birthday party. The party had just begun, and everyone was talking about how they had been taking advantage of the beautiful weather in Seattle. Meanwhile, I was seething. Of course on the outside I conveyed nothing of the sort. I acted as if I was happy for them. But all I could think about was the work that I had to do that night as deadlines were approaching. In the midst of the party, I started to realize that I was losing my capacity to function socially as a result of the internal rage that was brewing within me. I couldn't hold conversations. I couldn't enjoy the people. I could hardly stand to look at them. So, I did what I had trained myself to do: I quietly exited and went to my office to drown myself in work. While my colleagues enjoyed the evening together, I worked well into the early morning hours, my bitterness and weariness growing side-by-side. How will it be possible for me to expose what it is I really need, while not hiding behind a façade of busyness?

That particular story encapsulates seven years of leadership experience for me. The Johari Window assessment tool helped me make sense of some of these experiences. I noticed that my "arena" was quite small, especially as it related to my superiors. I've had a very difficult time asking for help, and in the absence of help, I've grown bitter toward those whom I've seen as having the responsibility to give me the needed help. I've become resentful as I've felt abandoned and uncared for in the midst of much struggle.

My struggle has centered on feeling guilty about asking for help
or even making my needs known. I've made myself appear as
if I can handle everything, and therefore I'm continually taking
on more responsibility and not saying "no." When I look to the
future I become excited thinking about being in a leadership situation where I am really known. My past experience taught me that
my leaders don't really want to hear about my problems because
they've had their own issues to deal with. I know that I've treated
my employees like that as well. Allender's thoughts on our weaknesses actually being our strengths make a lot of sense to me.[2] This
seems to be the ultimate paradox of leadership—acknowledging
weakness can actually have a positive result. As my needs and
weaknesses are exposed, I'll be able to obtain the assistance I need,
freeing me to both serve and be served.

Speaking Up

A few years ago I co-led a small group of men through the
organization I worked for. The format was very open ended with
the topic for each week being flexible in order to meet the current
needs of the group. The other leader who led with me was very
vocal, steering the group in the way that he saw best. In my
opinion the way he led only skimmed over deeper issues that were
being surfaced and allowed him to give brief, spiritualized insights
that didn't leave much room for conversation. Most days after our
meetings I would be very frustrated at the direction of the group.
I blamed him for it and felt annoyed that he couldn't see how
the members of the group were not enjoying it or contributing.
I had a sense that I had some good things to say and contribute,
but I always ended up deferring to his voice and not trusting my
own. This group continued for a few months and then disbanded
as the members finished up their time with our organization and
dispersed. In the debriefing process for our small group, much of
the feedback was surprisingly directed toward me. The essence of
the feedback was that the members wanted to hear more from me.
They appreciated when I did speak, and they trusted my opinions
and thoughts. But they consistently wanted more from me. How

will I be able to learn to trust my voice and my instincts in the future?

In reviewing my results from the DiSC assessment, I recognized my very high *C* and *S* scores had a large impact on how I use my voice. I tend to be very precise in what I say, oftentimes waiting until I am sure of something before I speak up. However, the feedback I've received has made it clear that when I do speak in times of uncertainty or chaos, my voice is powerful and good. The process of learning to trust those words has been very difficult. Allender speaks to this: "A leader must be willing to jump into the fray without having a complete knowledge of what will be required of him."[3] This quote is the antithesis of the actions of Adam in Genesis, when he disappears from the scene as the serpent is tempting Eve. God asks him, "Adam, where are you?" This represents Adam's failure to enter into the chaos of the situation, leaving Eve to fend for herself. For me, I believe it's a matter of honoring the unique gifts that I possess and not suppressing them. A few weeks ago my pastor went so far as to say that I have gifts that are obvious to other people but I don't even see or know about them. A principal reason for this is that I tend to ignore compliments and absorb only negative feedback. Looking to the future, I see myself as a leader who speaks into silence even when the outcome is unknown. I don't desire to forego caution and wisdom, but I will also not allow fear to keep me from using my voice.

The Battle Against Self-Betrayal

A few years ago I had an employee named Mike who was continually performing below the standards that had been agreed to. Often, he arrived late to work. He didn't pay attention or contribute to meetings. He was distracting to students in our program. Altogether, his behavior was erratic and unacceptable. I was very aware of my sense that there were circumstances outside of work that were affecting his performance. But I didn't act on that intuition. Instead, I resorted to responding to his repeated failures with anger and passive-aggression. Instead of addressing his shortcoming directly, I would give him a dirty look to let him know what I thought of him. When I did address him directly, my words were terse, sharp, and meant to inflict harm. My main concern was the quality of the program I was running, not his personal issues that needed to be attended to. Even as I was berating him, I knew that I was betraying myself. I knew that there were things happening below the surface that needed attention. But I had decided that those should be handled elsewhere. I was a jerk. Years later, as my relationship with him grew, I came to understand that he had been in a state of severe depression. Work was the least of his concerns. Surviving every day was his chief goal. I had been in position to attend to some of those needs, but I was too busy worrying about practicalities, so I glossed over them. Is it possible to produce a high-quality product or service while attending to the needs of employees and co-workers?

I was very conscious of the fact that I was betraying myself, as I was not responding to my instincts regarding Mike's situation. Even though I knew self-betrayal was occurring, I felt that it was justified based on the needs of the organization. I simply felt like the organization's practical needs eclipsed Mike's personal needs, and it wasn't my responsibility to care for him in that manner. As this situation continued over the course of many months, I accumulated many self-justifying reasons for why it was acceptable for me to treat him this way. His behavior had become so detrimental to our team that I saw no reason to extend any grace to him. As Mike and I have discussed the situation in later years, we've both come to realize there was some collusion taking place. Just as I was betraying myself by not acting on my instincts to deepen the issues, he was betraying himself by not acting on his instinct to share some of those things that he knew would've helped the situation. In Galatians Paul illustrates the difficulty of speaking up and caring for each other: "Let us not become weary in doing good, for at the proper time we will reap a harvest if we do not give up."[4] Allender goes on to further illustrate the point: "[Paul] encourages us because he knew that caring for others is demanding; and far more than merely exhausting, it saps our hope."[5] Accumulating self-betrayals is a negligent way to deal with relational difficulties. I desire to be a leader who addresses things as I notice them, not one who brushes them aside and tries to ignore them. Often,

183

my assumption is that problems will go away if I ignore them long enough, but that is not how I desire to lead. I envision working in an organization where people speak truthfully to each other, naming issues directly instead of avoiding them. The reality is that relational difficulties will spill over into whatever product or service any organization is attempting to produce.

My tendency has been to only condemn the past and refuse to grieve it. Condemnation has only led to cynicism, which feels empty and shallow. It has also led to the feeling that I'm not "for" anything—only "against" everything. However, as I've grieved my story of leadership and owned the parts of the story that I've contributed to, I've allowed hope to enter the story. Hope enters as I consider my own contributions and how those conscious choices could be different in the future. As I think about leadership in the future, I'm realizing how much of my difficulty has been rooted in my inability to trust my instincts and voice. My hope gathers momentum as I consider this past year and all that I've learned about myself through classes and relationships. I believe that when I enter into leadership again, it will involve a choice to lead. My previous experiences of leading have stemmed from situations where I happened to be in the right place at the right time. I've stepped out of leadership by my own choosing, and when I enter back into leadership, it will be by my own choice. In looking to the future, I'm already in a position where I am much more aware of what I bring to leadership—all of my tendencies, strengths, and weaknesses. My desire is to bring all of who I am to the leadership setting and influence my peers, employees, and employers in a collaborative learning environment. I'm tired of traditional leadership styles that have failed me in the past. I'm hoping for a new, life-giving experience.

Troy

The word *leadership* is anything but sterile. It evokes intense thoughts and spirited emotions; seldom do those who hear it experience the word with little reaction. We hear the word and we are reminded of stories—stories of success, of overcoming obstacles, and of achieving goals. Our reactions to leadership are intertwined with these stories, and as a result, the word inspires passion, arouses desire, and stirs the imagination to dream. Unfortunately, our stories also hold our pain—where we have lost or fallen short, how others have failed us, and how we have failed others—and so the word *leadership* awakens fear, or repulsion, or intolerable pain. More likely, our stories contain both goodness and pain, and we are left feeling ambivalent about the nature of leadership.

My story is no different. Ambivalence permeates my visceral reactions to the word, and stories of both glory and depravity swirl throughout my mind. My personal journey with leadership began early in life, and my positive experiences only fueled a desire for more. By the time I arrived as a freshman in high school, I had established myself as successful in both academic and social life. So, it seemed natural that I join the student leadership council. Although planning activities was our primary responsibility, there was an underlying sense that we were people with influence. We were the representatives of our fellow students; we were the leaders of the school. I thrived on the popularity, and when elections for the following year arrived, I ran for president of my class. I won easily, and my confidence as a leader soared. I do not remember what I accomplished, but I know that I loved the prestige. I ran for reelection my Junior year, and my win came by default—no one ran against me. The perception among the student body was that I was unbeatable. "Why run against him when failure is virtually inevitable? May as well run for another position where you at least stand a fighting chance," was the sentiment echoed throughout the halls. My ego skyrocketed.

The message to me was clear: you are our leader; there is no one else. I stood out from the crowd, and I enthusiastically accepted the baton of leadership. Power, influence, and prestige were given to me, and I thrived on them for a few years. However, an ineluctable responsibility ended my tenure—the graduation speech traditionally delivered by the senior-class president. The speech was over a year away, but the fear of public failure was overwhelming. Other students encouraged me to run, but I refused to see in me what they believed me to be. They wanted me to lead; I chose to opt out of the election. In short, I feared the power of my own voice.

The irony is remarkable. Why would a leader, with a passionate discontent for the status quo and a desperation to be heard, choose to silence his or her own voice? Every leader carries wounds that are imbedded in his or her stories of betrayal, futility, loneliness, and exhaustion. Often, leading just does not seem worth the counted cost. So, we pack our bags, say our goodbyes, and head out the door in search of someplace else, anyplace else—hopefully, a place where our stories and our pain will be forgotten. Yet, our stories are a part of us, and it is these very stories that propel our discontentment and restlessness. It is these stories that drive our passion for change. We silence our voice to avoid the pain of leading, but in so doing, we simply intensify the illusion. A leader cannot abscond his or her agency for change, nor can he or she guarantee crisis-free leadership. Any dissenting thoughts are a chimera, a mythical illusion. In the end, the silencing of a leader's voice is an unnecessary tragedy.

So, what will it take for a leader to become disillusioned? What will it mean for a leader to find his or her voice? What will it mean for me to find mine? As I entered my undergraduate years at a small mid-western liberal arts university, my discontent began to take shape. My awareness of the global world increased, and I became aware of the distinct differences between other cultures and my culture founded on Western and American ideals. I grew frustrated with the structures of our society, namely, the consumeristic, achievement-oriented, success-driven rat race that exploited the weak and rewarded the haughty. The academic life I was emphasizing seemed pointless—I struggled for the best grades, so that I could graduate, find a notable job, make money, establish security, and retire at an early age, all so I could then do what I wanted to do, whatever it was I imagined that to be. "What is the point?!" was the question that raged within me. I was angry, and my anger turned to contempt. My contempt became divisive, the elevation of my ideas converted me into a dogmatic narcissist, and I lost all curiosity for the societal structures around me. All I knew to do was to judge the systems, dismiss others' opinions, and distance myself as much as possible.

Again, the irony is profound. My discontent and restlessness, two fundamental necessities needed to propel an influential leader, mutated into a violent contempt for our culture. No longer could I effect change from within, because I had distanced myself from the very cultural structures that I desired to transform. Practically, this meant that I replaced the drive for power and wealth with a desire for connection and intimacy through relationships. People became my primary focus in life, and I dismissed any constraints that did not lead toward this objective. A story from the spring semester of my Senior year illustrates my ideology: I was a second-year resident assistant, and I loved my job. My primary responsibility was to be available to the men on my floor, engage them in discipleship and mentoring, and create an environment that facilitated enriching relationships and a sense of belonging. Other aspects of the job existed, but they were secondary in importance to me. One particular evening, the residence life staff planned a continuing education program for all resident assistants on campus. After two years of attending such events and struggling to see their value, I decided to skip the program and attend a social gathering with the residents on my floor instead. The large group of guys piled into several vehicles and exited the parking lot. As we turned onto the campus street, we passed a sidewalk on which my resident director, my boss, was walking to the RA program.

"What are you doing?" he asked, surprised to see me leaving campus.

"I'm going out with the guys," I responded. I tried to exert confidence, but my response was sheepish; I knew I was caught.

"Did you remember the RA in-service?"

187

"Yes," I answered. I could not lie. I do not recall the ending to the conversation, but I know I blatantly ignored my boss and my responsibility, and I drove away.

My response was foolish, but my reaction to drive away was not atypical for someone with my personality style. On the DiSC personal profile system, my score revealed that I was an *I*, meaning my preferred style of leadership is "influence." An *I*-style on the DiSC profile will tend to generate enthusiasm, seek to establish connections with others, create motivating environments, and see the world optimistically. *I*'s prefer an environment with minimal constraints, gravitate toward popularity and acceptance, and have a propensity toward group activities. More specifically, the classical profile pattern of my graph identified me as a "promoter." Promoters prefer social interactions and activities and are less interested in accomplishing tasks. Promoters are especially resistant to solitary environments where their enthusiasm and gregariousness is squandered.

If this description is accurate (and it's astounding how accurate I believe it is), it is no wonder that my response was to drive away. Weighing the option between an educational meeting and the opportunity for a social gathering, of course my desire was to participate in the activity with my guys—it is how I am wired. Unfortunately, I had not taken the DiSC assessment at the time, and I did not know that an *I* style of leadership also needs to improve certain aspects of life in order to be more effective. Setting priorities and deadlines, making objective decisions, and following through on promises and tasks are a few of these suggestions highlighted in the DiSC assessment. In short, I was living as a classic *I*, but I was not living as an effective leader.

Thankfully, my resident director did not ignore my poor decision. The following day he knocked on my door, came in, sat down, and proceeded to express his disappointment with my decision. His words were harsh—and they were true. I was not responsible; I was not dependable. I wanted to see culture and structures transform, but I had chosen to reject the current systems and lead my own way—on my own. I tried to change the system from without rather than transform from within. The words from my boss were painful, but they were also essential. He recognized the potential of my voice, and he knew that my irresponsibility and poor decisions were effectively silencing that voice.

Our meeting stunned me. Here was my boss, a man who knew my heart and my potential, and he was telling me that something needed to change—I needed to change. I had become contemptuous in my discontent, and my contempt became divisive. I led without regard for others, and I missed any opportunity for my voice to be heard. If I wanted to lead effectively, I had some work to do.

In the years following this admonishment from my hall director, I labored to become a more effective leader through developing time management and organizational skills, setting priorities, and following through on tasks. I graduated from college, became a resident director myself, and was living well. I became dependable, responsible, and trustworthy. The man I left behind in college was no more than a silent shadow of the man I had become. However, something else also changed in this process. My responsibility and dependability became no more than mere compliance to the structures that once brought discontentment, and I seemingly lost my passion for something better. On the positive side, I was no longer violent, divisive, and contemptuous; instead, I was now merely apathetic, silent, and indifferent. In the struggle to become an effective leader, I unknowingly exchanged one set of problems for another.

It is a dilemma many leaders face—the war between their impulsive drives for change and their hopeless resignations when the vision seems insurmountable. Somewhere in the middle, there is a place where passion and conviction and imagination take shape, and it is in this place that leaders reside. My hope is that I discover this place—this place where my contempt and indifference can be molded into a passionate discontentment, and where my dogma or silence can transform into a voice—a voice that is loud, yet gracious; bold, yet kind; inspired by conviction, yet stimulated by curiosity.

Through the years I have been sidelined by the complexities, pain, and fear of leadership, and my story is not unlike the stories of many others. Our ambivalence toward our stories has knocked many of us out of the game. We watch from the bench, criticizing those on the field, and we imagine how we would be different. If generative change is to occur, the next generation of leaders must step into the game, despite their injuries. Our stories have told us that leadership is about perfection, or at least the striving for it. Yet, we live in an age of the *already* and the *not yet*. Yes, we are *already*, and so we should lead, with audacious passion, a loud voice, and restless discontent, but at the same time, to use Dan Allender's words, "I am not yet, nor are you. Therefore, when we are together, there will inevitably be tragic failures of love."[2] We retreat from leadership because we cannot face the certainty of failure, but our desire for perfection is yet another illusion created to mask our deep insecurities.

Leadership is not about the successful achievement of a charismatic or driven personality; rather, leadership is the passionate and restless voice of discontentment that generates transformation from within.

Chapter Six Questions for Reflection

1) Who are those muted leaders within your community? Who are those people that show glimpses of their potential?

2) What are some ways you can cultivate a space for these leaders to more deeply explore their giftings?

3) Where did you locate yourself amidst these stories of unexpected successes and spectacular failures? How do you respond to the paradox of their profound apathy and hopefulness?

4) If these stories seem familiar to you—if they portray something of your own struggle to lead—where can you create space in your current context to explore your potential? Where can you be given a place to experiment with your growing awareness of your own leadership?

Chapter 7

Stories of Humanity: When Weakness is Made Strong

Therefore I will boast all the more gladly about my weaknesses, so that Christ's power may rest on me. That is why, for Christ's sake, I delight in weaknesses, in insults, in hardships, in persecutions, in difficulties. For when I am weak, then I am strong.
—2 Corinthians 12:9-10

As suggested in chapter 3, knowing your leadership limitations helps make you a more credible and authentic leader. But having discovered your flat sides, those areas where you are most prone to fail, then what? Most modernistic views of leadership would invite an aggressive plan of "development" to "fix" those shortfalls, or at least get them under enough control so they don't get you into too much trouble. Whether fixing them, or subduing them, the typical answer when it comes to your own humanity is "hide it."

But what, then, did Jesus mean when he said, "In your weakness I am strong . . . my power is perfected in your weakness?" These young leaders seem to be suggesting that there is something beautiful in our humanity and that, more than just fixing it, we need to embrace it. Campbell puts it quite well: "People want perfect leaders. After the tragedy of Eden, however, one of the most significant hallmarks of humanity is imperfection—the tension between the glory and depravity that reside together in the soul. Chasing the illusion of perfection is, in fact, dehumanizing as well as exhausting. Instead of hiding my humanity and feigning an aloof strength in leadership, my desire is to authentically reveal myself to others, including my weaknesses and fears. It is these universal human experiences that, rather than distancing me from others, actually brings us together in community. The cost of self-exposing honesty is trust, and the reward is the connection with others that I so desperately need."

In these stories you will hear these four leaders reflect on the cost of hiding our humanity and the destruction of trust that hiding can have, the importance and risk of confession as a mechanism of building trust, the role humility plays in leading us to discover our own and others' humanity, and how our failures lead to the authentic, albeit painful, discovery of our humanity, which in turn leads us to an entirely new perspective of others, not as objects or means to our ends, but as fellow humans.

Most modernistic theories of leadership have scrubbed out imperfections in favor of the all-knowing, charismatic, have-it-all-together leader that both exudes and invites confidence. Sure, while some leadership theorists would suggest that self-disclosure is an important aspect of being approachable and credible, ultimately, one mustn't ever let others see "too much" of one's flaws if one is to keep a healthy distance from the commoners.

This has been greatly pervasive in the church. The televangelist image of today's pastoral leader has left many troubled by what they perceive as inauthentic faith being proliferated by spiritual-sounding, highly emotional preachers selling Jesus across the airwaves. Add to that the litany of moral failures toppling the regimes of mega-church leaders, and you have a degree of cynicism that even the most genuinely authentic pastor-leader would struggle to penetrate. That may sound like an overly-harsh and too-broadly generalized indictment of the church. But it's important to understand that emerging leaders have been painfully influenced by the toxic effects of pop Christian culture, and many of them, too, are unfortunately throwing the baby out with the bathwater.

Jacob challenges this false notion of leadership well: "We want leaders to be inhuman. We want them to not feel what we, normal people, feel. We want them to have answers when it seems that questions are all that is present. We want an example to follow, at all times. We don't want to see our leaders struggle. We definitely don't want to give into the reality that life is complex and that leading is not as defined as we would like to believe. We wonder why it is that people cower and cringe away from leadership. It is because without any real critical analysis, the aura of the model leader is set. A false pretense is constructed and followed. Our characterization of a stoic leader is a hoax, and I would go so far to say that it is disastrous. Not only does it drive people from leading, but it causes leaders and their organizations harm."

May the stories ahead invite you to reconsider the fullness of your own humanity, daring you to embrace the great strengths you have been gifted with, as well as the flaws that display your full humanity through which God can best reveal his power and strength.

Buzz

"When I had journeyed half of our life's way, I found myself within a shadowed forest, for I had lost the path that does not stray." —Dante Alighieri from <u>The Great Inferno</u>

I feel that I'm at a crucial turning point in my life with my efforts to be a leader in the church. Taking the lead was something that came easy to me while growing up. From my elementary school years all the way through college, I was the captain of every sports team I joined and did well in the classroom. A natural at gaining the admiration and respect of the adults and peers in my life, I felt confident to "take on the world." Offsetting this, however, was my tendency to blend in at home and not really have a voice or be heard. Nonetheless, I was looking forward to becoming a strong leader as I prepared to enter the ministry.

Fast forward from my childhood and adolescence to my past fifteen years in youth ministry, where my efforts at being a leader in the church have not been as easily attained. I've found that the attitudes that made me so successful in my developmental years (mainly my boldness, passion, and enthusiasm) were not as valued in the "more conservative" confines of the church, and so I resigned myself to a fatalistic mindset. Yet, in my heart, I believe that many of the setbacks were the necessary byproducts for the process of sanctification to take root in my life. Come to find out, I could not exert my influence over the Holy Spirit by simply working harder and being charismatic. As a matter of fact, I've learned that it's better for the Spirit to exert her influence over me. Fortunately, I'm learning these lessons now, while I still have many years of ministry ahead of me. With my failures and broken-ness clearly in sight, I am now better prepared to serve God in a more humble, but still enthused, fashion.

How I Got Here: My Self-Assessment as a Leader

"The whole purpose of places like Starbucks is for people with no decision making capabilities whatsoever to make

*six decisions just to buy one cup of coffee. Tall, decaf,
cappuccino, et cetera. So people who don't know who on
earth they are, can for only $2.95, get not just a cup of
coffee, but an absolute defining sense of self.* —Joe, played
by Tom Hanks, from the movie *You've Got Mail*

The most common sort of lie is the one uttered to one's self.
—Friedrich Nietzsche

I was surprised to discover that my Personnel Relations Survey
results showed that I was a "Type A" personality, which signi-
fies an impersonal approach to interpersonal relationships. Such
a style indicates withdrawal and an aversion to risk taking on the
part of the leader due to interpersonal anxiety and safety seeking.
These are not the results I was expecting since I've always had
close relationships with the teens to whom I've ministered. But as
I thought about the test in light of my relationship to the church at
large, it unfortunately rang true. I grew up being the youngest in a
rather large family of sixteen children, twelve of them boys. To say
the least, it was hard to get a word in edge wise! When I did find
the courage to say something, it was usually shot down by one of
my more well-read and informed siblings. So, I was determined to
speak without using words by receiving high marks in the classroom and doing well on the athletic field.

I think this seen-and-not-heard mentality has carried over to my
work in churches. My leadership role in churches has always been
in the realm of youth ministry, a position infamous for its lack of
voice and stature in the community (even in the best of situations).
Through countless interactions I came to believe that my opinions,
convictions, and values really didn't amount to much. Thus, both
my family of origin and my voiceless position in churches helped
me understand my test results more readily.

Combine this closed-off outlook with the results of my DiSC
personal profile (which describes me as "a people mover" who is
good with words and inspirational) and you have the ingredients
for one frustrated individual. Talk about irony; talk about resignation! What comes to mind is an image of being lost in a big, empty

cathedral where my best conversations are with the walls due to the reflection of my own voice! What would it mean for me to leave the cathedral, stroll down the street, and make some conversation with the people I meet on the street? Would they take the time to listen? Would I take the time to listen? Would there be something meaningful in our interactions? Or would we walk past each other with the assumption that neither of us has something to offer the other?

Finding My Voice: Seen and Heard, See and Hear

At my first position as a youth minister, I was at an urban church on the outskirts of Detroit. In the beginning, the youth group's makeup was a few "church" kids and about a dozen or so "street" kids. It didn't take long for me to realize that if the youth ministry was going to thrive, it was going to happen through the integration of these two groups.

I made the effort to communicate to our church that referring to the unchurched youth as "street" kids was not very helpful or welcoming (especially since none of them lived on the streets). I communicated to the teens how important it is for us to reach out to one another. It wasn't long before we had a teen-initiated tutoring program, along with a basketball outreach called "Hang Time." In fact, we had dozens of youth attending our youth group in a very short period of time. There was so much growth that I believe the church was frightened by so many "street" kids in and around the church. Plus, they failed to recognize the passion and commitment that their own youth were displaying in their efforts to reach out to their peers.

It wasn't long before the leaders of our church tried to regain some control over the situation. They suggested that I no longer use gospel rap (a talent I possess) to reach out to the urban youth and that there had to be a dress code for our basketball outreach program. To retain a sense of integrity with the youth, I felt I was given no choice but to resign.

This event, among many, many others, has brought me to a place of frustration and has fed the gnawing feeling that any changes I am able to bring are just momentary blips in how churches typically run. Something that may help alleviate the tendency for some of my ideas to ultimately fail are to make some of my changes at a slower pace and to include young and old alike to get things accomplished. If an idea is slowly built up then people won't be as shell-shocked by the changes that take place, and I'll be more likely to get more people involved. Moreover, I need to simply realize that even though my voice may not be as valued as others, it is still very important that I'm heard.

My inspirational nature must be tempered with a realization that it takes time for people to change, that others must be an integral part of the process, and that I need to continue to take chances knowing that I won't always be embraced or accepted. After all, as someone who was raised in the church, I can leave the cathedral but the cathedral won't leave me. Like my family of origin, its presence in my life defines who I am. The church is still the organization that God uses to make his Kingdom come alive in this world and the next.

When I look closer at my stories, I see folly and failure, but I also see grace and purpose. What would it mean for this spineless visionary to find his voice and share it with others who desire to lead but may be afraid that what they think doesn't really matter or won't be received? What would it mean for me to find meaning in the times that I stuck out my head just to get it cut off? I do believe there is meaning in the shaming that leads to silence! Can I call others to account for the shame they bring upon others and myself, not return it, and call others to repentance? Will I recognize when my inspirational nature kicks in at the expense of others' values and input?

I have many questions because I know the role of leadership is risky business and wrought with trial and error. I need to keep reminding myself that there are reasons that I've stuck with it and still lead in churches. My outlook needs to switch from passively accepting the status quo to a belief in those around me, such that I can honestly share what I feel with the expectation that it will make a real difference. This will be displayed by caring for those around me so much that sharing my thoughts will be a spontaneous event. and I will be sharing what's in my heart. The humanity of those around me, and my own humanity, will be paramount.

A New Breed of Leaders: Taking it to the Streets and Back Again

> *These walls are funny. First you hate them, then you get used to them, enough time passes, you get so you depend on them. That's institutionalized.* —Red, played by Morgan Freeman, from the movie *The Shawshank Redemption*

My hope is that a new breed of leaders will rise up in the church, people who don't have thick lines of separation between the "streets" (or the unchurched) and the church. My hope is that they feel free to mix in both environments knowing full well that they both belong to God and that God is already present wherever we find ourselves. Psalm 24:1 states, "The earth is the Lord's and everything in it, the world, and all who live in it." My hope is that these leaders will still possess the knowledge to differentiate between cultures and will seek to be sensitive and speak the language of those with whom they interact.

This incarnational posture will mirror Christ's stance toward humanity. He was equally at home with "sinners" and the "religious" life in the temple (Luke 5:29-32; Matt. 26:55). Philippians 2:6-8 portrays Christ's stark humanity in this way: "Who, being in very nature God, did not consider equality with God something to be grasped, but made himself nothing, taking the very nature of a servant, being made in human likeness. And being found in appearance as a man, he humbled himself and became obedient to death- even death on a cross." Christ's example of being a servant-leader is a nod toward possessing an all-out commitment that will always involve tremendous heartache and pain.

I hope for a new breed of leaders who are able to get beyond the dichotomy of the "social" gospel and the "old-time" gospel, who are passionate about evangelism as well as discipleship, and who are careful to not ignore those in the margins while freely sharing the salvation message with them. In doing so we will wipe out the whole mentality of liberal churches just being concerned with

200

the poor and conservatives just focused on personal professions of faith. Churches, in the spirit of the great commission (Matthew 28:19-21) will care for the whole person: mind, body, and spirit!

In my journal for this leadership class, I chose to observe the leadership aspects of presidential candidate John McCain. What drew me to McCain was his ability to cross the political divide and accomplish things with those who have different political views (I believe the same possibility is the draw for Barack Obama as well). I find it ironic that my example of the best leader I've known personally was an older pastor who had some of the same qualities as McCain. What separates these leaders from the pack is the personal courage they displayed for those who could potentially turn on them. Personal courage is often grandiose and selfish unless it is undergirded with a stance toward others that is filled with compassion and faith. Underlying all of our efforts must be a heart for the other.

When I think about it, my desire to cross borders and bring people together is enmeshed in my desire for my voice to cross the divide of my own heart and make itself known, to not only the world, but to myself. Could it be that my heart for those who are marginalized stems from the deepest recesses of a "punk kid" who doesn't know any better? Tell me, who's better qualified to speak to a church who has lost its voice in our world? Let it be heard—no one! My hope and dream is to join my voice with others as we call out to the world and to God for his Kingdom to come!

2 Corinthians 5:18-21: And all of this is a gift from God, who brought us back to himself through Christ. And God has given us this task of reconciling people to him. For God was in Christ, reconciling the world to himself, no longer counting people's sins against them. And he gave us this wonderful message of reconciliation. So we are Christ's ambassadors; God is making his appeal through us. We speak for Christ when we plead, "Come back to God!" For God made Christ, who never sinned, to be the offering for our sin, so that we could be made right with God through Christ.

Campbell

Disillusionment has come swiftly and easily to me in recent years. The empty shadows where I searched frantically for self-worth have all fallen away in turn. In spite of all my past successes, or perhaps because of them, recent times have found me feeling more like a lost child than a fearless leader. Uncertainty, a feeling I would normally flee from like the plague, has become my usual companion. This may not be all bad. Indeed, it may be the best place to start the path that lies before me. Disillusionment is where I have to start, because it is where I am. It is not where I want to end.

As I survey my long track record of leadership opportunities, I am forced to come to a simple and difficult conclusion: most of the time, I was a fake. To all who were watching, I appeared self-confident, energetic, and effective. While those traits are a part of who I am, they also hide a deeper reservoir of fear, loneliness, and desire. I tried desperately to hide these powerful places from others and myself, and because I was good at it, I was made a leader. People want perfect leaders. After the tragedy of Eden, however, one of the most significant hallmarks of humanity is imperfection—the tension between the glory and depravity that reside together in the soul. Chasing the illusion of perfection is, in fact, dehumanizing as well as exhausting.

Now, the winds of change are blowing, or maybe it is the gentle breath of God that I am sensing. In any case, it is God's story that will move me forward into a new future of leadership, and it is telling the truth that will set me free to lead with authenticity, generosity, and patience.

My wrestling with disillusionment and uncertainty has left me desiring a new name, a new way of being. Disillusionment must give way to clarity, an ability and courage to see myself accurately and to let others see me as well. Now that is scary! It is scary for me because I have trained myself to need no one, to trust no one. I thought that was what a strong leader was like. This is clearly evidenced by my Johari Window results. My arena is small, confined to the upper left-hand corner and providing space for a gaping façade and blindspot. This indicates that for most of my life, I have been an island, unwilling or unable to expose myself to others and afraid to really hear how they perceived me. It is so very difficult for me to trust anybody.

My high school soccer coach handed me a card as I came down from the stage after receiving the team's MVP award during my senior season. I was expecting a feel-good note thanking me for four years of blood and sweat, league titles and state tournaments. What I got was a piece of advice that set my blood on fire. He did acknowledge my effort, but finished the note by urging me to learn to trust my teammates and share the load. He said words that I have now come to regard as prophetic: "Campbell, you can't do it all alone." I would spend the next decade trying to prove him wrong. I knew I had been seen, and it infuriated and scared me.

The only way out of this lonely "corner" is courage and honesty, which in many respects have become synonymous for me. To courageously tell the truth about who you are is called authenticity, and I have come to see this trait as foundational to the kind of leader I want to be. Even more, it is the kind of human I want to be. Dan Allender insightfully comments, "Becoming more human involves confessing one's need for others . . . the confession that we need each other is almost nonexistent in the formal structure of leadership."[1]

Instead of hiding my humanity and feigning an aloof strength in leadership, my desire is to authentically reveal myself to others, including my weaknesses and fears. It is these universal human experiences that, rather than distancing us from others, actually brings us together in community. The cost of self-exposing honesty is trust, and the reward is the connection with others that I so desperately need. Authenticity is the solid ground I have always longed for. It frees me from maintaining the pretense that I am perfect, which in turn frees others to stop pretending as well. An authentic leader has the power to create a humble and honest community that can pour its collective energy into doing good work rather than maintaining useless illusions. Authentic leadership begins by hearing the call and responding with Isaiah's simple "Here am I";[2] this is the confession that what I have to offer is simply who I am—the person that God created and that my story has thus far shaped. If this is not enough, then there is no hope for real leadership.

With authenticity established as the only firm and sustainable foundation for my renewed vision of leadership, it is possible to move boldly toward the second characteristic of a true leader—generosity. What would it look like to live with my possessions and my needs held loosely in an open palm? At first glance, it appears dangerous. Indeed, true generosity in a fallen world is a great risk. If we actually do live in a closed system with limited resources, then grabbing what you can and hoarding it is certainly the wisest course, especially for a leader. The apostle Paul, however, cautions us against "looking only on the surface of things."[3] God's reality is deeper than the world we see, and God is the great opener of "closed systems." It is Jesus himself who introduces us to the paradox of laying down our lives in order that we might gain true life.[4]

Generosity is countercultural. The world we live in tells us to grab all we can and guard it against others. Look out for number one. A leader is in a unique position to radically change culture by taking the first step in a new direction. The early church in the book of Acts paints a radical and beautiful picture of reciprocal generosity. These people trusted each other because they trusted the God who was doing something new in their midst. What if I were to take the things that God has given me—money, time, skills, connections, hopes—and put them on the table as an offering to anyone who might need them? Would I lose these things? Would I run out? Possibly, but then I hear the promise of Jesus to those who would follow him: "Do not worry, saying, 'What shall we eat?' or 'What shall we drink' or 'What shall we wear?' . . . but seek first his kingdom and his righteousness, all these things will be given to you as well."[5]

A distrustful heart will kill generosity before it ever has a chance to grow. But if I can learn to trust both God and others, then I can radically share what has been given to me, and that generosity has the chance to become contagious and reciprocal. Either way, I cannot control the outcome. The question is, do I believe that God is in control or not? The world offers closed systems, limited resources, and binary conflicts. If, however, God's story is the true one, then leaders can move beyond these dead ends and anything might be possible. Generosity thrusts me into a world where others are just as important as myself.

Once leadership ceases to be a venue for meeting my narcissistic needs, then I am free to see others as whole human beings as well. The Arbinger Institute calls this living "out of the box." If a leader succumbs to the pressure to appear perfect, then he or she must endlessly justify choices and blame others for shortcomings. People cease to be people, and are reduced to being props to support a deeply entrenched self-deception. The secret antidote is simple and surprisingly difficult. I have to move beyond myself and into the world of others, trusting that our stories are more similar than they are different, and that others are capable of responding to the real me with respect and care. It may actually be as simple as "love your neighbor as yourself."[6]

I have often found myself, while crawling north on Interstate 5 toward the Mercer Street exit in downtown Seattle, looking around at the multitude of people-filled cars that are sharing the congested road with me. In these moments, when life literally forces me to slow down and stop frantically rushing around, my mind begins to contemplate the reality that each person is a complex universe of hopes and regrets, memories and desires, responsibilities and anxieties, successes and failures—just like me. They are whole people with stories that bear the marks of a bigger story, and souls that bear the image of their Creator—just like me. This can be overwhelming because it means that to God, each of them is just as important as I am. Living in this open-hearted, open-handed reality can also be the key to generous leadership. Unfortunately, learning to be authentic and generous can take a lot of time.

The final characteristic of true leadership that I hope to move toward is patience. Patience for me means the ability to slow down. I have competed in track and field my whole life, so it feels very natural to try and finish everything as quickly as possible, removing all obstacles to efficiency and success. Impatience has also fit my internal makeup very well, since you can ignore a lot of hard truths about yourself if you keep moving fast enough.

As a leader, patience provides time to reflect. When I resist the tyranny of the urgent, I create space and opportunity to explore solutions together with other people. Patience is the key to avoiding reactionary decisions—"a man's wisdom gives him patience; it his glory to overlook an offense."[7] A leader needs time to pursue truth instead of assumptions and to really listen to feedback. Patience makes room for others to join in the process, and this can only strengthen the final outcome.

Patience also provides time to pray. Prayer is one of the fundamental responsibilities of a true leader, and yet most leaders do not find the time. By prayer I do not mean reporting to God what God already knows about a given situation, then offering advice on how best to rectify it. Though I still struggle to pray for myself and others, I know now that prayer begins in one of two places: pain or gratitude. When I sit in these feelings, in response to my own story or the stories of others, I sense that I am sharing something real with God, and that God is listening intently to my heart. Samuel, the last great judge of Israel in the Old Testament, portrays the distinct role of prayer in the life of a leader when he tells Saul, "Far be it from me that I should sin against the Lord by failing to pray for you."[8] I want to be a leader who prays without ceasing for the people who have entrusted me with power.

When I think of the kind of leader I hope to be, my mind moves toward a vision of my old friend and mentor, Vern. He was my director on a nonprofit project in the public schools of Spokane. Having read some of Jim Collins's work, I now recognize that Vern is a Level 5 leader—tenaciously committed to achieving good goals yet radically humble in the role he played to get there.[9] Vern was ferociously dedicated to the vision of helping kids develop a healthy and safe sexuality while in high school. He never backed down from a debate, and no challenge was left untackled, no matter how daunting. At the same time, Vern was incredibly kind and sensitive. He was ridiculously generous to anyone in need. He and his wife, Sylvia, even kept a separate bank account that they would regularly put money in for the sole purpose of being ready should they encounter someone who was in need. Sometimes the person in need was me. In the midst of the madness that was our daily mission, Vern never seemed to lack the time to invest in me personally. He was strong and strategic, but it was his soft heart that caught my attention. I had never seen a man cry before. The way he vulnerably allowed others to affect him and move him was scary, convicting, and inspiring. I am still searching for that kind of emotional security and strength. My vision of Vern is forever grafted into my definition of true leadership.

In the end, it all comes down to our vision. A leader has to be able to see well. Seeing yourself well leads to authenticity. Seeing others well leads to generosity. Slowing down enough to see anything well leads to patience. My first prayer of future leadership will be for new eyes. I desire eyes that see beyond the surface—of myself, of others, of the problems I face and the illusions that tempt me. I desire vision that can see into the heart of God, where my new name is whispered to me alone.

Jacob

We have constructed a strange, idealistic picture of a leader. Humorously, the first thing I envision is the branding image of my new favorite bar, The Saint. On their coasters, billboard, and menus sits the image of a man with a sword raised high riding a horse that seems to be galloping or trotting atop a huge stone. It gives an intensely stoic feeling, as though he is leading a battalion of men into war with a heart full of courage and devoid of fear. While this may be humorous to me, I know that this is not too detached from what many hold as good leadership—a steady beacon in times of turbulence. While this may encompass some leaders, I believe that this picture informs our expectations of all leaders.

We want leaders to be inhuman; we don't want them to feel what normal people feel. We want them to have answers when it seems that questions are all that is present. We want an example to follow at all times. We don't want to see our leaders struggle. And we definitely don't want to face the reality that life is complex and that leading is not as defined as we would like to believe.[1]

Given these expectations, one shouldn't wonder why people cower and cringe away from leadership. Without any real critical analysis of the aura, our model of a leader is set, filled with false pretenses that we perpetuate and followed. If I could draw a diagram to help illustrate this notion, I would draw two platforms. One would be at ground level, and the other would be way in the sky. Then, I would draw a circle around the space that lies between the two platforms. This circle and the space within would represent the gulf that we believe lies between leaders and normal people. The pretense of this circle is what must be called into question. People are hesitant to lead because they believe that the gap within the circle is real. Our characterization of a stoic leader is a hoax, and I would even say that it is disastrous. Not only does it drive people from leading, but it causes leaders and their organizations harm.

One simple example of this would be leaders and their use of power. I have seen the pretense of this stoic leader in full action. I know a leader that does not want to be a leader, yet finds himself as one. Combine that with the very real pretense of stoic leadership, and you have a man that lives with a very destructive façade. He surrounds himself with those who help maintain this façade and who serve to perpetuate it, two very different things. I believe that the perpetuation of his façade will eventually cause him to self-destruct and, sadly, also to destroy his company.

Despite my fear of sounding too much like an idealist, I will nevertheless say we are in need of a change. It is not that all leaders are like this, it is just that this is still a more than prominent understanding of leadership. But, if change on a massive front is in order, then we must establish an alternative to move toward. If stoicism casts an inhuman shadow on leadership, then I purpose (along with our class) a more fully human leadership model.

In our stoic example the leader would be unable to show things like emotion, fatigue, and questioning. But, these are things that it means to be human. No one is emotionless. Everyone is affected in one way or another. Everyone becomes tired. Nobody possesses endless strength and stamina. And life, ironically, seems to have more questions than answers. So, why would it be logically wrong to question and wrestle intensely? Thus, what if our leaders displayed these characteristics not carelessly but intently?

If leadership were still conducted from the top down, then I want to believe that this would produce a more lively organization. Primarily because what it means to be alive for us as humans is not the negation of our humanness but the acting and living into it. I would argue that this would translate into the flourishing of an organization rather than the demise of it.

I know a leader that lives a stoic façade much like the one I've described. Because this leader, the owner and most influential person of the company, acts within this façade, others have to cater to it, primarily by putting on a façade to interact with his façade. Instead of holistic people interacting, they have to maintain the perpetuation of this truncated self while in the work environment. I do not think that it is difficult to understand the devastation that this could cause for organization. On top of whatever stresses the job might already require, the employees need to sustain an image that is not completely them, nor does it represent them truly.

I am not naïve enough to say that owners and leaders of companies always set the precedent for their company, but they often do. If leaders adapted into a more fully human role and intently showed characteristics that are traditionally seen as unfit, the effect would be great. I think immediately about times that should cause fear. Think about the difference between the leader who acts as if there is no justification for fear and the leader who acts in the acknowledgement that there is a terrifying situation yet must move forward. What does it do for those who are being led? I believe that it sets a foundation to flourish.

By not denying that fear is reasonable, the leader is actually communicating to the organization that it can exist holistically. The organization has the room to work openly in the expression of what it means to be more fully human. I think that a space like this could eventually lead to the acknowledgment that there are people in the organization that are different, and this could be a liberating thing.

When the stoic façade is diminished and the need for all those in the organization to create a matching façade is dismissed, it could lead to healthy examination and display that people are constructed differently. They could therefore operate differently and be used differently to suit their own characteristics and hopefully become more alive in their position within the organization. An organization that pays attention to these types of intimate intricacies will flourish as a whole.

To this point I have tried to show the harm and difficulty of a stoic leadership model. Also, I have tried to present a more fully human model and the effects that would have on an organization. In no way do I want to say that this is restricted to Christians. I believe that this type of model is and should be appealing to all. However, for the Christian, I want to believe that our beliefs incline us toward this model. Our Lord and Savior, Jesus, did not come to abolish our humanity but to work through it. Thus, more than just an inclination, as Christians we must not be satisfied with any type of model of leadership that does not embrace the entirety of what it means to be human for an organization.

Stuart

Leadership, for me and my generation, has generally been looked on as something to be feared and avoided. Leadership has been mysterious and unreal; it has been something that is taught with flashy, meaningless language, such as networking, getting people on/off the bus, good-to-great, touching base, et cetera. It's not that my generation does not understand the value of quality leadership—in fact, we deeply desire it—but what we have witnessed from our leaders is power cloaked by spin, meaningless words, and a drive for perfection and money. And it has wounded us. It is inevitable that my generation will someday take on the leadership roles that we have witnessed and disliked, and in doing so it is my hope that we will reform and redeem the nature of what it means to be leaders by first focusing on ourselves and our humanity.

In order to best know ourselves and our tendencies toward leadership, we must begin the often daunting task of understanding our stories and how those stories inform our perspective and experience of leadership. For example, through the assessments of the Johari Window and the DiSC, I have gained a lot of insight into the ways in which I operate in the workplace as well as the ways in which I am prone to interact with those that I work with and for. The Johari Window has shown me that I relate to others in very impersonal ways that are self-protective and do not allow my insecurities to be threatened or exposed. Instead, for me, there is a large element of the unknown. What is unknown is both my understanding of myself and my understanding of others. The consequence of this broad unknown is that I have the tendency to react to people and situations rather than explore a more studied or informed response. What is perhaps most unnerving about this revelation is the fact that it results in large amounts of unrealized potential and creativity and, furthermore, gives rise to an aversions to take risks, as well as increases my potential to respond with rigidity. I find this to be contrary to my view of myself in that I feel as though I am a risk taker and a very creative person; however, my ability and desire to take risks or explore my creativity is typically mitigated by anxiety, and the Johari results demonstrate the fact that anxiety, for me, is my primary motivation for how I relate and respond in the workplace.

The DiSC assessment has shown me a different and broader picture of my relational style as well. I fall largely into the category of dominance, with a pattern of creativity. Some of the implications of these categories are making quick decisions, questioning the status quo, solving problems, and initiating change, all of which seem quite desirable for leadership. However, like Johari, the DiSC has shown me that I need to improve my own understanding of others, to use my voice more effectively, and to relax more.

Coupling the two assessments offers me a surprising look into the inner workings of my relational style as well as the ways in which I can use my strengths and expose my weaknesses. While acting as an independent agent seems preferable to me, I understand that this is largely due to my tendency to react to others and judge them by my standards. This proclivity combined with my disregard for social norms exhibits to others that I am somewhat aloof and am apt to be quite blunt when delivering my opinions on matters. If such understanding were to remain unknown by me, it would present (and has presented) difficulties for me in working environments and relationships. However, even in beginning to consider these assessments, change is possible. For me, the most glaring revelation that I have seen is the fact that I need people. Not only do I need them interpersonally in order to help me better relate and communicate, but I also need them as a leader. Without recognizing this fact, I could enter leadership positions as a rigid, aloof superior who is an ineffective communicator who operates with a great deal of dominance. This is neither what I want in those who lead me nor the type of leader I wish to be. Even this brief look at myself through the lenses of a couple of basic assessments shows me my own mortality as well as how necessary it is for me to integrate this knowledge into both my personal and professional life.

My experience of being led also plays a vital role in informing my ideas of leadership. I recently wrote a journal about one of my current leaders by observing her interact with her employees in a variety of situations; this is something that I would recommend to anyone exploring what makes for an effective leader. Day-to-day experiences usually come and go without much thought or reflection about the intricacies of those experiences and the ways in which they inspire us; on the contrary, what is usually memorable is the ways in which we have been slighted or failed by our superiors. Journaling about these seemingly mundane day-to-day interactions can provide great insight into what leadership means and what we desire to gain from our leaders. What stood out to me most about my supervisor was the fact that she treats me as a human, as a peer in life, not merely an employee. What I found was that my manager was quick to admit her own faults and limitations, and just as quick to show gratitude for a job well done. Observing and reflecting upon such things demonstrated to me that I was desired as an employee and that my needs were important. My performance was not judged on results alone, but on my *character* and what that offers to the workplace. The product of such leadership was, and is, such that it completely alleviates my anxiety and makes me feel valued as a human.

If a leader is to be effective, they must look into their own humanity and recognize the humanity of others. Anyone who refuses to do this, or does so flippantly, is setting a course for disaster, one that produces a cold and inhumane environment in which the strengths and creativity of their employees will never be fully realized. Instead, things such as narcissism and rigidity become predominant.

I once worked for a small law firm as the executive assistant to the principal of the firm; I will refer to him as "Lewis." I was very good at my job and in small ways was able to help the firm run more efficiently. However, it quickly became clear that Lewis did not appreciate my pro-action and wished for things to remain as they had always been. At first, I would initiate changes on my own—changes that were directly related to my day-to-day ability to do my job well. I felt as though I was helping both myself and the firm attain smoother results. When Lewis discovered these subtleties, he rebuked me for acting independently and insisted that I revert to the previous way of operating. As time passed I grew more jaded with the routine of the job and felt that my creativity was neither desired nor welcome. I would still make suggestions on how to improve things, but Lewis met those with equal fervor and rigidity to the extent that my voice was eventually silenced. Fortunately, I am not one to remain silent, and even though my voice was waning, there was the occasional time that I would speak up for myself.

I remember one specific occasion where Lewis and I were discussing his delay delivering the firm's paychecks. This delay was not uncommon, and I had previously attempted to create a system that would eliminate this from occurring again. I remember the moment like it was yesterday. I was not getting paid, the other employees were not getting paid, and Lewis responded by telling me not to worry and that he had my best interests in mind. My reaction of disbelief to this statement must have been blatant because he instantly asked me whether or not I believed what he had said. I bluntly told him that I did not believe him, and he asked me to leave his office. About an hour after this exchange, I was called into a meeting with Lewis and his friend "Alex," who was the managing principle of a capital firm in the next office suite. Lewis told the details of what had happened and was clearly upset that I had not believed his statement. Alex proceeded to "arbitrate" the scenario, but the subject matter was less about the situation at hand and more about my perceived insubordination. The meeting ended with the basic statement to me that I should either respect Lewis's decisions or begin looking for another employer. I left crushed and feeling as though my needs and my opinions did not matter at all. Best interests indeed.

What is clear to me now is that Lewis may have thought that he had my best interests in mind—which somewhat explains his visceral reaction to my bluntness—but the *reality* is that he knew me so little, so impersonally, that he could not have the first clue what my best interests, or any of my interests, really were. Lewis was self-deceived in thinking that he knew what was best for me. In fact, in his self-deception, what he claimed to be in my best interest conveniently served his best interests. This self-deception is something that all of us must face because it produces the

inability to see that one has a problem.[1] James Hollis exposes the
nature of self-deception when talking about organizations when
he states, "Underneath the civilizing fantasies of any institution
lie the archaic issues of anxiety management and self-interest."[2]
Furthermore, this anxiety is a result of our uncertainty and thus
formulates our reactions to that uncertainty. Again, Hollis states,
"Any slippage in our moral or intellectual certainty sets off the
compensatory swings toward rigid, unswerving conviction."[3]

When we are self-deceived, our perceptions become distorted,
and over time, the distortion becomes systematic.[4] In this self-
deception we cannot hear the needs of others seriously, or see what
we are doing that perverts our thinking into self-justification and
thus invites more of the same; this is a vicious cycle of leadership
in which we are forced to invest more emotional capital in our
efforts to alleviate or mitigate our anxiety, which ironically results
in situations that produce more of the same anxiety.[5] In our narcissism and self-deception, we attempt to control the world in order
to limit its inherent ambiguity and complexity.[6] This in turn modi-
fies us into a suspicious and manipulative people who do not allow
ourselves to be wrong or to even confess that we are wrong when
we know that we are. Why should anyone have to be governed by
someone else's emotional immaturity, someone else's inability to
tolerate the ambiguities of life?[7]

It is therefore essential that we look into ourselves and our
stories and find the ways in which we are prone to self-deception and the ways that our self-deception and self-betrayal have
marred our ability to recognize and uphold the humanity of others.
When we expose these unknown truths—what I will refer to as our
shadow side—within ourselves, we are then capable of operating
in a new way. This new way of operating—of relating—is such
that we are no longer controlled by our shadows, but instead live
with our shadows and are able to use our knowledge of the previously unknown. Otherwise, we are doomed to lead in fundamen-
talist ways that leave us rigid and unable to understand what the
best interests of our employees, and our companies, actually are.
Leadership is not beyond redemption, but that redemption must
begin within us.

Imagine again my story of Lewis. What if Lewis had been open to my ideas for change? What if Lewis had worked with me to change the way the firm operated? What if Lewis, instead of being threatened by my creativity, had not responded with rigidity but with curiosity and a willingness to explore the new options that were presented to him? Things can be different. I imagine that had Lewis been willing to look beyond his own narcissism and rigidity that two things would have been different. First, I would have felt that my contributions to the firm were honored and respected, and second, Lewis may have found that a new way of operating would benefit both him and his employees. Regarding the payroll issue, what would have been my experience if Lewis had admitted that he had made a mistake and apologized for it? Instead of accusing me of not believing him, perhaps I would have been more understanding and we could have worked together to resolve the issue. This is a very different picture indeed.

The call of leadership is one that we must enter into boldly, but not without humility. We must shed the illusory images we have that leaders should be perfect stalwarts and instead make them human again. Leadership is not a destructive force motivated by power, but one that should generate relationships as well as results. Without relationships there is no chance for generativity or transformation.[8] Things such as cynicism, rigidity, and narcissism are too destructive to have a place in leadership. Cynicism undermines creativity and daring, arrogance snuffs out curiosity, and callousness shuts out compassion. I doubt anyone would choose to lead in a place where things like creativity, daring, curiosity, and compassion do not exist. Thus we must eliminate things like cynicism, arrogance, and callousness from our roles as leaders. Without such things the door opens for a new breed of leadership to be born. This new leadership, the leadership of the future, is gracious, generous, human. DePree, in his book *Leadership Jazz*, tells us "a love, a true love, of what you're doing results in real competence and real intimacy."[9] If we love what we do and the people that we lead, we will honor them with our gratitude. The consequence of this is not only results but also relationships. Exodus 15:13 states, "In your unfailing love you will lead the people you have

redeemed, in your strength you will guide them to holy dwelling."
What I gain from this is that loving the people you lead is primary
to leadership, not secondary. When we love, truly love, those that
we lead, our companies and the people who are part of them, will
be led to a holier future.

This holier future is not defined by the typical definition of
wealth and success—although these things may come as well—but
by people being loved and cherished in their humanity, which
produces the best possible results. Namely, the best is brought
out of them. To expect the best of people is one thing, to inspire
it another. Leaders who are unable to explore their own faults and
limitations will find those faults and limitations in the ones that
they lead. Entering into a position of leadership without humility
and hope and love is a recipe for disaster. I will leave you with a
quote from C. S. Lewis's *Prince Caspian*, which I feel sums up the
character of leadership quite well. Aslan, the kingly lion is about to
bestow kingship on Caspian when he asks, "Do you feel yourself
sufficient to take up the Kingship of Narnia?" Caspian responds
by saying, "I—I don't think I do, Sir. I'm only a kid." Aslan's
response is telling, "Good. If you had felt yourself sufficient, it
would have been proof that you were not."[10]

Chapter Seven Questions for Reflection

1) How have your views of a leader's weakness been formed? What do you believe about your own leadership shortfalls?

2) What ways have you tried to hide your weaknesses from others? How has that affected your relationship with them?

3) How did these stories challenge your views of humility and relationship?

4) What risks might you take to allow others more visibility into your full humanity, and how might that affect the influence you are able to extend within the context you lead?

Chapter 8

Stories of Next:
Envisioning a New Way Forward

Your attitude should be the same as that of Christ Jesus:
Who, being in very nature God,
did not consider equality with God
something to be grasped,
but made himself nothing,
taking the very nature of a servant
being made in human likeness.
—Philippians 2:5-7

We've journeyed a considerable distance together, and our journey has been filled with voices of longing, contempt, creativity, and honest reflection about the costs of leadership. We've seen some students long to run from leadership altogether, fed up with the whole enterprise and the damage it perpetuates. And we've seen some suffer from the ambivalence of knowing their voices have much to offer and yet feeling as though they don't yet know how best to offer it. And we've seen leaders for whom rediscovering their very humanity is essential to what leadership lies ahead for them.

Hopefully, you've been able to garner bits and pieces of what these young leaders are truly hoping for through their honest and, at times, gut-wrenching reflections on leadership. What lies ahead for you in this last chapter, however, are the clearest essays yet that capture "Leadership Stories from Tomorrow." The essays you're about to read develop the last chapter's emphasis on leadership embracing our humanity and call for each of us to lead from a centered place of knowing ourselves. It could be said that these students are after a three-pronged approach to leadership, grounded in authenticity to one's self, authenticity to one's community, and rooted most deeply in the dramatic symbol and action of the cross. What they offer is both innovative and pragmatic, creative and counterintuitive.

They offer a way forward that, on our best days, asks us to model the person of Christ in our leadership by sacrificing the very power we're given. Indeed, if Christ teaches us anything about leadership, we see that leaders are not people who assume the power in a community but are those people who are constantly relinquishing their power in the service of others discovering their own power. In other words, leaders are the ones who are most thoroughly emptying themselves for others. In many ways this is what our students are after, this sacrificial model that undermines much of our traditional leadership sciences from the last fifty years. And yet, as you'll see, this way forward is multifaceted in its approach and deeply complex. The men and women in these essays earnestly wrestle with this way forward because of its counterintuitive nature but hold out hope that it can be profoundly transformative. As David so clearly names,

> The future of leadership involves paradox. In fact, in order for a leader to work well with what she is entrusted with, she will have to learn to navigate a paradoxical world that claims such audacious ideals as "the first shall be last" and "weak is the new strong." The beginning of leadership is paradoxical in that leaders of the future will only function well in their environment to the degree that they recognize and live into their own weaknesses. For when one lives into one's weaknesses, one will find an exorbitant amount of strength.

What grows from this paradoxical stance is a beautiful humility and a chance to lead far differently than we've typically been led. Listen to Rachel as she carves a beautiful space for her leadership future,

> Personally, I long to Sabbath well, laugh generously, play vigorously, and hope radically. I believe that in the years to come, it will be necessary for pastors to lead with faithful simplicity and wise humility. I hope to be a good steward of the word and take seriously the responsibility of teaching and speaking. I hope I never come to a place where what I have experienced of the gospel is enough. There is always another day, another chance for redemption, for healing, for deliverance, and mutual liberation.

Despite their critiques, these leaders truly do have a latent hope for leadership buried deep within them. Our task—as readers, co-leaders, and peers—is to call this hope from them, continually fanning the flames of desire they have for a future leadership that sparks something deep within them. As you work your way through this next chapter, our students will be asking you to lead in ways that are difficult and unorthodox. But we invite you to be patient, be kind, and, most of all, participate in their journey.

Rachel

The light shines in the darkness, and the darkness has
not overcome it.
—John (1:5, ESV)

Hope Is the Thing with Feathers

It takes tremendous courage to enter the deafening silence of ambivalence and find the place where grief and anger meet, especially with regard to leadership. For weeks I have wrestled in the deep, trying to learn something of myself, something of my story, and something of this paralyzing quiet. Many times I was tempted to retreat and write a cheap story with borrowed hope, but I cannot help but love the truth, and so I waited in the dark. Never before has such a simple writing project prompted so much and yet so little. Throughout the next few pages, I hope to reflect honestly and compassionately on this journey into my reflections, fears, and hopes concerning leadership, particularly pastoral leadership.

Ambivalence prohibits movement and often leads to unrelenting contempt, and yet it is seemingly impossible to circumvent.[1] Initially, just below the surface of my ambivalence concerning pastoral leadership, I found two obvious narratives. First, I am a twenty-six-year-old single woman pursuing a master of divinity with hopes of becoming a pastor, teacher, and social justice advocate who happens to be a recovering Southern Baptist. Although God is a gracious God who redeems even the most broken things, I have so many stories of heartache with regard to my Southern Baptist upbringing that even now I hardly know the depth. So much needs to be reconciled, but what has been most damaging are the messages I received concerning women in leadership: masculine, ugly, seductive, sinful, arrogant, asexual, dangerous, and unwanted. Secondly, I have grown up as the oldest of four with a father who cannot bear my glory, so he leaves, and a mother who needs me to be her savior, so she consumes. Of course I do not want to be a leader, let alone a pastor.

I just want to be human size. I don't want to be left by men who cannot bear my strength, yet fail to see my need, desire, and vulnerability. I don't want to be consumed by those who mistake my glory for that of God's. I don't want to be a hero, or a savior, or a little god. I want to be vulnerable and real. That is where the work of grace comes to play. I don't want to lead in a way that creates an environment in which I have no need for God. Only Jesus saves. I don't. I am a woman, and I lead differently than a man—is that ok? I don't want to be seen as ugly or masculine or rogue or dangerous. I want to be seen as beautiful, feminine, kind, bold, strong, vulnerable, fallible, and lovely. I want to be loved, needed, desired, protected, cared for, and held. And yet, despite all of this, I know that I am called to hold, to teach, to love, to shepherd, to exhort, to admonish, to invite, and to journey with. So of course I deeply desire to be a leader, to be a pastor. Thus I have waited in the deep and let the tears of sorrow and rage begin to flood.

As I have continued to contemplate the instrumentation we used during class, I can clearly see parallels to my personal narrative and the results of my tests. With regard to my Johari Window, I am fairly guarded on all sides: exposure and feedback. Across all three sections my window is similar with slight variances. This makes a lot of sense to me. When I am exposed honestly and authentically, I have traditionally been left or consumed. I am a brilliant editor, and this tends to heighten in the presence of authority. I am a recovering perfectionist, and when survival "appears" to depend on the ability to perform, feedback can be "life-threatening." I am so grateful for the ways in which I have experienced redemption as my more playful and childlike parts are finding ways to coexist. All that to say, my windows are fairly small, and I am convinced that the farther I step into community, the greater this window will continue to expand.

My DiSC profile was somewhat surprising to me, and after further reflection, I think I may have discovered the root of the discrepancy. I scored a fairly strong *S* (steadiness) with a close *I* (influence). My lowest percentage was *D* (dominance). Although I agree that steadiness fits my personal style of leadership fairly well, as well as influence, my dominance score was highly suspicious. After spending time grieving, I began to realize that I purposely avoided dominance while I took the profile test, because I know deep down women are not "supposed" to be dominant. Here is where my church upbringing and the unresolved pain of being a woman in a Southern Baptist environment reared its ugly head. I do believe that some of the dominant characteristics, such as boldness, determination, restlessness, and persistence do speak truth to my leadership style. And yet, with regard to steadiness, I am a great listener and am very loyal. I love working with groups of people and calling out their gifting and casting vision. There are parts of steadiness that I believe will help me be a great pastor. Hopefully, the more I am affirmed in my calling, the more comfortable I will be with the more dominant parts of myself, and maybe, just maybe, I will come to know them as beautiful.

So often leadership is talked about as if it is an abstract role that can be systematized, but leadership is embodied, contextualized, and lived out. In some ways every human being has the capacity to lead someone. Children are some of the most underappreciated and profound leaders in the world with their simplicity, imagination, and intuition. For example, the other day I was riding the bus and a group of about fifteen four-year-olds got on. In their excitement they rushed and giggled and occupied half of the bus. Most of the other passengers scowled at such an inconvenience. When we reached Ballard High School, a group of mentally impaired students clumsily stumbled on, looking for seats. Most passengers stared and squirmed with discomfort. From the back I heard a sweet voice shout out, "Hey, you can sit with me, and you can even have the window seat." I cannot think of a more beautiful picture of leadership or a more beautiful expression of the kingdom of God.

When I think about Kingdom leadership, I cannot help but think about the foolishness of God and the servant leadership of Jesus. I love what Paul says about foolishness in 1 Corinthians: "God chose what is foolish in the world to shame the wise; God chose what is weak in the world to shame the strong; God chose what is low and despised in the world, things that are not, to reduce to nothing things that are."[2] It does not fit the power structures of our empires and corporate conglomerates. Jesus subverted worldly power structures in many ways, but most directly by submitting to the cross and joining our history not only through the Incarnation but also through the suffering. Jesus's leadership was defined by love: love of God and love of others. When the disciples ask Jesus who is greatest in the kingdom of heaven, this is his response: "Truly I tell you, unless you change and become like children, you will never enter the kingdom of heaven. Whoever becomes humble like this child is greatest in the kingdom of heaven."[3] What a tremendous paradox: we are called to lead and invite in strength and the power of the Holy Spirit through the humble service of love.

When I think about servant leadership as a pastor, I have many hopes for the days ahead. I hope for a more holistic approach to leadership in which pastors can see themselves in the whole of the kingdom as one part of the body. I hope for leaders to become more authentic in their relationships, able to ask for help, reveal vulnerability, and create a context in which there is still a need for a saving God. My true belief is that the more we as leaders can embrace our own humanity, the more we will know of the depths of God's love and forgiveness, and thus will empower those we lead to know more and more of the depth of God's love.

Personally, I long to Sabbath well, laugh generously, play vigorously, and hope radically. I believe that in the years to come, it will be necessary for pastors to lead with faithful simplicity and wise humility. I hope to be a good steward of the word and take seriously the responsibility of teaching and speaking. I hope I never come to a place where what I have experienced of the gospel is enough. There is always another day, another chance for redemption, healing, deliverance, and mutual liberation. I hope for a day when men and women can lead together with their embodied differences, just as I hope that more and more voices will join the chorus of the gospel, giving it more color, more vibrancy, and more of the wild space of God's great imagination, a day when my African and Indian brothers and sisters have just as much interpretive authority as the white Western man. All of these things will come as we embrace our differences as gifts that bless the whole. Above all, I just want to be human size and know something of love, something of community, and something of the gospel.

Sue

Let me relate a story that has impacted me. It's about Myani, who lives in a peaceful village in Uganda, Africa. The village is prosperous by some standards; it is hard to maintain crops in a difficult and barren soil, yet village people have gotten along by hard work. Things have changed in recent years as a wasting illness has begun to spread. So many are affected by HIV/AIDS now that only a few can work the crops.

Working the ground is women's work, and Myani tended the ground from sunup to sundown just to maintain a meager living for her family. Her husband, John, was becoming weaker and experiencing pains in his body. He couldn't move without help anymore. The ulcers in his mouth were raw and made him not want to eat even the meager porridge they all share. No one wanted to help John, they were all afraid of him. Sometimes Myani heard him crying in the night.

Then, last Friday, John died. She probably knew he would die, but she blocked it out of her mind. She began to feel distraught about her future and that of their four children. Her own health was becoming a problem and the baby had a persistent rash. John's family insisted on the customary practice of his brothers inheriting his widow. This included their home, fields, and children. His brothers were harsh with their women. If only she and John had talked about things; if only he had made a will so his family could not take the land. Fear and panic were closing in on Myani.[1]

The story of this village woman reflects the stories of a multitude of widows throughout Africa. Their plight became known to me firsthand about five years ago. Since then, I have returned several times to the continent and can say that now I sense a growing long-term commitment to participate in efforts to enable indigenous churches to minister effectively in the context of the HIV/AIDS pandemic.

A response is taking shape in my thoughts, and I share this humbly with you. It has caused me to explore my own theology, my potential as well as my weaknesses in leadership, how I work with others, and where and how I choose to let my voice be heard. I am wondering how God will lead in it all.

The root of my commitment to friendship, work, and ministry is undergirded by the interweaving theological motifs of *imago Dei*, the Great Commandment, and the Great Commission. In these I find alliance with an incarnational mission that facilitates positive change in the whole of human life, with dignity, where I will invite others to join me to defend human flourishing and to speak out on behalf of the orphan, the widow, and the stranger. This paper strives to flesh out these concepts in a meaningful way as well as explore my potential role of leadership in this setting.

It is my hope to step into an international ministry that is committed to assisting the local faith community in Africa to address HIV/AIDS. At the time of writing, a job description has come to my attention for an international monitoring and evaluation coordinator. The stated goal is to facilitate

transformed individuals and communities resulting in a reduction in the impact of the AIDS pandemic in the target regions. •HIV/AIDS ministries with churches and other partners that focus on care, hope, and compassion. •Enable churches to be strengthened, growing, and having a greater impact on their society. Within this program, Field Offices and Partners create their own country strategy in response to their specific situation, needs, and partnerships. It is desired that the Coordinator speak some French.

The programme provides an overall framework where four key strategic directions guide individual country strategies: Home based care; Orphan care; Prevention; and Enabling churches and partners. At an international level, the XXX AIDS Coordination Team provides services in coordination between countries, with networking, resource development, public relations, communications, capacity building, including the sharing of best practice, and monitoring and evaluation. The Monitoring and Evaluation Coordinator will be an integral member of this team.[2]

Yes, this is for me, I'm thinking excitedly. I have begun discussion with an international ministry about this type of work. I'm captivated with the idea, emboldened, smiling at God's plan, both resting and excited in divine sovereignty, and also scared that I might be found wanting. It's not far beyond my experience and ability but I am waffling—do I want to lead again? Do I want to extend myself at this level again? Will they want me?

In this setting, the leadership role would require some or all of the following capacities: the ability to work alone and self-initiate; network on a broad scale in several countries; be part of a coordinating team and international project system; train other coordinators, project managers, and emerging leadership; participate in writing funding proposals; develop and implement systems for regional communications; enjoy new learning experiences; give attention to detail; be able to apply principles to a variety of situations; be willing to travel for significant periods of time; monitor, evaluate, and report; engage in PR and resource development; and have the capacity to function with limited resources

I have been there before. Africa can be demanding—power shortages, limited resources, language barriers, water shortages, limited training, et cetera. In the United States I've stood in the role of a leader/manager/director in a grassroots ministry. I've also lost the wind in my sails—my husband is gone now, and I'm a widow. I've made mistakes, been broken, disappointed people, and I've held back when asked to lead again.

My resume lists former positions as director, coordinator, manager, leader, and board member. Now, I'm none of these. I've been heard to say, "I want never to lead again." But now, after visiting Africa and entering into graduate studies, I've regained my footing a bit. My dependence is more solely on the Spirit of God. The wind is returning to my sails. I am pondering, *What will it look like to be moved by the wind as a leader?* I see how volunteer work and advocacy have been part of my life story. In fact, I'm amazed that my story (including my weaknesses) shapes my thinking, my behavior, my internal responses, and how I relate to others in the work of ministry.

In the sixties I was a young adult in formation. Civil rights issues were often at the fore of our thinking. I remember arguing with my father in favor of interracial marriage and bringing minority populations (and women) fairly into the work place. After college and marriage, our second child was born with disabilities. Her struggles shaped much of our family life for years to come. Eventually, we learned that advocacy and intervention were highly important to ensure good heath and good education for her. Before that era, education would not have been ensured to children with her needs. Further, on a spiritual and social level, I came to understand that her value was not based on her abilities, her beauty, or her intellect. Her value is as a fellow human, made in God's image, and she is part of our family.

For some people this is automatic; they accept everyone easily and compassionately. Not me. I was selfish and bought into society's skewed ideas of worth and value. Now, life circumstances were changing my values. As Molly became older, my mother came to live with us. Mom was dying from brain cancer, was in a wheelchair, and needed round-the-clock care. Caring for her was not fun and was the hardest thing I ever did. Yet I have no regrets. Conscientious choices and a commitment to the well being of others who could not speak for themselves were becoming central to my lifestyle.

Later, I began working with a Christian nonprofit agency to assist women in unplanned pregnancies—women who were at risk for considering abortion, and in need of support. The issues to me were focused on the unborn, who had no choice, and the pregnant mom, who had little or no support no matter what her choice was. In this setting I came to know that I would not be a public mouthpiece of tight rhetoric and accusations, but the one behind the scenes to be there to help the young woman if she wanted it. I wanted to see something positive happen for her, to be someone to listen with compassion, to agonize with her, to explore with her the God of intimate relations, and to make viable alternatives available.

I became executive director for the three centers, set policy, worked with a board, trained volunteers, raised funds, became known among many nonprofits, churches, and to individuals who cared. I was surprised to find that I enjoyed the administrative side of things

It helps me to recite this story, because in it I see patterns of choices and decisions. Honestly, I don't see myself as highly compassionate or a good counselor, but others do. I don't think I'm very smart or capable, but others do. I like to take a vision and develop it when many won't go there. Can I be honest? From my perspective, some leaders shouldn't be leading. I haven't quite fit it all together.

Observing a female leader from afar, a woman in the public eye of ministry with media attention to her commitment to global AIDS, I wonder what's behind her public demeanor? Studying and journaling all I can find online, I discover she thinks of herself as an ordinary woman, a mother, a wife, and a breast cancer survivor. She says she's been changed by a Damascus road experience and knows she is to be an advocate on a global scale for those suffering with HIV/AIDS.

Now my discernment kicks up a notch. *Why*, I ask, *am I put off when listening to her rhetoric?* She's a driven person in her actions and her words; her approach is ardent, and her words sound strident. She uses highly religious language, calls herself a prophet, and she holds a strongly conservative view. It's too much for me to appreciate. Softening my defense, I realize, *I am not her, yet I'm called to a similar mission.* Hmmm, now I see the possibility of God's diverse approach in reaching the AIDS orphan, widow, and stranger—through various imperfect but willing vessels. Sovereignty means God can do what God wants, however, and with whomever. I'm not God, basically.

Ultimately, at this point in my thinking, I can say that I have a better feel for my theology of leadership because I have lived and worked through defining experiences that have given me the chance to make mistakes and explore what's important to me.

As a leader, I know these things about myself: I am conscientious, courteous, careful, diplomatic, and I seek out facts; my steadiness shows itself as deliberate, amiable, stable, relaxed, and not very demonstrative; when I dominate, I feel self-assured, inquisitive, and adventuresome. Another part of me avoids seeking to influence others directly, which comes across as being aloof, self-conscious, and reticent. Get me stressed, and I will draw inward. The ups and downs, it's all my story.

In recent years, as a potential employee, a testing firm returned the following assessment which I find agreeable.

> Although she is an independent thinker who seeks to maintain her own options, she is also a consensus seeker who can fit in almost anywhere. Has made a career for herself that is consistent more for her determined steadfastness than because she has excelled or stayed long in any one job or with any one organization.
>
> Strives to get along, but matter-of-factly takes things in stride and is more attentive than apprehensive when she encounters a bump in the road. Respects authority, but has learned to trust her own judgment. Does not let her genuine affection for others—and this includes most of the people she knows—diminish the clarity of her vision when it comes to making judgments about them.[3]

So, now, I'm not surprised that the sovereign Lord is directing me to step into leadership of some sort again. While the role of a leader has been stretching and sometimes disappointing, it's part of who I am created to be. It's something I've struggled against, but I'm beginning to think that it's my loving Creator that makes sure that leadership finds me again.

When in Ghana a few years ago, Naomi came to see me. I was the counselor who broke the news to her that she tested HIV-positive.

For Naomi, what the church in her village near Manya Krobo would do about AIDS was a life-and-death matter to her personally. Her nursing baby now lay sleeping in the crook of her arm as she pulled at the shoulders of her two young boys standing by her knees. Gazing quietly beyond the workers, she had much to ponder, and a crisis to face.

231

She lived in a region where antiretroviral medications were not yet available. Her husband traveled and was likely the carrier of the disease, yet according to his traditional cultural and spiritual practices, she would be turned out with the baby and shunned by him and her people. There was a 30 percent chance that her baby also had the virus.[4]

She trusted no one with her news. Her neighbors were afraid of catching the wasting disease, and she would be shunned. Neither her pastor nor the small village church congregation were prepared to respond compassionately or willing to face the stigma and discrimination that prevailed among them.

Much stigma is based on fear and lack of knowledge. In religious groups, stigma is also related to labeling one who is sick as one who has sinned, omitting a response of grace and restoration. Local church practices are culturally influenced and sexual practices are imbedded in culture. Compounding the issues, African cultures generally display a reluctance to discuss sex, death, and dying.

Naomi and her baby girl would likely face the disease alone.[5]

This experience in Ghana was an earthquake event to my soul. Since leaving Naomi, I've been drawn to the issues of how the indigenous church in sub-Saharan Africa is struggling to respond to the pandemic on a grassroots level. I am asking God to allow me to go again, this time in a long-term capacity. Can it be? I am compelled to respond in my heart and by something that is part of the leader in me.

Naomi and her baby girl are made in the image of God, they are of value to God, to all of humankind, to me, to her family. The Great Commandment exhorts, "Love the Lord your God with all you heart, soul, mind, and strength. And, love your neighbor as yourself." I love God and look to the Lord as the lover of my soul. I believe I am asked by the Eternal to love Naomi and her daughter. The Great Commission directs us to "go into all the world and make disciples." As I am going along the way, I will look for ways to share the Gospel of Jesus Christ with people like Naomi.

I consider the mission I step into as incarnational—indwelt by the life, presence, and power of Christ. And I believe it is part of the divine plan to care for the whole of human life—the spiritual and the physical together as one whole. For everyone, Naomi's orphan child, the widow Myani, and the stranger among us. The whole person matters to God and therefore matters to me. I seek to step into transformational development and Christian witness that honors God and humankind.

If others hear my voice, it may be because of my determination, my hope for transformation, my love for God. The willingness to remain honest and open to speaking of this vocational direction has a leadership quality to it too. It invites others to examine what Parker Palmer describes as "the life that wants to live in me."[6] While the development of leadership is an active process, responding to this *call* has an organic sense to it. Yet, even in sensing the nudging of the Spirit, there exists the choice to participate or not. Does it resonate with something within others that God is naming in their own story?

I must allow Naomi's life to impact mine. I have a choice to allow my voice to be heard—it won't be heard until I open my mouth, pick up my pen, and step out.

David

Tyson is the lead pastor of a large, evangelical mega-church in a mid-sized Midwestern city. Roughly nine years ago, Tyson, along with his family and fifty other families, were sent off by their home church on the established south side of town to plant a church on the newly developing north side of town. They began meeting in a local elementary school with the intention of focusing their ministry on small-group gatherings in homes with a monthly large-group worship celebration. Word of this new church spread quickly among the new subdivisions and, within six months, their little church experiment had grown in numerical size to almost six hundred people. They abandoned their original vision of small gatherings in order to meet the demand for a weekly corporate worship service. By year two more than fifteen hundred folks from the north side of town had joined up with this suburban church. Tyson consulted his elder board and other area pastors for advice on what to do with such a large crowd. It was decided that the next step in the life of the church would be a capital campaign to raise money for a permanent structure that could house an exploding number of churchgoers.

Fast forward three years and Tyson is having a harder time than ever convincing the church community to give more money toward the capital campaign. The original design for the building has gone through numerous revisions due to less than ample giving, yet numerically more people than ever are coming to the Sunday morning gatherings. As Tyson suggests yet another sermon series on giving, the elder board and staff are becoming more disgruntled with the direction the church is headed. Tyson is determined to raise money for his building and sees anyone standing in his way as dispensable. Many who question the direction of the church over the coming months find new positions elsewhere or are told that the funding for their current role has been cut indefinitely. Relationships are broken, vision is squelched, and many are silenced over the next few months as the church finally secures the loan that they need in order to begin construction. Eight years after the original team started their new church experiment, the building is opened to the congregation, but many of the truth tellers and question askers are absent from the ceremonies. They have quietly, or not so quietly, found homes in other congregations where their voices matter.

This story is a complex maze of relationships, logistics, details, and passion. It is the story of a real place with real people. It is my story. Tyson (whose name has been changed) is technically my former "boss." As more and more people kept coming through the church's doors on Sunday morning, the attention of our staff meetings quickly went from "How can we best serve the community around us?" to "How can we keep our numbers up?" When Tyson made numerical success the focus of our organization, he stopped listening to the hopes and dreams of those around him. Voices were silenced, creativity was stifled, and eventually, in the face of a complex situation, dogmatic rules were applied to decide whether one was for or against the vision of the church. Those deemed to be swimming upstream against the vision of Tyson were ultimately left to fend for themselves.

This is the story of many in my generation. In our youth we have become the refugees of organizational leadership, especially within theological and ecclesiological structures. This essay is my attempt at dreaming up a different world where leadership is no longer authoritative or hierarchical. This is my hope for the future of leadership, and it begins with a sobering thought.

The future of leadership is complex. It cannot be summed up in a short list nor can it be packaged in a few principles that will sell well at the next leadership conference. The future of leadership involves paradox. In fact, in order for a leader to work well with what she is entrusted with, she will have to learn to navigate a paradoxical world that claims such audacious ideals as "the first shall be last" and "weak is the new strong." The beginning of leadership is paradoxical in that leaders of the future will only function well in their environment to the degree that they recognize and live into their own weaknesses. For when one lives into one's weaknesses, one will find an exorbitant amount of strength.

Tyson is a man who, for all of his good intentions, worked incredibly hard at hiding himself from the rest of his leadership team. He was afraid of showing his weaknesses to the rest of us, lest we lose our confidence in him. In reality, the effect this had on those closest to him was that of distance and loss of trust as opposed to creating a perception of strength.

The future of leadership involves recognizing that one leader cannot do the bulk of the work on his own. When a leader believes he is more qualified and better equipped to do everything on his own, that leader only robs himself of the gift of community. *We* are always better together when we accompany one another on the journey. When my weaknesses are laid out for my colleagues to see, then they will know that I am (1) honest, and (2) in need of help. What we can create together as a community is overwhelmingly more creative, sustainable, and holistic than what I can create on my own. Leaders in the future will not simply value the voices of others, they will treat them as indispensable, knowing full well that the day they abandon those voices is the day they become ineffective at leading. To hear these voices is to tap into the hopes, dreams, and passions of those around you. What better way to create something of substance together than to enlist the passion and full-heartedness of those with which you work?

Along with hearing the hopes and dreams of those around them, leaders of the future will also be quick to hear from those who have the courage to tell the truth to those in power. Whenever one has power it is inevitable that one will, at some point, use that power to abuse someone else. Usually, those who have been marginalized by the powerful have a unique perspective on the life of an organization. They are usually those who have the most prophetic things to speak into the life of the community.

Leaders of the future will invite the voices of the marginalized into their midst, knowing full well that it is these folks who have the most important truths to speak into the leaders life. Tyson was so determined to pursue his goal of building a church home for his congregation that he failed to take seriously the voices of trusted friends and colleagues who were calling him to see something different. Maybe building a six-million-dollar structure was not the best investment of their resources when other existing structures could be renovated for much less money? Maybe their focus on maintaining and increasing their numerical growth had blinded them from creating a community where long-term transformation of individual lives was the norm and not the exception? Maybe their focus on attracting people to their worship gatherings was actually turning a large number of people away who were looking for an expression of the Christian faith that had more substance to it? These questions were commonly asked by a number of key leaders close to Tyson. Yet his responses to these types of questions revealed his dogmatism in the face of complexity. He had begun a capital campaign and to change course in the middle of such a campaign would make him seem weak in the eyes of the congregation. Furthermore, spiritual transformation *was* taking place because so many people were being introduced to the message of the gospel. And those who were looking for more substance could join a small group. Over months of being asked questions like these, Tyson became firmer with his answers. His trajectory was set in stone, and you were either with him or against him. Those who disagreed with him usually left the church. And those who stayed knew to keep their mouths shut if they wanted to keep their jobs.

The truth is painful—anyone can tell you that. The journey to maturity is always painful. Yet people are looking to follow someone who can live into their weaknesses and thereby work toward maturity. Tyson refused to give up the comfort of a numerically large congregation and all the prestige that came with it in order to gain long-term spiritual transformation for the life of the body. He gave up a church full of diverse people who would tell the truth for a church full of yes men. Certainly God can still work wonders through a church like this, yet the more Tyson grabbed to control the organization, the more he squeezed the life right out of it.

Leaders of the future will not only live into their weaknesses and listen to the voices of the marginalized, but they will also be those who seek out healthy interpersonal relationships with those around them. Leaders are only strong to the degree that they have honest, open, truth-telling and trusting relationships with those who they live and move with. Leadership is indeed a lonely endeavor. With all of the demand and responsibility that leaders face, one can definitely understand the tendency to isolate. Yet isolation breeds not only loneliness but also narcissism. Isolation can lead one to believe that your way of seeing things is the only right way and any other way is wrong. If everyone always sees things your way, then you're probably setting yourself up for disaster. It is risky business to show up and be yourself in front of those you lead, yet the payoff is trust and genuine relationship. To be known by others is the gift of relationship. Ultimately, leadership, just like all of life, is a spiritual act. To lead is to invite those around you to wellness, to wholeness. One cannot take people where they have not gone themselves; therefore, to lead is to be in active pursuit of one's own wellness or wholeness. Leadership involves engaging in the hard work of self-discovery and holistic living and inviting others to do the same. Leadership of the future will be a relational act—one where voices are heard, weakness is embraced, and relationships are of the utmost importance. To be a leader, then, is to navigate the interpersonal realm with grace and beauty. It is in this realm that things of substance are born.

Fran

None of us questions our uniqueness. We don't need an authority, either secular or religious, to convince us. We know about sophisticated processes that are capable of ascertaining our identities. We are marked by such things as our fingerprints, retinas, DNA, voices, handwriting, and palm prints. We proclaim that we are individuals: we seek our own style and voice. We know that no one else has ever lived exactly the same life or been formed by the same experiences as ours. We have discovered the truth of what has been recorded in the Bible for hundreds of years. We are each one of a kind. But the biblical account tells us that the particular markers that define each of us are not the result of chance.

The Bible tells us that each of us is uniquely designed and shaped by a God who knows us so well that he knows the number of hairs on our heads.[1] Jeremiah knew this. God told Jeremiah that he had been uniquely formed, even before he was in the womb. In the first chapter of the book that bears his name, Jeremiah wrote, "The LORD gave me a message. He said, 'I knew you before I formed you in your mother's womb. Before you were born I set you apart and appointed you as my spokesman to the world.'"[2] And when we were in the womb, the psalmist tells us that our formation was guided and we were known by God. "You made all the delicate, inner parts of my body and knit me together in my mother's womb . . . You watched me as I was being formed in utter seclusion, as I was woven together in the dark of the womb. You saw me before I was born. Every day of my life was recorded in your book. Every moment was laid out before a single day had passed."[3]

For some of us, as we were being designed and shaped, leadership was written into our DNA. We can choose to deny, neglect, or cover this part of our design, but whether we seek or shy away from leadership roles, these roles will find us. Others will recognize the leader in us, even when we might deny it. We are marked as leaders, just as we are marked by our fingerprints. We will be revealed in an unguarded moment, or when we step into a vacuum created when no leaders appear to be on the horizon. Perhaps in a crisis we will reveal that we are designed to be leaders. Whether or not we seek to lead, we will at times find ourselves doing so, but if we refuse to embrace the leader within us and struggle against becoming who God designed us to be, we will lead badly or indirectly and discover a kind of fragmentation of our inner selves. Our wholeness depends on our embracing fully who God meant us to be.

I know this firsthand, for I have spent many years denying the leader in me. At some point in my life, I decided that it was more important for me to be the person I thought others would like than to discover and embrace the person whom God designed me to be. So I quieted the things in me that were looking for a voice and expression until eventually I lost hold of them. Yet, although I lost hold, they remained part of my design and would emerge unexpectedly. Since I was doing nothing to enable this part of me to mature, these appearances were often inappropriate, fumbling, misunderstood, and always lacked the highest possible level of positive impact. Most importantly, in my refusal to step into this part of my design, I failed to be the person God made me to be and to do what he designed me to do.

God's plan is bigger than my or your uniqueness. We see this in Peter's words to the early church when he writes "for you are a chosen people. You are a kingdom of priests, God's holy nation, his very own possession. This is so you can show others the goodness of God, for he called you out of the darkness into his wonderful light."[4] Peter is addressing first century Christians, but his words apply to today's Christians as well. We are part of a chosen people that God intends to use to reveal his glory and to usher in his kingdom. In *The Drama of Scripture*, Craig Bartholomew references the songwriter John Wierick, who suggests that today's Christians should consider themselves "Kingdom Professionals," who measure their success in ways consistent with Peter's words.

> Kingdom Professionals do not define success in terms of money, job or status. They do not seek to maximize their income or their security or their status, or to advance their careers. Instead they seek to maximize their impact on the people and places to which God has called them. . . . They

240

see themselves as successful to the extent they are doing what God has called them to do, in the place to which He has led them, in such a manner that their giftedness can be well utilized. Nothing less will suffice; not the shallowness of status, not the ephemeral illusions of wealth, not the corrosive effects of power. What matters to Kingdom Professionals is that there is congruence between their daily lives and the further in-breaking of God's Kingdom where they live and work . . . one must be a "stewardly entrepreneur," a steward of the opportunities, talents, time, and money given by God, dedicated to witnessing to his coming kingdom.[5]

With these words, we are challenged to step into the uniqueness God has formed in us, doing what God has called us to do in such a way as to utilize all that God has made us to be. What might this look like for those of us marked as leaders?

First, in order to become the leaders God expects us to be, we must develop a character that reveals and glorifies God. As believers, we have received the Holy Spirit, who is at work in each of us to transform us so that the character of God himself becomes more and more evident in who we are and how we live our lives. The effectiveness of our leadership will always be related to the quality of our character and the extent to which we reflect the person of God and represent him in this world. We become the kind of "out of the box" person described in *Leadership and Self-Deception* who sees "others straightforwardly as they are — as people like [ourselves]who have needs and desires as legitimate as [our] own. . . . We experience [ourselves]as a person among people."[6] We are no longer "self-deceived . . . blind to the truth about others and ourselves . . . blind to . . . how the box itself undercuts our every effort to obtain the outcomes we want."[7]

This formation and transformation of character does not come easily. Paul writes of the difficulties he faced as he stepped into the leader God meant him to be. He writes in 2 Corinthians, "We are pressed on every side by troubles, but we are not crushed and broken. We are perplexed, but we don't give up and quit. We are hunted down, but God never abandons us. We get knocked down, but we get up again and keep going. Through suffering, these bodies of ours constantly share in the death of Jesus so that the life of Jesus may also be seen in our bodies."[8]

We will also experience difficulties, suffering, and broken-ness as God undertakes to remake us. In the words immediately preceding those referenced above, Paul writes, "For it is the God who commanded light to shine out of darkness, who has shone in our hearts to *give* the light of the knowledge of the glory of God in the face of Jesus Christ. . . . we have this treasure in earthen vessels."[9] Paul uses an image of light enclosed in an opaque vessel. Yet this light is meant to be seen, for it represents God's glory. There is no way for it to be seen apart from somehow cracking the vessel that carries it. Similarly, for the character of God to be revealed in us, there will be a breaking that must occur. When we choose to step into becoming who God wants us to be, we will experience breaking, but we will come to know fullness of life. We need to remember Jesus's words in Luke: "If you try to keep your life for yourself, you will lose it. But if you give up your life for me, you will find true life."[10] It is in this process of transformation that I can anticipate seeing my DiSC profile being modified in the areas in which I need to grow in order to become a more effective leader.

Second, while allowing ourselves to have formed in us the character God desires, we need to learn to steward all that God has made us to be. Again we must ask, what might this look like for those of us marked as leaders?

Leadership is only one of our markings. God has marked us with all sorts of life experiences: educational, spiritual, wonderful, painful, relational. He has characterized us with unique personali-ties and temperaments as well. These are all things that God has used in our lives that teach us and mold us and shape us into the vessels he intends for us to be. All of these factors must be consid-ered as we seek ways to become effective leaders. For we will only be effective in a lasting way when we are the leaders God wants us to be.

"As God works through the gifts and inclinations that he himself has given . . . work becomes an opportunity for witness . . . Witness will mean embodying God's renewing power in politics and citizenship, economics and business, education and scholarship, family and neighborhood, media and art, leisure and play . . . the way we live as citizens, consumers, students, husbands, mothers, and friends witnesses to the restoring power of God."[11]

We were designed to glorify God. All that we are and have were not intended for our own glory. We were designed to proclaim his glory, in all we do and say. When I fully and courageously acknowledge and embrace all that he has made me to be, I position myself to become a "Kingdom Professional" and step into the life I was designed to live.

Josué

The Lie of Leadership

I remember the first time I was fired from a church leadership position. Because of an alcohol incident on a mission trip, I was asked to step down from heading my college ministry. Allowing people to drink on a mission trip was an obvious problem. But the way I was let go and how I simply allowed it to happen was also a major problem. There were errors made throughout the whole three-month experience. And it was the last ministry work I would do before I headed off to seminary.

This final job filled me with cynicism and contempt toward those powerful leaders and pity toward those who followed them. I continuously pushed blame off of myself and onto others in order to escape my inadequacies and missed an opportunity to lead through my failures. This fear of leadership has become a theme for not only me but also for others in my cohort. I do fine as a leader when left to my own devices but when exposed and brought into a community of followers, I become scared and cowardly.

This current generation of leaders is skeptical of much—and with good reason. In the last decade, we have experienced the Enron scandal, weapons of mass destruction and Abu Ghraib, the Lewinsky scandal and other lies from our top leaders, to speak nothing of the lies experienced throughout the global church and in our own scope of leading. Given these realities, of course we would be cynical of those in power. And of course we would be scared of being in those same positions. I believe that one of the greatest abilities of a leader, a skill that has been lost to us through the last generation, has been the ability to confess. Our need for confession runs deep into the Christian core of our theology, and yet we have left it for those who are weakest. How we understand confession, forgiveness, and reconciliation may be the most central aspect in becoming a new kind of leader for a people in deep desire for an authentic relation with their leaders.

Influence through Embrace

Confession is an art-form that seems to be lost on us. Admittance into our hearts is usually seen as a weakness so it is rarely seen. Or worse, it becomes an act or a deceptive maneuver to hide the truth of our selves. Sex scandals in the church have led to more hiding rather than full exposure and honesty. The issue with confession lies in our desire to fix the problem at hand. We are a people who believe our first response to an issue should be solution. Rather than working on behalf of each other, we work in order to resolve. There is a need to see leadership as a struggle. DePree states that "leaders need to learn not to inflict pain, but bear pain. It seems to me that if you're bearing pain properly as a leader, whether you're a preacher, a college professor, a parent, or a teacher, you ought to have the marks of the struggle. One ought to have bruised shins and skinned knees."[1]

What is different about the Christian story is that the exposure to our sin never leads us to fixing the issue, but takes us to confession. David's plight with Bathsheba is a perfect example of this. David's ongoing work to hide his initial sin forces him into more sin: covering up the pregnancy of Bathsheba and forcing her husband's death. It is only in the exposure of his sin through Nathan that he is free from the shackles of his hiddenness and may begin the arduous journey of reconciliation.[2]

As a nation, we are currently facing our own pandemic of guilt. The Green movement has brought about an anxiety to fix the problem of carbon emissions, with the Vatican stating that it would offset its carbon footprint through planting forests in Turkey.[3] While this gesture has great implication for understanding the damage we have done to the earth, the issue is still missed. It moves from problem to solution looking for the easiest out rather than examining the fullness of the situation and responding from the most heartfelt benefits. This is true for all leadership. When we work to see how we can quickly fix the problem in order to save our skin, we flagrantly disregard the people we are most trying to serve.

Miroslav Volf's opus of a book, *Exclusion and Embrace,* catalogues the necessity for reconciliation.[4] Through the metaphor of a hug, Volf explains how we are called to embrace the other through opening our arms, waiting for the other to enter in, embracing, and releasing. It is through these four movements that we see reconciliation happen in our world. My favorite step, albeit the least glamorous, is the second one, waiting upon the other. Volf shrewdly explains that the work of reconciliation is not in our time but in the time of those with whom we are trying to reconcile. The action of waiting may be the most difficult because of how quickly we breeze through it. It is important for us to see how waiting on the other is an essential part of leading in grace.

Looking back at my first experience with being fired, I can see how we all failed at truly embracing confession. I failed greatly by desiring to run and hide rather than allowing myself to be seen by others. My leaders failed by pushing for fixing the problem rather than patiently working through the situation. And we all failed the community by tiptoeing around the issue rather than allowing us all in the work or reconciliation.

Through our two in-class analysis exams, what I already believed made itself even more evident. First, my Johari Window showed my proclivity toward being known by others at the sake of knowing myself. Often, I trust more in the words of other leaders than in my own gut. For those who I lead and my peers, the Johari Window showed a pretty even square for my arena, although the skew was toward self-knowledge. But when I am faced with leaders above me, my self-knowledge shrinks away, and what is known by others grows immensely. This tendency to be liked, appreciated, and known by upper leaders exposes my fear in my own leadership. In truth, I am most likely emulating those leaders as I lead others.

When I first moved to Seattle, I immediately began the search for who could be my mentor. I tenaciously worked to be seen by professors and upper classmen in hopes that they would take me under their wing and guide me. But this parasitic tendency was not out of a desire to grow and learn. My need for a guide was because of the immense fear in my own leadership. I could not bear the idea of relying on myself to get through seminary. This desire still lingers as I begin to reimagine what kind of leader I hope to be.

This was also made true through my leadership journal. I experienced a sort of simple fascination with my mentor and believed he could do no wrong. Throughout my internship, there were many times I found myself effusively speaking of my mentor as if his leadership style was beyond any other style of leadership. This became a factor for me because I would hide behind my mentor. If I were able to build him up enough, I would not have to see my own inadequacies. My cowardice toward leading with tenacity becomes glaring when seen through the Johari Window.

The second test pointed out my high *I* personality with a secondary *D*. This exam reveals what I do with exposure. It is already seen how my tendency is to hide away any inadequacies I may have in leadership. But what happens when I am faced with these truths? My DiSC profile reveals that, when stressed, I become a high *D*. This reliance to work toward an end falls into every leader's dilemma: looking for the answer rather than discovering the full question. Through this profile analysis, I also see how my overly optimistic response can be both helpful to the community and detrimental to the health of the leader. This combination in my personality is a part of who I am and how I lead. There is no need to discount them. But it is important to realize how I rely on these tendencies to a fault at times.

The Rite and Privilege of Leadership

What does this mean for leading in grace and reconciliation? I think that it is important to see how my leadership style (and the leadership ability in all of us) leads me toward the grace of the gospel. The gospel message, in all of its elusiveness and mystery, pronounces itself within the context of community. For me, I am learning how the gospel is not a solo experience that I have and then lead others to have. The gospel is not a one-time rite of passage (like death is). Rather, the gospel continuously manifests and unfolds itself in our lives. We need to be aware of how the gospel is made real to us and offered to us. As a leader, I am seeing how this gospel truth is just as vital to my daily life as it is to those whom I lead. Grace, confession, and forgiveness are necessary elements in the life of a leader, perhaps more intrinsically so, because of the position of power handed to leaders.

Many Americans do not realize that driving is not a right that we have as citizens. It's not like free speech or voting. Rather, it is a privilege, one that we earn through driving tests and exams. There is a major difference in understanding driving as a right that I have and a privilege given to me by the government.

For leaders in the church, we are privileged with leadership. It is not a right we assume but a blessing offered us by the community. When we step into a position of power and responsibility, we must be aware that this responsibility for the community must also be held upon ourselves. When Jesus points out the piety in the prayer of the rabbi versus the desire for righteousness found in the tax collector, he observes that those who believe themselves to be beyond the need of grace are the ones missing the point.[5] As leaders, we often believe in the same way the Pharisee does, with foolish hearts convinced we know the grace offered to us. But it is when we fully embrace our understanding of what it means to confess and be forgiven that we can truly begin to lead.

Max DePree offers this advice, "Ask this question about your institution: What can grace enable us to be? Think of it as a choice."[6] I realize now, after reading through this paper, what kind of risk this calls from me. These are easy words to write but hard words to live. And yet I truly believe that leadership grounded in grace is a leader worth following. As for me, I believe that this experience can only last for a leader if he or she is in a community that is also dripping with grace. Thinking back on stories of my past, if I had been as tenacious as this paper calls, I would have been met with hostility and regret. The community of leaders that surround you need to be able to hold you in the midst of your failures. In the same way, may you also freely and readily offer grace to those who desire it. Do not use grace as a scapegoat to run from the heart of the problem, but rather, work through the questions with patience and understanding. Through this, we are made to struggle with the gospel message in ways that reveal more of who Christ is for us and for our world.

Paula

One Theology of Leadership

When I think of leadership I think of "leaders," and specifically two kinds of leaders. There are the iconic leaders such as Martin Luther King Jr., Mother Theresa, Mahatma Gandhi, or Desmond Tutu, who have been a catalyst for social change (I would add Jesus to the list, but to say that he was a "catalyst for social change" does not seem to capture the magnitude of the gospel). The other group of leaders are those who have been personally life changing for me. In the eyes of the world, they may not be seen as having contributed to the liberation of humankind, but they have contributed to my liberation. These people have taken a chance on deeply affecting me and being affected by me as well. Although my heart is stirred when it comes to social and systemic change, leadership must first begin with learning how to let myself be transformed by others and to participate in the transformation of others' lives around me.

Participating in this kind of transformation comes with a cost—the exposure and vulnerability for the sake of touching those around us, and being touched by others. The summer after my sophomore year in college, I traveled overseas with a Christian organization whose mission was to share Jesus's love with college students through relationships developed by a team of students. A week-long orientation with other teams preceded the trip. The beginning of the week was a simulation of everything that could go wrong or be hard when traveling overseas. Part of what this meant was that we did not shower for the first half of the week because "the well had run dry." The heat and humidity took its toll, and we quickly became dirty and smelly. In the midst of this, our team was given the task of washing one another's feet, just as Jesus washed his disciples' feet. I had never participated in something like this before, but it was an incredibly intimate, humbling, and exposing experience. My dirty, smelly feet were exposed to people I had no history with and barely knew. As I sat there getting ready to get my feet washed, I had to risk trusting that those washing my feet would see less of my dirty feet and more my need for the care and comfort a good foot washing would provide. What astonished me more than anything was the realization that I almost did not know which was harder, to have my dirty feet seen or to see the dirty feet of others. Could I offer them the care and comfort that I so desired? I was affected by their dirty feet just as much as they were affected by mine. Even the mere touch of foot washing was a sensual experience that exposed my desire for connection with others even though it was scary and risky. The intimacy of this act surprised me, and I became like a less humble Peter when he said, "you shall never wash my feet." But Jesus replied, "Unless I wash you, you have no part with me."[1] It takes connection to my human needs and desires, my humanity, to be a part of Jesus, to be seen and to experience more fully the humanity of myself and others in ways that exposes yet leads to deeper and more intimate relationships. Leadership begins with touching others, and being touched by others in a way that is exposing, intimate, scary, and risky. Will I dare see the feet of those I lead? And will I let them see my dirty feet?

The problem is that I fight really hard to make my feet look clean even if they are not. I work hard to not let myself have the very human place of having dirty feet. Dan Allender, in his book *Leading With a Limp,* states, "Honest hunger after truth requires us to remain open to everyone, including those with whom we disagree and have conflict . . . We may never agree, nor do we need to do so, but we need others—especially those who challenge us to dig deeper and become more human."[2] To be human. There is a community of friends who I have had the privilege of being a part of for many years. They have so often challenged me to be more human and to see their humanity at the same time. When, in my fervor about my opinion, I would be reckless with our relationship, they would come to me, inviting me into the deeper issues of my words and to see the effect my words had on them. They were committed enough to me and our relationship that they would seek to understand me while bringing themselves to the conversation. If, as a leader, I am simply about a cause, issue, or the bottom line, and my personhood is absent from that, I am simply a hollow shell leading and creating an environment that easily becomes homogenously robotic. It cannot even be about changing the status quo, which I so often default to. Leadership has to be about benefiting people and their ability to be in relationship with one another. Leadership must take into account the complexities of relationships and not try to neutralize the complexity while not letting the complexity paralyze us. And it takes seeing people as people and not as nuisances who are impeding one's own self-interest.[3] Leadership in the absence of humanity and relationship is hollow and useless. Desmond Tutu stated it well when he said that, "My humanity is bound up in yours, for we can only be human together."

Being bound together means knowing that I often give those I am bound to rope burns. About a year ago, my friends and I were talking about one of the hot topics of the day that had affected me in a very personal way. In the midst of this discussion, I became defensive when one of my closest friends, Erin, said something I felt threatened by. Instead of letting myself feel what was at the root of my defensiveness, the fear that our relationship would be threatened by this difference, I kept the discussion about the generic issue because it was easier and less vulnerable. We both ended the conversation angry, hurt and not engaged with each other. The next day, we came together to talk about our interaction. As we talked, I realized how, instead of keeping Erin and our relationship primary, I only saw our two opinions pitted against each other. We ended that time in a vastly different place than the night before. Our relationship deepened that day as we reaffirmed our desire for relationship. We invited each other to be more human in the midst of both of us fumbling through conflict and fear. I cannot be "more human" without deeply committed relationships. And sometimes that means apologizing and asking for forgiveness. And I cannot "lead" without my humanity or relationships; otherwise, I would turn into a manipulative and tyrannical robot of a person, friend, or leader. Without a community, I will be a reckless leader.

In seeing my own humanity, I am invited to see other's humanity as well. However, I do not always want to be confronted with the darkness that exists. When I was in the fifth grade, I read a story about an African American family in 1920s Mississippi who were sharecroppers. The stories of inequality, lynchings, and dehumanization infuriated me. I could not understand this side of humanity. Juxtapose that, though, with knowing I fail to speak on behalf of others or myself because I am too afraid to speak. It is so much easier to not have to deal with it, to not be faced with the dark side of humanity, my own or others. My attempts at offering a prophetic voice seem to be more defined by my non-attempts and silence than by courage and strength. I have hope, though, because even the people Jesus picked to be a part of his immediate community screwed up a lot. Perhaps because of this, and grace, they went on to help the community of Believers take shape and form an identity that would sustain them.

To be a human leader, I have power that can be used to bless or to curse those I lead or those I follow. It is a choice. It is not, however, a choice to either "give power away" or to keep it. We have it. I have it, although I do not always want it. Now, what do I do with it? I do not always know because I am afraid of my power. I fear exposure, failure, being alone, being seen, and not being enough. I am afraid to let others see me in my full humanity. However, as Dan Allender puts it, "The more a leader lets fear be his driving force, the emptier his heart becomes and more suspicious he is of those with whom he works." He goes on to say that fear "creates a growing emptiness in the leader, which results in a self-fulfilling loop of paranoia and perceived betrayal. The cycle convinces the leader that she is alone and that the only workable solution is to manipulate the world so she can gain a small degree of safety."[4] Over time, I have developed strategies for being closed off in the midst of my personality being one of seeming openness. Being good at faking openness combined with fear of exposure is the perfect trajectory for becoming a manipulative leader. And I am someone to whom others look for leadership. There is power in that. How can I steward that power that is not manipulative? As Allender says, "Honesty is not just saying what we feel or think; it is seeking to be laid bare before the eyes of truth to see as we are seen."[5] Again, to be seen by a committed community of people where I am known is essential to not using manipulation to hide in my leadership.

Humans get tired and need rest. As a woman who has been raised to see her worth in herself as a *human doing* instead of *human being,* it is easy for me to minimize the need for rest. Coupled with a desire for social change, this makes me a great candidate for professions that require an immense amount of work and emotional energy that, in turn, makes me a great candidate for burnout, because I feel like I must fight *every* battle that comes along. I have had the opportunity of talking with a wise woman who has spent her adult life working in a male-dominated profession that can be hostile to women in leadership. As she recounted her stories, it became clear to me that this was a woman who had fought many battles, but who had come to a place where she picked her battles instead of letting the battles pick her. She told me that if I was created to fight battles and could sustain spiritually, then to do it, but to be cultivating spiritual practices now that would provide sustenance. She earnestly encouraged me to first and foremost seek "beauty and goodness" in this lifetime and to fight battles on the side. If I did not have spiritual sustenance or rest, I could become bitter and mean. I know myself somewhat well enough to know that my tendency is to see how things are not what they should be and to enter those battles without heed to the cost. I can live in the sorrow that Allender defines as "the space between the already and the not yet" without also acknowledging the beauty of the present.[6] I am again at a fork in the road in how I choose to develop my life, my character, and my practices in such a way that either minimizes my humanity or encourages it. Community and Christ-centered friendships invite me to see the beauty and the hope in the midst of the sorrow.

Part of spiritual sustenance for me is rest. Someone told me once that "it is no doubt you will lead people through hard things, but can you do it with rest and kindness, because that is what people will need in the midst of those hard things?" I have no idea what prompted him to say this, but again, it invited me to look at my life and how I choose to develop my sense of rest and play. It is stewardship of my personal resources in order to grow into the person I am created to be and for the good of those I will lead today and tomorrow. Jesus models this for us in the New

Testament. When the crowds became overwhelming, Jesus withdrew to "lonely places and prayed."[7]

In the need for rest, there is death to the way I have most often found worth, which has been to outwork everyone else. This takes a daily death to a superficial sense of worth and competence. And death is a daily part of living and leading. There is death to the need for an immediate solution for my sorrow, death to self-preservation and hiding, and death to control. Second Corinthians states,

> But we have this treasure in earthen vessels, so that the surpassing greatness of the power will be of God and not from ourselves; we are afflicted in every way, but not crushed; perplexed, but not despairing; persecuted, but not forsaken; struck down, but not destroyed; always carrying about in the body the dying of Jesus, so that the life of Jesus also may be manifested in our body. For we who live are constantly being delivered over to death for Jesus's sake, so that the life of Jesus also may be manifested in our mortal flesh. So, death works in us, but life in you.[8]

There is hope in the possibility to be a part of a "people of faith who can look death boldly in the face" and be sustained through it.[9]

What I hope for is to be an honest, forthright, courageous, and compassionate leader who knows the cost of leadership, is aware of my power and able to use it well, and can admit when I do not. I want to laugh and cry, and to be affected and not be hardened. I hope to be a leader who can engage playfully yet live as a person with a deep sense of my core and my center. I do not want to give in to the temptation of shunning the responsibility of leadership because of fear of failure. I hope there is a process that increases my grace, patience, and character that can bear hope, glory, and sorrow for myself and on behalf of others in a way that leads to generative change. To be human and in community, to rest and to play, to work and to pray, to forgive and be forgiven. This is the task of leadership.

Mark

It was officially winter in Chicago and the first snow was around the corner. This was my first position as youth pastor. I had been hired right out of college. I had finally begun to feel accepted, and it started to feel like home.

Coming out of college, I knew that I would need to find a church where I would be given the permission to learn, make mistakes, and grow as both a man and a pastor. I interviewed at many churches all over the Midwest, but when I met Bob, I knew I had found the right church. Immediately, our personalities clicked. We both liked coffee and beer, basketball and Dave Matthews. As a pastor, Bob was a great speaker, was able to connect with people, and the staff he led was full of amazing people. I instantly thought he would be a great mentor, a person I would want to follow.

I realized very quickly that I had no idea how to be a youth pastor. I found myself in a new place, with no friends, and in a profession where I felt clueless. Bob became a close friend and mentor. He encouraged me to set goals in ministry, gave me books to read, challenged my abilities, and provided opportunities for me to succeed. As time passed, I began to become more confident in myself, and I began to dream about the future.

Yet, this night was a particularly cold night. I had come to the church early in order to prepare for an upcoming youth trip. I wanted to get there early to make sure all the details were smoothed out before any student arrived. As I sat in my office going over the details, I heard the door of the church open and close. My office was at the end of the hallway, and I could hear him walk up the stairs. I looked up from my desk and watched Bob walk by my door. He nodded his head and walked by with his usual swagger. Within thirty minutes I heard his voice echoing down the hallway, asking me to come to his office. While walking down the hallway, I imagined the reason he was beckoning me. Does he want to pray with me and wish me well on our trip? Is he going to give me some more work to do? I entered his office and sat in a chair, like I had done hundreds of times before. I remember saying something I thought was funny, and noticing the expression

255

on his face was blank and white. His words hit me like a smack in the face, "I wanted to let you know that I am stepping down from the senior pastor position." I sat there with shock in my eyes and unable to move my mouth. He then hit me with the crucial blow, "I have committed a moral failure, and I cannot tell you any more."

The news of Bob's secrets brought about the worst of the winter's storms. I chose to work at this church because I knew that it would stretch me and challenge me, but I had no clue it would be to this extreme. I wanted to work with Bob because I felt that he could be a great leader and mentor, yet I didn't think the lessons he would teach me would be so difficult and so real.

Assuming that the staff and congregation could move past Bob's departure, we attempted to carve a way forward for the church. This attempt proved to be futile, and it created even more troubling issues. I want to believe that I left this church with a happy ending and that things were resolved with grace and love, but that wouldn't be true. The church was built upon the personality and charisma of Bob, and without him the church could not and did not survive. Within a year of Bob's departure from the community, the church closed its doors. Unfortunately, this story is but one of many with similar outcomes. Too often we hear stories of prominent leaders who, whether it be moral failures, embezzlements, or abuses of power, have done great harm to individuals and communities.

As we enter this post-Christian, postmodern era, there is still a cry for leaders, but these leaders must look different, smell different, and taste different. Most organizational contexts have a defined hierarchical structure of power and leadership in which everyone has a defined space and location that resembles the structure of a standard organizational chart. This type of leadership is top-down driven, and if a piece is removed, particularly a top piece, the entire structure is vulnerable, as it was with Bob. I wish to explore and develop a new organizational and leadership structure that will hopefully look more like an interlocking Venn diagram, more fluid than rigid, more horizontal than hierarchical, and more complex than defined.

Future leaders will not be able to follow the paths or strategies of previous leaders but must forge unique, adaptive, and relational practices. Searching for a single model of effective leadership will do more harm than good. Attempts to capture leadership strategies within a few simple steps or laws fails to capture the complexity and uniqueness of every leadership context. So, rather than paint another leadership strategy or law, I would like to suggest a leadership trajectory.

A trajectory does not necessarily determine the exact path or steps a leader might or must take, but rather gives a general direction and allows for the freedom and necessity of adaptation within their unique contexts. The leadership model portrayed in figure 1 above is commonly described as the CEO model of leadership. The leadership trajectory I wish to present describes a leader as a facilitator rather than CEO. There are three clues to this type of leadership, which I would like to explore: servanthood, shared values and outcomes, and the dissemination of power.[1]

"Leaders are servants." This statement has been used and abused, but it is no less true. Servanthood is often confused with things we ought to do rather than focusing on the person we ought to be. It's important to understand that servants are called, not elected.[2] Servants are raised up by God, not by a vote or hiring process. Servants naturally respond to human needs by choice, instead of being asked.

This type of leadership will question the false dichotomies of laity/clergy and volunteer/staff.[2] These distinctions create systems that devalue most of the people in the Body of Christ. New leaders will remove this distinctions and cultivate a community identity that understands itself as the servant people of God.

Some leadership models encourage the leader to develop a vision and subsequently work to motivate people to achieve this vision. In ecclesial settings this often results in a pastor sitting at her desk writing a mission statement, vision, and a list of the church's top ten values. Yet, leadership is not something that is done in isolation but as a fellow journeyer with shared values and outcomes that result from a shared vision. Acts 20:28 uses the metaphor of shepherd for those left in leadership positions.[3]

A shepherd lives with her sheep, eats, sleeps, and walks with her sheep. A shepherd knows her sheep and the sheep know her. This type of leader will allow vision, mission, and values to permeate out of a communal passions and desires. Leading in this way is not simple, easy, or timely, but necessary.

The final clue I want to examine is the dissemination of power. In a traditional model of leadership, power originates from the leadership on the top of the chart and flows down. Leaders higher up the chart are given more power and more responsibility for certain decisions. In contrast, leaders who understand themselves fundamentally as facilitators are always looking for opportunities to give away power and desire for others to lead and develop their gifts and talents. This allows for communities to see their need for one another, and difference becomes a strong communal value. Often times this is understood as chaos or anarchy, but anarchy is often confused with freedom.[2] People will blossom when leaders give them freedom in the Spirit. Power can be a difficult dynamic to navigate, but allowing others the freedom to flourish in leadership roles is a sign of true health and stability.

Sustainable leadership in our changing culture will look, think, and feel differently from leadership of the past. New leaders will emerge who understand the world, reality, and leadership in a way no one else has before. They will be poets, artists, theologians, and philosophers. These leaders will be more fluid than rigid or controlling, more horizontal than hierarchical, and more complex than defined. These leaders will use new metaphors, draw new pictures, and build new communities with the dream of changing the world.

Mary

A healthy leadership theology should call leaders to look within themselves in order to look out for others. A healthy leader should understand their own personal leadership capabilities, personal preferences for influencing others, and what type of character fuels these tendencies. With a healthy grasp of these, leaders can then better see how their leadership sets the context for leadership as relationship. I have observed and experienced many church leaders who seemed to have little awareness of their own selves, much less their leadership tendencies. Their lack of desire to know these things created train wrecks of relationships and congregations. For much of my life, I've been keenly interested in my own leadership skills, almost as if it were a prerequisite for my pastoral calling. From the experience of being a congregant, I could only hope that every pastor engages in a study of their own leadership tendencies and the effect those tendencies have on those who are following them.

My own work began by examining my supervisor at work. Little did I know that I would not only be paying attention to her but also tracing the outlines of my own leadership tendencies. My journal proved itself to be its own personal profile system. My journal was a combination of my DiSC and Johari profiles described through my interactions and perceptions of people and situations at my job. Though my administrator was the journalistic focus, I also shared the spotlight and clearly displayed my DiSC behavioral tendency of influencing.

Both my DiSC profile and Johari Window had remarkable insights into my behavior. I am an influencer. I see myself as a persuader while I see others as perceiving me as an appraiser. I am an appraiser under stress. I believe that others expect me to be an appraiser. I found that I definitely follow these patterns in situations at work. Generally, I carry a larger façade than is considered balanced with all co-workers. My façade is at its lowest with superiors, though I overuse exposure while receiving little feedback. With employees I garner more feedback with limited exposure, and with colleagues my feedback and exposure are very limited.

Most concerning for me is how I am controlling of the information between myself and my co-workers, and how this affects the quality of our relationships and work. The Johari tool states, "Mutual understanding and shared information is the assumption that productivity and interpersonal effectiveness are directly related to the amount of mutually held information, and, therefore, the larger region 1 (arena) becomes, the more rewarding, effective, and productive the relationship can be."[1]

The Johari tool empowers me to realize I can influence the type of relationships I am having (and therefore our productivity) by examining the areas of the arena, blindspot, façade, and the unknown. The tool brought to light for me the fact that the shape of the arena has "implications for feelings which are likely to be experienced by parties to a relationship . . . the quality of production is largely a function of those feelings."[2] This then infers that the feelings my co-workers have toward me can be determined from the shape of my arena. These probable feelings set off an alarm for me. To my colleagues I come across rigid and aloof with the possibility of some hostility felt toward me. With employees I could be felt untrustworthy with a side of anxiety and hostility toward me. My profile with supervisors lends itself to feelings of hostility, insecurity, and resentment.

As mentioned before, the findings of the DiSC and Johari Window tools were not simply characteristics deduced in a questionnaire, but they also revealed themselves in my journal. Though my intensity varied in my journal, I was fault-finding, critical, and demanding of higher standards. I analyze and appraise situations on the basis of what has happened, what is happening, what will happen, and what should have been done in the first place. Regardless of the situation, I have an internal drive to look good. My journal definitely showed that when I am under pressure, I become impatient and critical. I journaled my need for more analysis and data regarding situations at work before the next actions can be taken. When I am operating in a stressful environment, I have the need for public recognition for my ability in tough situations. My journal described someone with a large façade that probably comes across as semi-supportive to co-workers. I saw in myself a person who has trouble trusting others. This lack of trust creates the need for more exposure and feedback with all of my co-workers.

In my journals, I also reviewed the behavioral characteristics I saw in my supervisor. A major topic of my journal was the hiring of a reception person. I saw my supervisor needing to be more realistic when appraising others in the hiring process. It has been like a rotating door for the reception position, and I feel there could be a possible blindspot for hiring the same type of employee without enough feedback from other colleagues regarding the issue. At the same time, I saw my supervisor's more spontaneous, impulsive, and impatient side when deciding to fire someone—it was done quickly. When things are tense at work, she definitely becomes restless, impatient, and critical. For example, in a stressful time, another employee was having her own internal struggles at work, and my supervisor somewhat hounded her impatiently until she told her what was going on. The employee said later she would have preferred a little time to think through things before having to talk it out with our supervisor. I saw in my journal that my supervisor does have the desire to get along with others and make good impressions. In my journal she frequently bought lunches for employees. Overall, I saw that my supervisor had a larger arena but did not get a lot of feedback and clung to her own opinions and authority. Just this week, our receptionist submitted her two-week notice.

When I look to the future of leadership, I hope for an environment where a two-week notice is not an imminent threat for employees or supervisors. I hope that a place of leading and following is fertile ground for productive collaboration where what is produced is beneficial for the over-arching goal of an organization but also provides healthy interpersonal growth for leaders and followers alike. For all involved, these byproducts of good leadership will have a ripple effect into the relationships of all involved, other co-workers, families, and friends, to name a few.

I hope that leadership in the future will be seen similarly as environmentalism is now. True and healthy leadership is for the benefit our world. People will be valued, value themselves, value others, and value our world. Leadership is saying to the world that someone and everyone is important. Someone is important enough for me to strive to be a better leader and a better person for the benefit of all. Leaders of the future will realize that when they value one person, they are valuing all peoples of the past, present, and future.

I call leaders to know themselves and strive to be comfortable with who they are. I desire them to know that in their own process of transformation lies the beginning of the transformation of those around them. Transformation of the world starts with transformation of the self, and leadership is taking on the transformation of the world through one person. When more and more people in our world participate in leadership as a tool for the betterment of our world, our world will show it.

When I look at my future of being a leader and following Christ, I see a well-worn path ahead. Christ was an ultimate leader for the betterment of the world around him. In his knowledge of the greater needs of the world, he attended to the needs of individuals as though their need was the only need. Christ I believe calls leaders to be fully human and, in doing so, to exist within the big and small needs of the world we exist in. Our world is a community where Christ repeatedly calls us to act on the behalf of others. As we are created in God's image, it is naturally within us to take on God's character and God's characteristics to act on the behalf of others.

Matt

> *No young kid growing up ever dreams of someday*
> *becoming a businessman. He wants to be a fireman, a*
> *sponsored athlete or a forest ranger. The Lee Iacoccas,*
> *Donald Trumps, and Jack Welches of the business world*
> *are heroes to no one except other businessmen with similar*
> *values. I wanted to be a fur trapper when I grew up.*
> —Yvon Chouinard, from *Let my People Go Surfing*

Cruciformity as Leadership

Growing up in a white collar suburban area had it advantages and disadvantages. Good schools, nice people, and plenty of public places to play free from fear are just some of the advantages I enjoyed. As for disadvantages, I grew up with a notion of leadership (including pastoral) that saw its ultimate goals in the shape of Iacocca, Trump, and Welch. But, in the style of Patagonia founder Yvon Chouinard, when I grew up I wanted to be a mystic. Yet, life itself is not quite as simple. So often what we grow up wanting to be gets turned toward something else, and as God would have it, I didn't become a mystic; however, God would use that desire to turn me into a reluctant pastor.

One area of critical concern for me as I develop a theology of what it means to be a leader is the notion that a good leader can be separated from what it means to be a faithful Christian. For instance, as a Mennonite I am also a pacifist. I am not a pacifist because I believe that it is the most effective foreign policy, or because it would solve all the world's problems, but rather because I believe being a disciple of Christ in a world as violent as ours offers no other way to faithfully live. This might suggest that to be a good leader, we need to renounce effectiveness, but this is not true. As John Howard notes:

> Then to follow Jesus does not mean renouncing effectiveness. It does not mean sacrificing concern for liberation within the social process in favor of delayed gratification in heaven, or abandoning efficacy in favor of purity. It

means that in Jesus we have a clue to which kinds of causa-
tion, which kinds of community-building, which kinds of
conflict management, go with the grain of the cosmos, of
which we know, as Caesar does not, that Jesus is both the
Word (the inner logic of things) and the Lord ("sitting at
the right hand"). It is not that we begin with a mechanistic
universe and then look for cracks and chinks where a little
creative freedom might sneak in (for which we would then
give God credit): it is that we confess the deterministic
world to be enclosed within, smaller than, the sovereignty
of the God of the Resurrection and Ascension.[1]

With this focus, it becomes impossible to ask if the means must
meet the ends, but somehow the ends are embodied in the means.
Therefore, as I seek the question of what it means to be a leader in
an emerging context, it cannot be done with some universalized set
of expressions, but only through the shape of the cross.

While growing up in the suburbs may have had some indica-
tion on my desire to find and develop a distinct form of leadership,
growing up with a learning disability most certainly has some
impact on the leadership direction I hope to take. To be honest,
though I am not quite sure the shape this takes, my DiSC type and
PRI instrument might shed some light upon the ways this shapes
me.

Reading the words describing my DiSC type is an exercise in
self-exposure. Being a high *I* with a high *D*, I find great hope in
words like *risk-taker*, *adventuresome*, *enthusiastic*, and *persuasive*.
And yet, on the other end, with my high *I* words like *rebellious*,
spontaneous, and *defiant* appear, to which I responded to my group
with "I don't understand how those are bad things." The group was
kind to respond with the fact that "We need people like that . . .
sometimes." Combine this with the PRI arena, and it is easy to find
a distrust of authority, a rebellious spirit, and someone who avoids
feedback, both positive and negative. To say that this is because
of the endless critique I received growing up with my learning
disability and somehow always believing I am the underdog is to
let myself off too easy.

The truth is, I need other people to help me still to this day, no matter how much I might want to write off their feedback. They make me a better person, more aware, and kinder. As Rowan Williams has put in words that have become emblazed in my memory, "Self-dependence is . . . a mechanism of self-destruction; to cling to it in the face of God's invitation to trust is a thinly veiled self-hatred."[2] To consider myself a self-styled underdog who has beaten back his demon in the form of a learning disability is perhaps the slightest form of self-destruction and, not even creatively, a way to sabotage myself. Yet the invitation of the cross-shaped community that God provides for me to trust in forms me into a more faithful person and dispenses a mighty force called grace. This is exactly what I hope to create, but it means that if I continue in my old patterns, it is exactly self-hatred. To use the language of the PRI, I need to grow my arena, which means that as a Christian I need to make myself available to be formed into a faithful disciple of Christ by those whom I offer my life to so that they can speak truthfully to me.

Sitting in class recently, the professor decided to read the Sermon on the Mount aloud. This professor, who has one of the kindest demeanors, read the section of Matthew in a way that was in stark contrast to how many of us have heard the voice of Jesus in the past. Taking the words from a stance of doom and hellfire to a stance of kindness and love allowed people to hear the voice of Christ in a new way. While this is certainly true in the way many hear the voice of Christ, those who have voiced Paul in my life have often been those leaders who, to put it kindly, I found wanting. For them it was possible to do things with Paul's writings that they couldn't do with Christ, and it allowed them to lead in ways that are hardly compatible to the way of the cross. So, with that, I decided Paul was a relic of a theologian hardly needed.

As mentioned above, God has a way of shaping us differently than we might shape ourselves, and soon God had sent a book that would radically shock my view of Paul and give me answers to the question, What should the shape of Christian leadership be? The title of the book is *Cruciformity*, written by Michael J. Gorman. Simply defined, cruciformity means, "conformity to the crucified

Christ."[3] However, Gorman uses the term to uncover "what Paul means by conformity to the crucified Christ, showing that this conformity is a dynamic correspondence in daily life to the strange story of Christ crucified as the primary way of experiencing the love and grace of God."[4] While the book aims to uncover Paul's narrative spirituality of the cross, it also serves as a new paradigm for understanding the shape leadership should take.

I have never been involved in a discussion about Christian leadership that at some point didn't involve the hymn or poem from Philippians 2. Gorman's book takes seriously what Philippians 2 says about faith, hope, and love, and interestingly adds power. First, cruciform faith is faith that allows you to surrender yourself to God, abandoning all attempts to save yourself. It is often in the call to be a leader that we feel as if we are the ones in control, or that if we let go, the whole system will fall part. In short, we as leaders often think far too much of ourselves. Cruciform leadership begins with the knowledge that it is not we who have control. When we learn to let go of this control, options that seemed unavailable to us before will begin to take shape because the church doesn't rest upon our effectiveness.

Cruciform love is an aspect that enables leaders to be downwardly mobile and reject the "status indicators" of our culture. As leaders this enables us to make decisions based on those who are lowly. This means that we ask two questions about roles as leaders: How might the exercise of my privileges or rights be harming others, and How might I reconfigure or even renounce the spiritual and material benefits of my statues for the good of others.[5] Cruciform love frees leaders to live into an other-centered sense of leading, which allows for creating a community that is mutually seeking the benefit of others rather than the benefit of those at the top, and which allows that community to freely give social power and grace.

Cruciform hope is "confident in the triumph of God because of God's victory, not only in the cross but also the resurrection."[6] This kind of hope enables Christian leaders with knowledge that is unique to the church: in the end, the ultimate arch of the universe is toward cruciformity, and even death has not defeated that. It personally allows for the leader to live not only in joy but also in cultivated peace and to be free from the totalitarian demands of the world. Christian leaders who embrace this kind of hope are able to Sabbath, to let go, and be aware that the defeat of principalities and powers they seek to defeat have already been relinquished of their power in the cross and resurrection of Jesus.

Finally, cruciform power is "not imperial power; it is not domineering or violent."[7] The cross for Christian leaders is enduring because it is where Christ endured suffering and death, along with the misuse of power.[8] It is through the cross that those called to power understand how to be free from imperial temptations and violence, and learn to live in self-giving sacrifice exemplified by Christ. This is no small move, but it is the great critique of what has been wrong with abuses of power in the past.

Of all the insights gained during the time I spent watching a pastor in public, the most important came from discussing how their church operates with the chair of the leadership team. Instead of attempting to ground church politics in Robert's Rules of Order, or some other system of church polity, they seek to move forward in their conversations through consensus. What this means for the pastor is that in the decision-making process, he must listen to all voices and not buy into a notion of majority rule that silences all minorities. This notion of major decision making is critically aware of the fact that as people formed under the rule of God, all we have is time. If we don't make a decision this week, God will still be God and the spirit will still continue to move in our midst.

But as we leaders of the next century move into more critically formed visions of leadership, we must also remain aware of its faults. For instance, our society assumes that good discussions are those that begin together and end together, but as we move into new paradigms for leadership, disagreement must be a marked character in conversations. The false sense of tolerance that we often give to discussions is often more manipulative than it is helpful. Michael Quirk explains this well:

It is the cardinal error of political liberalism to think that conflict on important matters can be domesticated, privatized, smoothed over, without losing something very important in the process—namely, a sense of the meaning and worthiness of our lives. Argument does not deny but confirms one's faith in the good will of one's interlocutor: to fail to engage one in argument, when it is not simple squeamishness, is often the grossest sign of disrespect, and a missed opportunity to forge a consensus that might enrich the lives of everyone involved.[9]

As leaders we must be willing to break into honest conversation that airs real opinions and disagreements, not just so that better options might emerge, but because if we fail to do so, our faith will only be as radical as the half-baked consensus we reach.

A phrase I have become more apt to say is seen as an affront to many within carefully constructed Christian communities. The phrase *Extra Ecclesiam nulla salus*, translated as "No salvation outside the church," comes from the Roman Catholic tradition, but I feel is a deeply needed sentiment in our postmodern, fractured world. I truly believe that the form salvation will come in is with the people we make our lives vulnerable to and the practices those groups use for formation. How often we practice elements like confession, communion, truth telling, and baptism will have a profound effect upon how we live our faith. The church is God's instrument for helping us in this lived-faith, and for shaping us as one body; therefore, the statement "No Salvation outside the church" is not condemning of those who don't attend church, but a call to radically acknowledge that in our communities, we will find salvation defined and lived.

This kind of thought about the church should point to the fact that one of the central challenges of cruciformity that leaders must face is that it is intrinsically communal. In the following quote, though Stanley Hauerwas and William Willimon are referring to the Ten Commandments, they very well could also be referring to cruciform leadership: "Apart from this community [the church], the commands of God appear heroic, impossible, idealistic, or just odd. Church, a community of the forgiven, a people who keep coming together to worship a God, makes the commandments intelligible. In fact, we might put on the Decalogue a warning: *Don't try to obey any of these commandments alone.*[10] Leaders need to acknowledge not only that doing this alone will lead to destruction but also that there is a great use in doing cruciform leadership with a community, which makes intelligible our lives and the expressions of our faith.

In conclusion, to be leaders influenced by cruciform leadership means that we first must acknowledge that we have failed and will continue to fail. But these past failings, our own and those of the leaders who have failed before us, expose something deeper about the universe. Given a worldly perspective, our efforts will seem hard and most likely futile on a grand scale. Yet, with Christian eschatology, we learn that those who attempt to shape the world through the misuse of power, the silencing of others, and the use of the sword are not as powerful as we think. As John Howard Yoder states, "It is that people who bear crosses are working with the grain of the universe. One does not come to that belief by reducing social process to mechanical and statistical models, nor by winning some of one's battles for the control of one's own corner of the fallen world. One comes to it by sharing the life of those who sing about the Resurrection of the slain Lamb."[11]

Chapter Eight Questions for Reflection

1) What are some ways you currently embody the future of leadership that these students long for? How do you know this? Would your peers (or those you lead) say the same things?

2) How do think you can pursue the young leaders in your midst to uncover the hope within them?

3) If you are an emerging leader, what are some ways for you to genuinely engage traditional leaders with your frustrations and hopes? How can a space be created for the two of you to learn from each other?

Epilogue

It's very likely that you are exhausted now. Hopefully, exhausted in a very energized way. You have had the rare and precious privilege of an up-close, intimate encounter with the souls of tomorrow's leaders. You have had an uncommon glimpse into what the future might look like. And, hopefully, you have been changed along the way.

We hope that you will return to some of these stories many times. The ones that especially pierced you or confounded you are the ones you need to engage even more. Because they are likely the stories of those who you encounter every day. The women and men whose stories you have just experienced have gifted you with a worldview of leadership that you can now invite from others and from yourself. Make your time with their stories count for more than just the passing of reading time. Let what has penetrated you stick, and let it permeate your relationships with other leaders, especially those you are trying to help prepare for future leadership.

We recently received this email from a very gifted young leader with boundless potential:

> In the middle of the meeting, the boss asked us for our thoughts on how to resolve a major conflict between two departments in our organization. We had spent the morning in silent prayer, reading, and in what he called "discernment" about what we might do about this. Everyone sitting in the room knew exactly what the issue was, but nobody

was willing to say anything. He practically pleaded with us, saying, "Please, if you have ideas, I really want to hear them." So I decided to take the plunge and speak up. Maybe I didn't do it in the most eloquent way, but I tried my best. When I was done, there was silence—everyone was pretty uncomfortable. It felt like hours passed before he spoke even though it was only about a minute. All he said was, "Does anyone else have any ideas?" Nobody said anything. Then he said, in a very condescending tone, "Do any of you actually agree with this assessment of the problem?" It was clear what he wanted people to say, and most everyone caved and said they didn't agree. Hung out to dry, I was now alone and without my voice and my credibility. I should have known he really didn't want the truth. I wonder if anybody really does ever want the truth. Leaders who want to "mentor" us tell us to speak up and share our views, but what they really mean is "tell me what I want to hear and make it feel good." Honestly, I'm not sure it's really worth it. Maybe after all the old farts die off we'll have a shot. But not likely before then. I'm sure as heck not gonna stick my neck out anymore, that's for sure.

Your first reaction may be one of self-righteous piety—"I would never do that to someone." Or one of dismissal—"That's an extreme example, that stuff doesn't really happen that often."

To both responses we would resoundingly say, "Yes, you would, and yes it does." The voices of tomorrow's leaders are being muted with the best of intentions. Even by you.

But now you have new choices. You have more options. Hopefully, you have a more tender heart, a more supple mind, a more loving posture, and deeper convictions about the important role you can play in preparing tomorrow's leaders. Whether they are younger than you or your peers, you can still play an essential role in ushering in a generation of leaders more equipped to change the world than they would otherwise be left on their own. We hope that having heard their voices and peeked into their dreams, you have a great desire to do so.

In John 17 we read Jesus's legacy prayer—his accounting for his life. Notice he doesn't list the endless accomplishments to sum up his life's work. He would have been well within his right to boast to his Father of all the great work he had done. What does he hold up as the trophies that represent his life's greatest accomplishment? Those he loved.

What—or who—lines the trophy rooms of your heart? Is it the great results you've achieved? The empire you've built? The buildings you've erected? The policies you've crafted? The sermons you've preached? The programs you've grown? Or is it the faces of those you have loved well?

You get to decide what it is that will signify your leadership journey. Having engaged the stories in this book, our prayer is that it will be the stories of tomorrow's leaders, which you have the privilege and opportunity to shape for great good.

Whose story awaits your imprint?

Notes

Chapter 1
Carl

1. Jacques Derrida, *Of Grammatology*, trans. G. Spivak (Baltimore: Johns Hopkins University Press, 1976), 158.
2. Genesis 1:27-31 (TNIV).
3. Psalm 139:14 (TNIV).
4. Jurgen Moltmann, *God in Creation*, trans. M. Kohl (Minneapolis: Fortress Press, 1985), 218-19.
5. David Benner, *The Gift of Being Yourself: The Sacred Call to Self Discovery* (Downers Grove, IL: Intervarsity Press, 2004), 20-23.
6. Dan Allender, lecture given at Mars Hill Graduate School, Sept 10, 2008.
7. Air Jordan Legacy, "Michael Jordan Quotes," http://www.airjordanlegacy.com/michael-jordan-quotes/ (accessed June 24, 2008).
8. Søren Kierkegaard, *Fear and Trembling*, trans. A. Hannay (New York: Penguin, 1985), 41.
9. Jim Collins, "Level 5 Leadership," *The Harvard Business Review* 73 (January 2001):67-76.
10. In preparation for this paper, I interviewed the lead pastor at a local church and observed this person, both in the pulpit and via blog postings, over the course of one month. The church has grown rapidly over the last three years, and this pastor would be considered by some to be an effective leader. My observations were mixed. Although this leader

seemed to have a sense of voice, movement, and risk, my assessment was there was a lack of self-examination and humility. This leader seemed to pay particular attention to physical appearance (dress, self-portraits on blog site, etc.). In addition, I got the sense this pastor wants to be seen as funny — very subjective, I know, but that was my impression. Because of my perception of this leader as wanting to impress, plus the lack of perceived humility, I found this would be a leader I would have difficulty trusting.

11. 2 Corinthians 12:9 (TNIV).

Daniel
1. Phillipians 2:6-8.
2. Flannery O'Connor, "A Good Man is Hard to Find," in *A Good Man is Hard to Find and Other Stories* (Orlando, FL: Harcourt Brace, 1955).

Joshua
1. 1 Corinthians 3:21-23 (TNIV).

Chapter 3
Steve
1. DiSC, 15.

Tyson
1. DiSC, 15.
2. Jurgen, Moltmann, *God in Creation* (New York: Harper and Row, 1985).
3. Ray S. Anderson, "A Theological Perspective on Cure of Souls" in *On Being Human* (Pasadena, CA: Fuller Seminary Press, 1982), 194-206.
4. Ron Carucci, "Leadership 1: Personal Influence in Service," lecture given at MHGS, June 2008.

Chapter Four
Beth
1. Allender, *Leading with a Limp*, 132.

2. Allender, "Intimate Allies," marriage seminar in Grand Rapids, MI, 2005.

Shannon

1. Jay Hall and Martha S. Williams, "Personnel Relations Survey" (Waco, TX: Teleometrics International, 2000).

Chapter Five
Greg

1. Mark 9:35.
2. DePree, *Leadership Jazz*, 69.
3. Arbinger, *Leadership and Self-Deception*, 168.
4. DePree, *Leadership Jazz*, 57.
5. Allender, *Leading with a Limp*, 138.

Jeannette

1. Allender, *Leading with a Limp*, 171.
2. Ibid., 59.
3. Ibid., 161.
4. DePree, *Leadership Jazz,* 63-64.

Laura

1. Shoshana Zuboff and James Maxmin, *The Support Economy* (New York: Viking, 2002), as published in Franklin Covey Leadership Classic Organizer, "Leadership: The Problem and Solution" tab, 2008.
2. Arbinger, *Leadership and Self-Deception*, 104-114.
3. Execution Qutent [xQ] questionnaire, conducted by Harris Interactive for Franklin Covey 2003, as published in Franklin Covey Leadership Classic Organizer, "Leadership: The Problem and Solution" tab, 2008.
4. Proverbs 29:18 (KJV).
5. Luke 10:17.
6. Luke 10:19.
7. DePree, *Leadership Jazz*, 22.

8. Marsha Jackson, "In Pursuit to Recruit," *Evansville Journal*, Volume 6, Issue 5 (2007) http://www.evansvillebusiness. com/current/1206/cover.html (accessed October 28, 2007).
9. Jan den Ouden, "Trends in Mission," http://www.postmission. com/articles/trendsdenouden.pdf (accessed October 27, 2007).

Tamara
1. Allender, lecture given at MHGS, June 13, 2008.
2. Matthew 16:24.
3. Arbinger, *Leadership and self-deception*, 39.
4. Allender, *Leading with a Limp*, 28.
5. 1 John 4:16; DePree, *Leadership Jazz*, 60.
6. Depree, *Leadership Jazz*, 188.
7. Ibid., 165.

Chapter 6
Caroline
1. Depree, *Leadership Jazz*, 5.
2. James A. Autry, *Love and Profit: The Art of Caring Leadership* (New York: Avon Books, 1991).
3. Ibid., 80.
4. Arbinger, *Leadership and Self-Deception*, 64-80.
5. Ibid., 76-77.
6. James A. Autry, *Life & Work: A Manager's Search for Meaning* (New York: Avon Books, 1994), 255.
7. Stephen R. Covey, *Seven habits of Highly Effective People: Restoring the Character Ethic* (New York: Simon and Schuster, 1989), 235.
8. Depree, *Leadership Jazz*, 220-25.

Jeremy
1. Allender, *Leading with a Limp*, 173.
2. Depree, *Leadership Jazz*, 190.
3. Roy Barsness, "Surrender and Transcendence in the Therapeutic Encounter," *Journal of Psychology and Christianity* 25, no. 1 (2006): 47.

Jessi

1. Moveon.org is a group of organizations bringing real Americans back into the political process. The goal is to encourage people to get involved in the process of creating progressive politics in the USA.

2. The trickster is an alchemist, a magician, creating realities in the duality of time and illusion. The trickster is an important archetype in the history of man. He is a god, yet he is not. He is the wise-fool. It is he, through his creations, that destroys, points out the flaws in carefully constructed societies of man. He rebels against authority, pokes fun at the overly serious, creates convoluted schemes that may or may not work, plays with the Laws of the Universe and is sometimes his own worst enemy. He exists to question, to cause us to question, not accept things blindly. He appears when a way of thinking becomes outmoded, needs to be torn down, built anew. Description taken from http://www.crystalinks. com/trickster.html.

3. 2 Samuel 12.

4. Barabara Nicolosi, "Toward a Christian Cinema," *Behind the Screen: Hollywood Insiders on Faith, Film and Culture* (Grand Rapids, MI: Baker Books, 2005), 124.

5. Allender, lecture given at MHGS, Fall 2005.

Zach

1. Allender, *Leading with a Limp*, 135.

2. Ibid., 55.

3. Ibid., 59.

4. Galatians 6:9-10.

5. Allender, *Leading with a Limp*, 34.

Troy

1. Allender, *Leading with a Limp*, 29.

2. Ibid., 177.

Campbell

1. Allender, *Leading with a Limp*, 120, 122.
2. Isaiah. 6:8.
3. 2 Corinthians 10:7.
4. Matthew 16:25.
5. Matthew 6:31, 33.
6. Luke 10:27.
7. Proverbs 19:11.
8. 1 Samuel 12:23.
9. Jim Collins, "Level 5 Leadership: The Triumph of Humility and Fierce Resolve," *Harvard Business Review* 73 (January 2001): 67-76.

Jacob

1. I am using "we" here and throughout to demonstrate my participation in this as well.

Stuart

1. Arbinger, *Leadership and Self-Deception*, 16.
2. James Hollis, *Why Good People Do Bad Things* (New York: Gotham Books, 2007),132.
3. Hollis, *Why Good People*, 133.
4. Arbinger, *Leadership and Self-Deception*, 75.
5. Ibid., 85, 87, 96.
6. Allender, *Leading with a Limp*, 6, 5, 41.
7. Hollis, *Why Good People,* 140.
8. Carucci, "Leadership 1: Personal Influence in Service," lecture given at MHGS, June 2008.
9. DePree, *Leadership Jazz*, 188.
10. C. S. Lewis, *Prince Caspian* (New York: Macmilian, 1951), 200.

Chapter 8
Rachel

Title is inspired by a line from an Emily Dickinson poem.
1. Ambivalence: a state of having emotions of both positive and negative valence or of having thoughts or actions

in contradiction with each other, when they are related to the same object, idea or person (for example, feeling both love and hatred for someone or something). The term is also commonly used to refer to situations where 'mixed feelings' of a more general sort are experienced or where a person experiences uncertainty or indecisiveness concerning something. www.wikipedia.org/wiki/ambivalence. Accessed April 30, 2008.

2. 1 Corinthians 1:27-28 (NRSV).
3. Matthew 18:2-4 (NRSV).

Sue

1. Adapted from Joy Thomas and Ray Thomas, *I'm Not at Risk, Am I?* (South Africa: OM Books, 2005).
2. Adapted from a well-established international mission agency, posted 2008.
3. Report to employer modified from original, 2006.
4. UNAIDS, 2006 Report on the Global AIDS Epidemic, Executive Summary, http://data.unaids.org/pub/GlobalReport/2006/2006_GR-ExecutiveSummary_en.pdf (downloaded May 5, 2008).
5. "Soul Earthquake, Stirring Beginnings," www.sueinafrica.blog.com, December 2007.
6. Parker Palmer, *Let Your Life Speak: Listening for the Voice of Vocation* (San Francisco, CA: Jossey Bass, 2000).

Fran

1. Matthew 10:30 (NLT).
2. Jeremiah 1:4 (NLT).
3. Psalm 139:13-16 (NLT).
4. 1 Peter 2:9 (NLT).
5. Craig G. Bartholomew and Michael W. Goheen, *The Drama of Scripture* (Grand Rapids, MI: Baker Academic, 2004), 202-3.
6. Arbinger, *Leadership and Self Deception*, 35.
7. Arbinger, *Leadership and Self Deception*, 100.
8. 2 Corinthians 4:8-10 (NLT).

9. 2 Corinthians 4:6-7 (NKJV).
10. Luke 9:24 (NLT).
11. Bartholomew and Goheen, *The Drama*, 201,204.

Josué
1. DePree, *Leadership Jazz*, 139.
2. 2 Samuel 11.
3. Elisabeth Rosenthal, "Vatican Agrees to a Carbon Offset Scheme," *International Herald Tribune* http://www.iht.com/articles/2007/09/03/business/carbon.php (April 30, 2008).
4. Miroslav Volf, *Exclusion & Embrace* (Nashville: Abingdon Press, 1996).
5. Luke 18:9-14.
6. DePree, *Leadership Jazz*, 87.

Paula
1. John 13 contains the story of Jesus washing the feet of his disciples.
2. Allender, *Leading with a Limp*, 121.
3. Arbinger, *Leadership and Self-Deception*, 104-114.
4. Allender, *Leading with a Limp*, 142.
5. Ibid, 120.
6. Allender, "Leadership 1," lecture given at MHGS, June 15, 2008.
7. Luke 5:16.
8. 2 Corinthians 4:7-12.
9. Tom Ryan, "Leadership 1," lecture given at MHGS, June 14, 2008.

Mark
1. See DePree, *Leadership Jazz*.
2. See Bill Easum, *Leadership on the Other Side* (Nashville, TN: Abingdon Press, 2000).
3. See Dan Kimball, *The Emerging Church: Vintage Christianity for New Generations* (Grand Rapids, MI: Zondervan, 2003).

Mary

1. Jay Hall and Martha S. Williams, Personnel Relations Survey, (Waco:Teleometrics International Inc., 2000).
2. Ibid.

Matt

1. John Howard Yoder, *The Politics of Jesus* (Grand Rapids, MI: WB Eerdmans, 1972), 246-47.
2. Rowan Williams, *The Wound of Knowledge* (Lanham, MD: Cowley, 2003), 100.
3. Michael J. Gorman, *Cruciformity* (Grand Rapids, MI: WB Eerdmans, 2001), 4.
4. Ibid., 5.
5. Ibid., 390.
6. Ibid., 397.
7. Ibid., 395.
8. Ibid., 395.
9. Michael J. Quirk, "Stanley Hauerwas: An Interview," CrossCurrents June 2002 http://www.crosscurrents.org/ Hauerwasspring2002.htm.
10. Stanley Hauerwas and William Willimon, *The Truth About God: The Ten Commandments in Christian Life* (Nashville: Abingdon, 1996), 19.
11. John Howard Yoder, "Armaments and Eschatology," *Studies in Christian Ethics* 1 (1988): 58.

Breinigsville, PA USA
15 November 2009
227578BV00002B/1/P

9 781615 792719